THE TIES THAT BIND

THE HISTORY OF SUTHERLAND ASBILL & BRENNAN LLP

∼

Published by Sutherland Asbill & Brennan LLP

ISBN: 978-0-9790943-0-9

Written by Joe Renouard
Edited by Robert Somerville
Designed by Dana Magsumbol

Special Contributors: Tina Taylor T2design,
Jane A. Martin (Photo Research), Judy Lyon Davis (Index)
Photo Credits are listed on page 240

Printed in Canada by Friesens
10 9 8 7 6 5 4 3 2 1

THE TIES THAT BIND

THE HISTORY OF SUTHERLAND ASBILL & BRENNAN LLP

~

WRITTEN BY JOE RENOUARD

FOREWORD BY
MARK D. WASSERMAN AND JAMES L. HENDERSON III

ACKNOWLEDGMENTS

This book would not have been possible without the thoughtful contributions of several Sutherland firm employees and family members. I would like to thank the following for granting interviews or for otherwise giving generously of their time and knowledge: (in alphabetical order) Al Adams, Bill Barwick, John Bonds, Bill Bradley, Tom Byrne, John Chandler, Nick Christakos, George Cohen, Carey DeDeyn, Connie Echols, Mike Egan, Alan Elsas, Edith Elsas, John Fleming, Ed Grenier, Jim Groton, Ed Hales, Fraser Harbutt, Jim Heffernan, Jerry Libin, Al Lindseth, Keith McCrea, John Mobley, John North, Pat Patterson, Jim Paulk, Kim Perret, Peter Rodgers, Teresa Wynn Roseborough, Steve Roth, Steuart Thomsen, Randolph Thrower, Jim Wilson, and Walter Wingfield.

I would also like to acknowledge a few others who were closely involved with the project from the start. I am grateful to Jim Henderson for effectively "turning me loose" with the firm's historical documents and encouraging me to write the story as I saw fit. J.D. Fleming gave first-rate advice and assistance throughout, and on several occasions he went beyond the call of duty by proofreading chapters and sending detailed replies to my queries. I also want to note my appreciation for the previous work of Joe Brennan, which I consulted at many points while I was researching this book. Although I never met him, my many sojourns into his notes gave me a deeper appreciation for the considerable talents of the Sutherland firm's founding generation. And finally, thanks to Jennifer Orth for taking on the thankless task of reading the entire manuscript, even the boring parts (of which I hope there are few). While I have relied on many people for assistance with this project, I take full responsibility for any errors in the text.

Joe Renouard
Atlanta, GA
December 2006

CONTENTS

FOREWORD

This firm history project began about two years ago. Through his connections at Emory University, J. D. Fleming helped us find Joe Renouard, a Ph.D. candidate in History at Emory, who undertook the project. It was determined that the history would focus primarily on the early years and lawyers, describing the foundations of our current practices and fast-forwarding the last twenty-five years, and on particular cases, matters, and personalities that would be of historical interest to a general reader.

The book is intended for the firm's family and friends. It is not a comprehensive description of all our practices, achievements or (the few) foibles. It is not the product of a committee. It is not a marketing piece. It reflects a single author's narrative of the firm's history based on his research of publicly available materials, the firm's own records and the writings of our partners about the firm, and on interviews with a number of our partners and others.

In reading this book for the first time, we were struck by several things. First, great law firms are not built by timid people. Second, while good fortune is indeed very important, so are hard work, perseverance, a commitment to excellence, and goodwill. Third, we have, and our reputation is enhanced by, a rich and ongoing tradition of active public service and engagement with the times in which we find ourselves.

Finally, and most importantly, we realize how fortunate and privileged we have been to be part of something much larger than ourselves. In an organization always being built on the achievement of talented and ambitious individuals, it is often easy to underestimate the value of our legacy. It is a rich legacy. It is these ties that bind for which we are most grateful.

December 2006
Mark D. Wasserman, *Managing Partner*
James L. Henderson III,
Of Counsel and Former Managing Partner

William A. Sutherland, Mac Asbill, Sr., and Joseph B. Brennan (left to right)

*Particularly in the early years, the
partners exerted a great deal of effort on
matters that yielded no immediate
profit, but which provided them with the
experience they would need to ensure
future expansion.*

CHAPTER ONE

THE FOUNDING GENERATION

THE FOUNDERS' PLAN

To paraphrase Charles Dickens, the early 20th century in America was the best and the worst of times. It was the machine age, when the horse was giving way to the automobile and laborers were working long hours for short pay. This was the America of Henry Ford and Theodore Roosevelt, of women's suffragists, progressive reformers, and 12-hour factory shifts. Tycoons like Rockefeller and Hearst were holding court over their empires, while muckrakers like Upton Sinclair were exposing the dark side of the industrial revolution. These were the growing pains of modernity, a time of opportunity for some and hard times for many.

The founders of the Sutherland firm – Bill Sutherland, Elbert Tuttle, and Mac Asbill, Sr. – came of age in this rapidly changing world. Although in many ways these young men were typical of their generation, they were also exceptional. They grew up in stable, hardworking families; far outside the Northeastern corridors of power, perhaps, but relatively comfortable. At a time when few studied past high school, they were able to excel in the nation's finest universities and law schools, and their experiences as young men opened their eyes to the prospects of the world around them. Above all, they possessed the kind of intellect and integrity necessary to establish and sustain a top law practice, and their considerable foresight and skills would carry them through long, distinguished careers. They became active participants in the process whereby the law kept pace with the demands of the American people, and in their remarkable journey they made their mark on the pages of the nation's legal and social history.

Early in his life, Bill Sutherland, a native of Coweta County, Georgia, proved himself a prodigy on a par with Orson Welles. Owing to his unusual upbringing (his father was in the timber business, so young Bill grew up in sawmill towns with names like Number Six, South Carolina), he studied under private tutors before entering the University of Florida at the remarkable age of 14. He transferred to the University of Virginia and received his A.B. there in 1914 at the age of 17. He then sped through Harvard Law School, graduating with honors as part of the famous class of 1917, and soon thereafter spent two years as a clerk to Supreme Court Justice Louis D. Brandeis. During the summers he carried out graduate study at the University of Wisconsin, eventually receiving the A.M. degree in 1919. So by the ripe age of 23, not only had he received his A.B., A.M., and J.D. degrees, but he had also been admitted to the District of Columbia bar and clerked at the highest court in the land.[1]

Justice Brandeis

Justice Brandeis – one of the luminaries of the latter years of the Progressive Era – saw potential in the new federal regulatory agencies, and he suggested to the young Sutherland that he begin his career in a government bureau. Sutherland took the justice's comments to heart and decided to work as an attorney and examiner for the fledgling Federal Trade Commission in 1919 and 1920. There he learned the ins and outs of the Washington bureaucracy, which was knowledge that would serve him well when he permanently relocated to the city after World War II.[2]

But although this work was interesting, Sutherland had his sights set on an independent practice, and after 15 months at the FTC he moved to Atlanta to practice law. He was admitted to the Georgia bar and soon formed a loose association with the firms of Jones, Evins & Moore and Miller & Chevalier. In 1923 Sutherland married Sarah Hall of Newnan, Georgia, and the following year he and Elbert Tuttle founded the firm of Sutherland & Tuttle.[3]

Elbert Tuttle also had a rather unusual upbringing, which no doubt contributed to his later iconoclastic decisions as a jurist. Like Bill Sutherland's, Tuttle's childhood was exceptionally nomadic. He was born in Pasadena, California, in 1897 and lived for a brief time in Washington, DC, where his father, Guy Tuttle, worked as a clerk in the War Department. Guy later accepted a job documenting immigrants in Los Angeles, and in 1907 he signed on as an accountant with the Hawaii Sugar Planters Association. Elbert was 11 years old when the Tuttles made the long voyage to Honolulu via the SS *Sierra*.

Elbert and his brother, Malcolm, spent the rest of their formative years in Honolulu. They rode a motorcycle to the multiracial Punahou school every day, and they were among the first "mainland" Americans to surf regularly at Waikiki Beach (the 11-foot wooden longboard was then in vogue). The Tuttle brothers joined a group of other surfers in forming Hawaii's first prominent surfing club, the Outrigger Canoe Club, which nearly every important businessman in Honolulu eventually joined. Guy Tuttle served for many years as the Outrigger's president, and the club thrived throughout the 20th century.[4]

Elbert Tuttle came to the field of law after first studying journalism at Cornell

ATLANTA DIRECTORY LISTINGS

ROBERT P. JONES
SAMUEL NESBITT EVINS
JEROME MOORE
E. CLEM POWERS
ROBERT T. JONER, JR.
WILLIAM A. SUTHERLAND

WALLACE T. DALEY
OLIN M. FULLER
MARTIN P. FISHBACK
PAT C. BERRINGTON
JACKSON D. THOMAS
AUGUSTUS F. OWEN
RALPH WILLIAMS

Jones, Evins, Moore & Powers

COUNSELORS-AT-LAW

Walnut 7976

1318-28 Atlanta Trust Co. Bldg., Atlanta, Ga.

WILLIAM A. SUTHERLAND
ELBERT P. TUTTLE

CHESTER F. PRICE

LAW OFFICES OF

SUTHERLAND & TUTTLE

1315-17 Atlanta Trust Co. Bldg.   Atlanta, Ga.

*1927 — Jones, Evins, Moore & Powers
(with Sutherland)*

1927 — Sutherland & Tuttle

(A.B. 1918, LL.B. 1923), where he served as editor in chief of the *Cornell Daily Sun* and graduated first in his class. He had originally planned to attend Harvard, but owing to World War I and his marriage, he ended up forming a lifelong association with Cornell instead.[5] (Half a century later he would be awarded an honorary LL.D. from Harvard.) One of his colleagues at the *Daily Sun* was E.B. White, who later penned the classic children's books *Charlotte's Web* and *Stuart Little*, as well as the famed writing manual, Strunk & White's *The Elements of Style*; it was one of many connections Tuttle established at Cornell. Tuttle served a brief stint in the Aviation Section of the Army Signal Corps at the tail end of World War I, then worked on the news and editorial staffs of the *New York Evening World*, the *Army and Navy Journal*, and the *American Legion Weekly*. He later said that his early work in journalism helped him develop the facility for doing things crisply and quickly, talents that stayed with him throughout his legal career.

As if these many accomplishments did not make Tuttle enough of a Renaissance man, he also codesigned and oversaw the construction of an apartment building near the Cornell campus while he was an undergraduate. During travels in France, Tuttle had made a sketch of a chateau and given it to his friend, J. Larkin Baldridge, who was studying architecture. With the help of another classmate and the financial backing of their parents, Tuttle and Baldridge built and rented out the Tuttle Apartments, which were still standing as of the 1990s.[6]

Tuttle's first trip to the South turned out to be momentous, for it was here that he met both Bill Sutherland and Bill's sister, Sara, the woman who would become his wife of 75 years. (When he was in his 80s, Tuttle remarked that this marriage was one of the keys to his longevity). A friend's father had offered Tuttle a summer job in Florida, and the day Tuttle arrived, his friend arranged a double date at the beach with Sara. Later that summer Tuttle met Bill Sutherland and Bill's law school roommate, Mac Asbill. Sutherland and Asbill had become good friends in part because they were among the few Southerners at Harvard Law School. Tuttle later recalled that he did not form much of a bond with Bill and Mac at their first meeting because the two "elders" were Harvard Law students, while Tuttle was a lowly Cornell undergraduate.

The year 1919 was momentous for Sutherland, Tuttle, and Asbill for two reasons: first, because Elbert and Sara got married; second, because this was when the three young men formulated the idea of starting their own law firm. Fittingly, they hatched the plan while vacationing in Ponte Vedra, Florida, a stone's throw from where they had first met a few years earlier. Since Tuttle had not yet been to law school, the three decided that he would return to Cornell to study law in the hope that the trio could later establish a partnership in a city of their choosing. The promising Southern city of Atlanta was at the top of their list, for not only had the Sutherlands lived near the city for many years, but all three were accustomed to a warm climate.

The ambitious young men were fully intent on carrying out their partnership plan, but it took Asbill much longer to join into a law firm with the other two than any of them could have imagined. Like Sutherland and Tuttle, Asbill took a circuitous

The Founding Case

Bill Sutherland and Elbert Tuttle decided to launch the firm in 1924 when Sutherland earned the unusually large fee of $2,400 for winning the "impossible" *Hartley v. Nash* case in the Georgia Supreme Court (157 Ga. 402, 405 (121 S.E. 295)). In this case Neal Hartley sued Dekalb County commissioner L.T.Y. Nash for 7% interest on county warrants issued by Nash's predecessor. Sutherland persuaded the court to decide that holders of past due county warrants were entitled to interest, notwithstanding a provision of the Georgia Constitution that seemed to prohibit such interest as "new debt" in excess of authorized limits. Faced with apparently conflicting precedents, Chief Justice Russell wrote a classic opinion discussing the limitations on the doctrine of stare decisis, in which he stated, "Common honesty and good morals apply as much to any branch or subdivision of government as to a private individual."[17]

route to joining a private law practice. A native of Ridge Springs, South Carolina, he graduated from Wofford College (Spartanburg, South Carolina), then attended Harvard Law School. He was commissioned as an artillery officer during World War I, and after an honorary discharge he became an attorney for the U.S. government's alien property custodian. Among his other government duties, he handled tax matters and claims against foreign nations growing out of the war, and he tried cases in different sections of the country. Asbill was the first of the Sutherland/Tuttle/Asbill trio to relocate to Atlanta, and at the end of 1919 he cofounded the firm of Watkins, Russell & Asbill, later known as Watkins, Asbill & Watkins. When Tuttle and Sutherland formed their firm in 1924, Asbill, who was fairly well established in his practice, decided against joining them for the time being. Little did they know that the eventual realization of the Sutherland/Tuttle/Asbill partnership would have to wait another 25 years.[7]

While Asbill was with the Watkins firm, Sutherland and Tuttle spent the early 1920s building relationships in Atlanta and at Cornell. Just as Tuttle had distinguished himself at Cornell as an undergraduate, he also made a name for himself at Cornell Law, especially through his service as editor in chief of the *Cornell Law Quarterly*. After he graduated in 1923, the university offered him a job as assistant comptroller, but Sara Tuttle convinced him that he would never be happy if he did not practice law. Taking Sara's advice, Elbert turned down the Cornell job. He also passed up an offer from the New York firm of Sullivan & Cromwell and instead went to Atlanta to work at Anderson, Rountree & Crenshaw, where he earned the princely sum of $175 a month in his first associate position. Sutherland had meanwhile formed an association with the Washington, DC, firm of Miller & Chevalier, which was recognized as one of the country's leading tax law specialists.

This association came about through his handling of some important tax matters for clients of Jones, Evins & Moore (the firm of golf legend Bobby Jones).[8]

The impetus for founding Sutherland & Tuttle was the 1924 case of *Hartley v. Nash*. When Sutherland won the "enormous" fee of $2,400, he and Tuttle decided to take the plunge; assuming this money would last six months, they used it to form their partnership. In the meantime, Sutherland continued his association with Miller & Chevalier as the firm's "resident partner" in the South, and he continued to do occasional work for Jones, Evins & Moore. Sutherland was further inspired to start his own firm because, as was the custom in those days, his partnership with the Jones firm was unsalaried. He shared his fees with the Jones partners in exchange for some office space and the occasional referral. The lines separating Sutherland's associations were quite fluid, since all three firms had offices in the Atlanta Trust Company Building.[9]

EARLY GROWTH

Sutherland & Tuttle's first few decades were characterized by gradual growth. Particularly in the early years, the partners exerted a great deal of effort on matters that yielded no immediate profit, but which provided them with the experience they would need to ensure future expansion. Sutherland and Tuttle very quickly won recognition as bright lawyers who were imaginative enough to sustain their own law firm at such a young age. They spent these first few years building up their experience in general practice and handling civil matters as varied as breach of contract, divorce, corporate organization, bankruptcy, and wills and trusts.

Within a few years they began to lean toward tax and administrative law, and they quickly gained a reputation in federal tax matters. Some of these cases involved technical tax questions, while others concerned questions of substantive state law or federal practice and procedure. A few even included important constitutional issues that Sutherland and Tuttle argued in the U.S. Supreme Court. The decision to pursue tax law was rather unusual for its day. Lawyers at the time tended to look with some disdain on tax and administrative work because these were considered matters for accountants, and because the tax laws themselves

ATLANTA DIRECTORY LISTINGS

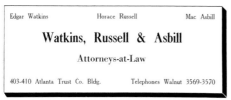

1923 — Watkins, Russell & Asbill

1925 — Anderson, Rountree & Crenshaw (with Tuttle)

changed so rapidly. The legal profession's disregard of tax law played right into Sutherland and Tuttle's hands, and the pair was able to succeed in this burgeoning field from the very beginning.[10]

Bill Sutherland's reputation as a tax lawyer developed naturally from his early participation in federal tax cases for clients of the Jones and Miller firms. One of these was arguably the most important federal tax case in the Southeast in the 1920s. When Jones client Atlantic Steel's income and excess profits taxes for the World War I years were in question, Sutherland helped handle the matter at the administrative level and in a later refund suit in the district court at Atlanta. He played the principal part in the preparation and trial of the case, which resulted in a jury's favorable verdict. The judgment rendered in 1927 for some $275,000 was the largest award secured in Georgia in a tax refund case up to that point.[11]

From then on Sutherland devoted most of his time to federal tax matters, while Tuttle engaged almost exclusively in general practice. They deliberately worked out this arrangement in order to avoid overspecializing in a limited area. The tax practice was fairly lucrative in the early days, but there was some question as to whether it would continue to be profitable after settlement of the cases involving World War I excess profits taxes. Equally important was the realization that a law firm could attain excellence in the practice of tax law only if it had a broad and well-rounded experience in a general law practice.[12]

The firm's general practice developed from various sources. Sutherland's early

Mac Asbill, Sr. Takes On Ty Cobb

Lawyers who joined the Sutherland firm in later years knew Mac Asbill, Sr. as an "old" man. Perhaps only a few of these latecomers were aware, then, that Asbill had had some interesting life experiences before he began his legal career. One story dating to his baseball-playing days at Wofford College is worth  repeating. One year, circa 1913, the Detroit Tigers had finished their spring training in Florida, and they were paying their traveling expenses back north with exhibition games in towns along the way. The Tigers scheduled a game with Wofford, and this gave Mac the opportunity to take on the legendary Ty Cobb. Asbill was playing second base, and the first time Cobb came to

Ty Cobb

bat he hit a ball to the outfield and rounded first, intent on getting a double. Despite Cobb's famed penchant for sliding with his cleats up, Asbill covered the base and blocked the Tiger's slide. Cobb, who was known for handling his fists as well as he handled the bat, brushed himself off and said menacingly, "Sonny, the next time I come around here, you'd better get outta my way!" Fortunately for Asbill, the rest of the game went off without incident.[33]

association with the Jones firm brought him the particularly close friendship and confidence of that firm's partners. These included Colonel Robert P. Jones (father of golfer Bobby Jones), Samuel N. Evins, and Rooney Moore, all of whom steered business to the young Sutherland firm and helped to build its reputation in the community. Sutherland's father-in-law, Hewlett A. Hall – attorney general of Georgia in 1910-1911 and a prominent member of the Georgia bar – was also responsible for getting the Sutherland firm into various matters.[13]

The Search for Clients

Bill Sutherland could be said to have been the one "wearing the pants" in the firm's early years, especially when it came to securing new clients. He utilized his considerable energy to gain clients whenever and wherever he saw an opportunity, although the customs of the day limited the extent to which he could market his services. Longtime firm partner Jim Wilson liked to reflect on an old story that helped explain Sutherland's acumen at gaining clients in the days before legal marketing became commonplace:

In those days the word "marketing" was a no-no in the practice of law, but a story illustrates Bill's approach to that. He would tell the story of the barber who asked a lawyer who came in for a haircut if his wife – the barber's wife – were injured in an accident, would the lawyer feel that he could come in and ask to represent her. And the lawyer said, "Oh no, that would be against my standard of ethics. But I certainly would come down to get a haircut." And Bill went all over the country getting haircuts, and was very successful.[14]

William A. Sutherland

Elbert Tuttle's talents and associations also brought in new clients. His early experience with Anderson, Rountree & Crenshaw helped establish his professional reputation in Atlanta. He also became active in the Georgia National Guard, and the personal contacts he made there proved very valuable in bringing some important matters to the firm. For example, Tuttle was made attorney for the Fulton County Board of Education shortly after he tried a case before Cam Dorsey as Master in Chancery. The Fulton board was the firm's first retainer client, and the representation brought a new measure of prestige. A few years later the board became a financially satisfactory client, beginning with the legal work involved in the issuance of bonds (see Ch. 8). Tuttle would also go on to make a name for himself in landmark civil liberties cases (see Ch. 4).[15]

The firm's timber practice also began in these early years. Because Bill Sutherland's father had worked in timber, young Bill came of age amid the sounds and smells of the sawmill. As timber producers and investors became embroiled in tax controversies over the federal Internal Revenue Code in the 1930s, Sutherland parlayed his knowledge into a viable timber and forest products practice. This eventually grew into a major set of national and international representations.

One of Sutherland and Tuttle's most propitious decisions in this period was their hiring of Joe Brennan (Georgetown A.B. 1925, Harvard LL.B. 1928) as the firm's first true associate in 1928. Brennan's acquisition was truly fortunate. If it had not been for South Georgia's dire economic troubles in the 1920s, Sutherland and Tuttle might never have met the Savannah native. Brennan had planned to return to South Georgia after law school, but economic circumstances there limited his career opportunities. His two brothers' Savannah practice was suffering as a result of the boll weevil epidemic, which had decimated the South Georgia economy. They could not give their brother a job, so when a friend recommended a St. Louis firm, young Joe headed out to the Mississippi country.[16]

Because Brennan had to pass through Atlanta on his way to St. Louis, he decided to take the time to talk to some Atlanta firms in the hope that a stroke of luck would keep him in the South. Sutherland & Tuttle was on his list, but naturally he chose to visit the big firms first. Although the established firms' partners could not give Brennan steady work, several of them noted how impressed they were with the efforts of the two bright young men in the Trust Company Building. Brennan therefore conferred with Sutherland and Tuttle on the off chance that they would be interested, and the three men immediately hit it off. They hired Brennan, and within a matter of months their new associate was briefing a case in the U.S. Supreme Court. Brennan went on to become the firm's first "homegrown" partner in 1933, after which the firm moniker was changed to Sutherland, Tuttle & Brennan. Throughout Brennan's long career at the Sutherland firm, he would loom large as a renowned courtroom lawyer, particularly in tax and administrative cases.

The combination of the three men's talents and their burgeoning reputation as creative lawyers gave the young firm a great deal of potential going into the 1930s.

BIOGRAPHIES

WILLIAM A. SUTHERLAND (1896-1987)

Bill Sutherland's intellect, work ethic, and legal acumen within his law firm were matched by his service to the profession. Among his many professional roles, he served on the ABA's Council on Taxation and in the ABA House of Delegates. He also served as president of the board of directors of the ABA endowment. In 1976 he received an outstanding professional service award for 50 years' service from the fellows of the American Bar Foundation.[18]

The World War II years were pivotal for Sutherland and the firm. During the war, Sutherland and Joe Brennan were the only lawyers who remained in Atlanta to keep the enterprise afloat. After the others returned from their military service and readjusted to their old jobs, Sutherland made a dramatic move of his own by permanently relocating to Washington, DC, in 1946. This proved a sound decision in the long run, as his commanding presence anchored the considerable growth of the Washington practice.

Sutherland cut back on his duties in later years, but unlike many successful entrepreneurs, he did not quietly disappear into the executive ranks. Indeed, as many insiders will attest, he remained "The Boss." He retained final approval in the hiring process, leading many future partners to joke that they were glad they did not do anything amiss when they first met Bill Sutherland. When the Washington office was on Farragut Square, the semiretired Sutherland preferred taking the stairs to his office so he could stop at the second floor bar to have a drink and say hello to his friends. In his free time he also enjoyed riding his horse, which he kept in a stable near his Washington apartment.

Sutherland's philosophy on the practice of law permeated every facet of the firm's endeavors for many decades, and these principles continued to guide the firm through good times and bad. First and foremost, he sought to build a firm that was topflight in every aspect. He never tolerated second-class work; everything that left the office was to be of the very best quality, regardless of the fees involved. Sutherland also maintained observance of the highest ethical standards, a sense of professionalism, and a genuine interest in public service. As Sutherland himself summarized his attitude toward the practice of law: "Once you get into a matter, you do the very best work. Whatever it takes, you get the best results."[19]

ELBERT P. TUTTLE, SR. (1897-1996)

Elbert Tuttle was, quite simply, among the most important figures in 20th century American legal history. He wore many hats throughout his long life, from journalist and military leader to lawyer and jurist, yet despite his considerable accomplishments, he never forgot his humble roots and his many years at the Sutherland firm.

A brief look at Tuttle's long life shows that he was one of those rare individuals whose work can truly be said to have made a difference in the world. He served as an officer in the Georgia National Guard, and he returned to active duty in the Army for World War II, during which he was wounded in action in the Pacific Theater (see Ch. 5). He eventually achieved the rank of brigadier general.

Tuttle's political activities propelled him into his second career as a judge. In 1952 he served as state chairman of the Georgia Republican Party, and he counted among his acquaintances most of the notable Republicans of the day. When Dwight Eisenhower was elected president, he appointed Tuttle general counsel to the Treasury Department. Tuttle was happy to accept this assignment, though it meant having to leave the Sutherland firm. (Tuttle did keep some professional contact with the firm for many years in order to help administer the trusts the firm had established in the 1930s and 1940s.) Two years later Eisenhower appointed the 57-year-old Tuttle to the U.S. Court of Appeals for the Fifth Circuit, which in those days stretched from Savannah to El Paso. Tuttle accepted, and the Fifth Circuit bench soon found itself at the center of the desegregation controversy (see Ch.7).[20]

Tuttle made President Eisenhower's short list of prospective Supreme Court appointees in 1958, when the president was faced with the imminent retirement of Associate Justice Harold Hitz Burton. Eisenhower wrote to Attorney General William P. Rogers in reference to Tuttle, "It is possible that it would be a good idea to have two southerners on the court, and I think [Hugo] Black is the only one now who would be classed in that category."[21] In fact, at this time the Washington legal community widely considered Tuttle to be "next in line" in the event that Justice Black retired.[22] Yet although Tuttle was not nominated to the Supreme Court, he became the chief judge of the Fifth Circuit court in 1960. His far-reaching decisions in this court prompted Chief Justice Earl Warren to call Tuttle "one of the greatest judges of the era."[23] Tuttle retired in 1967 at the mandatory retirement age of 70, though he continued as senior judge for the Fifth Circuit until 1981. He was then reassigned to the position of senior judge for the U.S. Court of Appeals for the 11th District, where he served well into his 90s.

As a judge, Tuttle was known for writing succinct opinions that went straight to the heart of an issue. His colleague on the Fifth Circuit bench, Judge John Minor Wisdom, said that Tuttle wrote "lean, strong English. He [had] a purist's feeling for the right word and correct syntax, a reporter's

Elbert Tuttle on Professional Service

Those who knew Elbert Tuttle were consistently awed by his professionalism. In 1957 Tuttle delivered a commencement speech at Emory University in which he explained his concept of the professional. This speech became a favorite of his colleagues in the years that followed, and excerpts have been widely quoted by law professors and lawyers alike:[31]

The professional man is in essence one who provides service. But the service he renders is something more than that of the laborer, even the skilled laborer. It is a service that wells up from the entire complex of his personality. True, some specialized and highly developed techniques may be included, but their mode of expression is given its deepest meaning by the personality of the practitioner. In a very real sense his professional service cannot be separate from his personal being. He has no goods to sell, no land to till. His only asset is himself. It turns out that there is no right price for service, for what is a share of a man worth? If he does not contain the quality of integrity, he is worthless. If he does, he is priceless. The value is either nothing or it is infinite.

So do not try to set a price on yourselves. Do not measure out your professional services on an apothecaries' scale and say, "Only this much for so much." Do not debase yourselves by equating your souls to what they will bring in the market. Do not be a miser, hoarding your talents and abilities and knowledge, either among yourselves or in your dealings with your clients, patients, students, or flock.

Rather be reckless and spendthrift, pouring out your talent to all to whom it can be of service! Throw it away, waste it, and in the spending it will be increased. Do not keep a watchful eye lest you slip, and give away a little bit of what you might have sold. Do not censor your thoughts to gain a wider audience. Like love, talent is only useful in its expenditure, and it is never exhausted. Certain it is that man must eat; so set what price you must on your service. But never confuse the performance, which is great, with the compensation, be it money, power, or fame, which is trivial.[32]

> *Shortly before Tuttle died in 1996 at the age of 98, the Atlanta Constitution called him "perhaps the most influential civil rights judge in Southern history."*

discriminating eye for significant details, and an editor's eye for logical order." When Tuttle was in his 90s, he could still recite page references and highly specific historical detail. He once told an interviewer that he believed in the theory of common law development, "that the law develops to meet changing needs and according to changes in our moral precepts."[24]

Those who knew Tuttle noted that he was quiet, modest, and unfailingly courteous – in short, an almost perfect counterpart to the more volatile Bill Sutherland. He lived by a conservative moral code and eschewed alcohol and tobacco. In fact, as a member of the Second Sunday Club, a diverse group of Atlanta intellectuals that met monthly as a discussion group, Tuttle sent notes to the other members before his turn as host to remind them that he did not serve liquor in his home. This is not to say that Tuttle lived a sedentary or predictable life, however. He enjoyed athletic pursuits throughout his life; as a young lawyer he and four other National Guard officers bought horses and played polo in their spare time in an area of Atlanta that later became Ansley Mall.[25]

Elbert Tuttle authored over 1,400 decisions over the course of his long career. In 1981 President Jimmy Carter awarded him the Medal of Freedom, which the judge self-effacingly placed in a cabinet beneath his television set. Tuttle also received many honorary degrees, including an LL.D. from Harvard University in 1965. In 1990 the Fifth Circuit Court of Appeals building was named after him, an honor that prompted one journalist to suggest that "[Tuttle's] real monuments have been his judgments, which will outlast even the liveliest memories of his modesty, wit, decency, and courage." While on the 11th Circuit bench in the 1990s he became the oldest working federal judge in American history. He authored his last decision in 1995, though he continued to help the overburdened 11th Circuit Court screen cases. Shortly before Tuttle died in 1996 at the age of 98, the *Atlanta Constitution* called him "perhaps the most influential civil rights judge in Southern history."[26] Sutherland partner Randolph Thrower gave a fitting summary of Tuttle's personality and his juridical style when he said, "Unlike the other partners, he never asked me to find out what the law was. He told me what the law should be."[27]

JOSEPH B. BRENNAN (1903-1991)

Joe Brennan was hired as the firm's first true associate in 1928, and he became its first homegrown partner in 1933. Over the course of his many years at the firm, he was renowned for his love of the law. In longtime partner Randolph Thrower's words, Brennan was "a lawyer's lawyer who really didn't want to be bothered with anything else. He just wanted the tough matters put in front of him. He had a perfect library between his ears and a perfect computer system for recalling it." Brennan was equally admired for his tax work and his courtroom acumen. "He was more than just a tax specialist," said partner Jim Wilson, "he was a great trial lawyer. He took command of a courtroom like a man leading a team of horses on a stagecoach. He had a strong voice that just filled the courtroom."[28]

The Savannah native's considerable intellect was a constant source of inspiration to the younger associates and partners. "Joe Brennan was an extremely brilliant man," said partner Pat Patterson. "He spoke fluent and frequent Latin. It wasn't just that he could quote some legal opinion; he could quote the references it came from. He had such an encyclopedic knowledge of the law, and particularly the tax law. He was such a great guy, a great lawyer." Firm partner Mike Egan agreed, calling Brennan "a great writer of briefs. I'd write something that I thought was as good as it could be and he had a way of marking it up with his red pen so that it ended up being nothing short of perfect."

Brennan's talents certainly complemented those of Bill Sutherland and Elbert Tuttle, but his personality leaned more toward Tuttle's. Brennan was both Savannah Irish and Southern, and his Low Country manner made him popular with clients and lawyers alike. Edith Elsas, the wife of longtime partner Herbert Elsas, said Brennan was "just the opposite, temperamentally, of Mr. Sutherland." Brennan was "very much the peacemaker in every way, and was equally brilliant, but in a much different fashion. He wasn't as evident about it. He didn't try to blow you down with how bright he was, but it was there."[29]

The Atlanta community also benefited from Brennan's service. He worked on the board of the American Red Cross and was national president of the Georgetown Alumni Association from 1954 to 1956. The Georgetown association went on to give him its John Carroll Award at the end of his presidential term. Brennan was also a member of the ABA and the Georgia and Atlanta bar associations. Interestingly, in light of Elbert Tuttle's close association with the Republican Party, Brennan was a lifelong Democrat. He died in 1991 at the age of 87.[30]

Elbert Tuttle and the Roots of Hawaiian Aviation

Although many stories from Elbert Tuttle's life are well known, few people have heard the tale of how Elbert and his brother, Malcolm, became the first to fly an aircraft over Hawaii.[34] In 1910, less than seven years after the Wright brothers' historic first flight in North Carolina, the Tuttles chose to study aviation as a class project. When they discovered that no one had flown an airplane over the Territory of Hawaii, they decided to try their hand at designing and flying a small-scale model airplane. Their first attempt, a bulky craft made of bamboo, silk, and wire, was capable of flying a short distance with a rudimentary rubber spring device, while their second model was a small-scale, motorized replica of the Wright brothers' "Flyer." The Tuttles' airplane designs soon caught the eye of the townspeople, as evidenced by a local newspaper headline from 1910: "Honolulu Youths Study Aviation: Tuttles May be Rivals of Wrights."

It was then that Elbert and Malcolm came across a magazine article that explained how to make a glider out of wood, cotton cloth, and piano wire. With some guidance from their father, the brothers built the craft as a summer project, and by October of 1910 it was ready for a test run. The 40-pound glider was 15 feet long and 18 feet across, with two overlaid wings separated by wooden supports. They brought the craft to a hill, and Malcolm took the first crack at placing his arms and shoulders into the bottom of the glider while Elbert held the tail upright. The pair ran down the hill, and when Elbert let go of the tail, the craft flew upward. Malcolm only traveled a few feet, but the brothers' distances improved as they traded turns with the craft. On Malcolm's third attempt he covered a distance of more than 40 feet before crashing. (By comparison, the Wright brothers' first flight – with a motor-driven propeller – covered 120 feet.) Malcolm was unhurt, but the glider needed repairs.

The Tuttle brothers, Malcolm and Elbert, with their scale model of the 1903 Wright brothers' biplane, June 1910.

Later that week, the Pacific Commercial Advertiser of Honolulu ran a story on the Tuttle brothers under the headline "Honolulu's First Bird-Men Take to the Air." The author of the article wrote, "The Tuttle brothers of Honolulu have become the contemporaries of the Wright Brothers of Dayton, Ohio, and their names will be perpetuated in history as the first aviators of the Hawaiian Islands." Shortly thereafter Elbert and Malcolm repaired the glider, then used it in a Christmas program at their school. About two months after the Tuttles' first glider flights, a professional aviator became the first to fly a motorized airplane over Hawaii. Thereafter, the Tuttles were too busy with their studies to continue pursuing aircraft construction. Elbert, however, would put his knowledge to good use when he served in the Aviation Section of the Army Signal Corps during World War I. Perhaps more important, the Tuttles' designs inspired several local youths to take up aviation, and many of these Hawaiians went on to become renowned aviators in their own right.

Randolph W. Thrower, Herbert R. Elsas, and Elbert P. Tuttle, Sr. (left to right)

In retrospect, one of the founders' shrewdest decisions in the 1930s was the opening of the Washington office in 1937.

CHAPTER TWO

THE TAX PRACTICE EMERGES AND THE WASHINGTON OFFICE OPENS

As the 1930s dawned, the promising future of the talented young trio of Sutherland, Tuttle, and Brennan was threatened by the nation's flagging economy. American industrial productivity and investor confidence plummeted in these years, while unemployment shot up to 25%. Americans had had economic depressions before, but by the time Franklin D. Roosevelt took the oath of office in 1933, they were already giving this economic downturn pride of place as the "Great" Depression. At the local level, the downturn in the Atlanta economy meant that Atlantans had less disposable income and thus a diminished ability to pay for legal services. The stagnant business environment threatened to halt the growth of the Sutherland firm in its tracks.

Yet despite the nation's dire economic circumstances, unexpected legal opportunities abounded, and this decade saw the partners make significant steps toward taking the firm to the next level. In May 1931 Sutherland & Tuttle moved its offices from the Atlanta Trust Company Building to the newly enlarged and remodeled First National Bank Building. These new quarters provided more room for physical expansion. As for the expansion of *human* capital, three more future partners joined in these years as associates: Edward R. Kane (1934), Herbert R. Elsas (1935), and Randolph W. Thrower (1936). Another new associate, C. Norman Stallings (Harvard LL.B. 1938, LL.M. 1940), came on board to succeed Thrower in the Washington office upon the latter's return to Atlanta at the end of the decade. Kane and Stallings would depart the firm in the late 1940s, but Elsas and Thrower would remain for their entire careers.

These lawyers took on many duties in the 1930s, and they were frequently in the courtroom. Tuttle handled a number of important civil liberties cases, while Sutherland and Brennan represented textile mills in connection with their resistance to heavy cotton processing taxes. Sutherland also worked briefly as the solicitor general for the Tennessee Valley Authority (TVA) in 1933 and 1934 (see Ch. 14). Kane served on Sutherland's legal staff at the TVA before joining the firm as an associate, and Elsas and Thrower assisted the partners in a wide variety of cases.[1]

The partners also hired two valuable secretaries to assist their legal work. Audrey Taylor (née Phillips) and Doris Buchanan (née McLean) joined upon graduation from Commercial High School in Atlanta, and both went on to devote their entire careers to the firm. Taylor was hired in 1926 and was both the firm's bookkeeper and its secretary until her retirement in 1963. Buchanan came to the firm in 1928 and served as Joe Brennan's secretary until she retired in 1977.[2]

HERBERT ELSAS AND
RANDOLPH THROWER COME ABOARD

The two acquisitions from this period who would have the greatest future impact were Herbert Elsas and Randolph Thrower. Elsas (Harvard A.B. 1932, LL.B. 1935) was hired as an associate upon graduating from law school in 1935, but the firm's partners had realized his value much earlier. Elsas was not only a "double Harvard" – attending both the college and the law school – but also an Atlanta native and a member of the family that owned Fulton Bag and Cotton Mills, an important firm client. Sutherland and Tuttle thus took him on as their first summer associate in 1934. He was admitted to the bar of the Supreme Court of Georgia in 1936, and he became the firm's fourth partner in 1940.

Elsas would go on to act as a stabilizing force in the early years of the firm, a voice of moderation to balance the hotter tempers of Bill Sutherland and Ed Kane. He also became, for many years, the firm's "business lawyer." Bill Sutherland and Joe Brennan had little interest in everyday business details, but Elsas was willing to get involved in business management and planning. Elsas's family connections gave him entry to Atlanta's inner circle of leaders, while his intellect led these leaders to seek his counsel in return. As one Sutherland partner said many years later, "Herbert always knew what was going on behind the scenes in Atlanta, and this helped the firm immeasurably." Elsas also established estate and business planning as a practice beginning in the 1930s, and he was active in this area throughout his career. He went on to be the firm's managing partner for more than 20 years, and he was the longest-serving member of the management committee.

As for Randolph Thrower, although in hindsight it was a stroke of great fortune for the firm that he came onto the scene, Thrower himself felt he barely made the cut when he approached Tuttle and Sutherland for summer work during law school. He found that his chances were particularly hampered by one of his college activities. In his words:

I talked to Elbert Tuttle, and I'm sure I did not make a very good impression on Elbert, who was at that time in the National Guard. There had been a group of students at Emory who were proposing to conduct a strike on the campus for an hour or two, an antiwar protest. The dean of students was concerned about it and spoke to me, as president of the student body, to see if I could do anything to divert it. I persuaded [the students] that, instead of fruitlessly protesting on the campus, they should secure signatures for a petition and make a presentation to Congress. So they organized a little group…and I agreed to be the honorary chairman of the organization if they would not strike. They didn't have the strike; instead they filed the petition. Elbert had read about it in the paper, and he obviously did not appreciate what the students were doing, and so he talked more about that than engaging me. In any event, he said they didn't have any room. As I came to know him better later, he may have been chiding me, but not too sternly.[3]

Because Thrower did not get the nod from Sutherland, Tuttle & Brennan, he did summer work for the firm of Jones, Fuller, Russell & Clapp. He met once again with Bill Sutherland the following year, but although Sutherland was clearly interested in Thrower, the firm had already engaged a law student from Yale. Thrower then found employment with yet another "Jones" firm, the Macon firm of Jones, Johnson, Russell & Sparks. (These Joneses were the father and grandfather of future Sutherland firm partner Baxter Jones, Jr., who was killed in the Orly plane crash of 1962.) In the brief period Thrower was in Macon, he found the quaint antebellum town a congenial place for a young lawyer. "The only drawback," he reflected, "was that it was a politically very conservative and highly regimented firm."[4]

After Thrower had spent several months in Macon, Granger Hansell, one of his Emory Law School professors, persuaded him to return to Atlanta. As Hansell saw it, two factors would invariably prevent Thrower from realizing his full potential in Macon. For one, the Jones practice was a family firm with limited growth opportunities for an outside associate. But perhaps more important, the town of Macon was equally unlikely to grow beyond its provincial bounds. Hansell's words on this point were prophetic: "What you see in Macon now, you'll see in 50 years. Atlanta is where the action is." Hansell then dealt Thrower his ace in the hole. Sutherland and Tuttle were now interested in Thrower because their Yale graduate had not worked out. After this conversation, Thrower consulted with a close colleague at the Jones firm, and he, too, agreed that the opportunities in Atlanta would likely be better than in Macon. When Thrower returned to Atlanta to meet with Sutherland, Tuttle, and their wives, he wisely concluded that they were a group worth joining. Thrower went on to work mainly with Joe Brennan in the early years, honing his skills in the areas that would become his specialties: federal taxation, civil and criminal tax controversies, litigation, and estate planning and administration. Over time he became widely regarded as one of the leading tax practitioners in the 11th Circuit.[5]

THE WASHINGTON OFFICE

In retrospect, one of the founders' shrewdest decisions in the 1930s was the opening of the Washington office in 1937. Bill Sutherland's good friend General Harry Semmes offered Sutherland some office space in the suite occupied by his firm of patent lawyers, Semmes, Keegin & Semmes, in the Investment Building at 15th and K Street, NW. In light of the Washington office's growth in the postwar years, its opening now seems a remarkably understated affair. As Randolph Thrower quipped, "It was not what you would call a grand opening." Indeed, for its first decade or so, the Washington office was largely an outpost to facilitate the handling of tax and other federal matters for the Atlanta office. It was manned sporadically and only included one full-time secretary.[6]

Despite the opportunities available in Washington, Bill Sutherland had a difficult time getting any of the firm's partners or associates to permanently relocate. Virtually all of the lawyers spent some time in the city, but none were willing to uproot themselves and their families and spend the rest of their careers there. Sutherland eventually realized that he had to tackle this problem with a bold move of his own. He permanently relocated to Washington after the Second World War, and the office grew steadily from that point on.

Randolph Thrower spent the years from 1937 to 1940 shuttling back and forth between the two cities, and he did more work in Washington at this time than any of the firm's other lawyers. He later recalled that his work in Washington had not been a matter of personal choice: "I was the youngest person on the totem pole…and no one else would go. All the others were married, and so I was not asked, I was sent!" But he added, "It was like throwing Brer Rabbit into the briar bushes. I had a wonderful time in Washington, and I was kept busy." Thrower relished the life of a young man in the bustling city, which was only then beginning to grow into Pierre-Charles L'Enfant's original design. But after marrying in 1939, Thrower found the commute between the two cities to be too demanding. He returned to Atlanta for good in 1940, which greatly upset Bill Sutherland. Thrower later noted that Sutherland was not at all shy about getting involved in his employees' personal affairs. Fortunately the partners were able to make up the shortfall by hiring C. Norman Stallings to man the Washington office.[7]

THE EARLY WORK ENVIRONMENT

The Sutherland work environment in the early years was largely defined by Bill Sutherland's personal intensity. Unlike the even-tempered Elbert Tuttle, Sutherland was somewhat volatile by nature. According to Edith Elsas, "Bill thought fast, talked fast, and even walked fast. And if he liked you, you had it made." Whatever else could be said about Sutherland, he undoubtedly expected the absolute best from those around him, and he was able to channel his own passion for the law into a rigorous intellectual environment. Randolph Thrower once described how this atmosphere impressed him as a young associate:

I'd say that Bill knew no barriers whatsoever when it came to things that needed to be done, whether it was to move the president, or the Supreme Court, or Congress, or some other law firm. And many of his ideas, I would say, needed to be screened, and he used the other lawyers as a sounding board. He might have four or five that were not practical for the situation, but then he would have one that would win the case or prevail in the matter. It was a debating society with limited application of the Queensberry rules. To argue about questions that were intellectually challenging, legal questions, you had to be prepared to be insulted, shouted down, and Bill would escalate to whatever decibel level. But on the whole, while he would shout, he was also listening. And he would accept the judgment, if it seemed sound, of anyone. Age and rank were of no moment to him at all.[8]

Thrower emphasized that "the shouting was not in bad humor," but "there would be times when it would escalate. Bill tended to think anyone who could not understand his reasoning and accept what he had to say was either a fool or a knave. And he would try to convince you of your foolishness."

The other lawyers responded to Sutherland's "debating society" in different ways. Elbert Tuttle was more placid and was known to be much more precise in his expression with respect to legal matters. Sutherland rarely argued with Tuttle about the kind of refined legal issues that he would argue so vigorously with the others. Joe Brennan, meanwhile, could match any of his peers intellectually, though he was less likely than Sutherland to shout his opinions. Ed Kane, on the other hand, who had a sharp temper to match Sutherland's, frequently got into heated debates with the senior partner. The early partners were men of varied talents and temperaments, but future Sutherland, Asbill & Brennan partner Pat Patterson was able to succinctly describe the one thing these men had in common throughout these debates: "All these guys were smart as hell."[9]

In addition to his renowned intellect, Bill Sutherland was also admired for being a tireless worker. In Randolph Thrower's words, "He enjoyed life and he enjoyed friends…but he simply worked day and night." It went without saying that the firm's secretaries, Doris Buchanan and Audrey Taylor, would not think of planning an activity in the evening, or even on weekends, without first consulting Sutherland. This schedule was taken for granted. Thrower's recollection of one particular case illustrates the intensity of Sutherland's work ethic. "The day that we lost the *Anniston Manufacturing Company* case (1937), which was so deflating that I thought everyone would close the office and take to drink or something, Bill was back at the office that night working on something else. Bill and Joe were workaholics, and Herbert [Elsas] and I tried to keep up." Thrower added, "It didn't seem oppressive because it really was so exciting and so challenging. We all enjoyed it."[10] Elbert Tuttle, by contrast, kept more of a regular schedule in the 1930s and 1940s. He arrived at the office in the morning, went through his mail, dictated letters, went to the courthouse at 10 o'clock, tried cases, and left in the late afternoon. Sutherland and the associates, meanwhile, would remain in the office well into the evening.[11]

Treasury Annex – Washington, DC

EARLY TAX CASES

At the beginning of the 1930s, most of the firm's federal tax practice involved controversies either at the administrative level or in litigation. Typically a tax case was referred to the firm after a revenue agent had examined a return and proposed additional tax. The taxpayer then had 30 days to protest the proposed adjustments. The protest went to the commissioner in Washington, and if the taxpayer requested a hearing or conference, it would be accorded in the National Office of the Bureau of Internal Revenue.[12]

Before Sutherland, Tuttle & Brennan opened its Washington office in 1937, it was not feasible for the partners to make a special trip to the capital city for a conference in every tax case. The sheer number of trips would have been prohibitively expensive and time-consuming. Instead they customarily accumulated a number of protested cases and scheduled them for hearings or conferences seriatim. Sutherland and Brennan would then take the train to Washington for a week or more, usually staying at the Washington Hotel across from the Treasury. In those days the hotel clerks would not only take telephone messages for the guests, but also give callers information as to the guests' whereabouts and how to reach them by telephone. The partners considered this arrangement the next best thing to having a Washington office.

Conferences in protested tax cases were usually held in the Treasury Annex, across Pennsylvania Avenue from the Treasury. The offices of the general counsel of the Bureau of Internal Revenue were located in a separate building, some distance away at 19th and New York Avenue, NW. The general counsel had a somewhat broader function than the chief counsel would later have. Lawyers from the general counsel's office defended refund suits in the district courts as well as cases in the Board of Tax Appeals. In such litigated cases, conferences and negotiations for stipulation or settlement were normally held with the general counsel's staff in Washington.

When tax refund suits were filed in the court of claims, the Justice Department handled the government's defense. In those days the Justice Department was located on Vermont Avenue just north of K Street, and taxpayers' lawyers had conferences there not only for court of claims cases, but also in matters under the jurisdiction of the solicitor general. On a number of occasions Sutherland and Brennan pressed the solicitor general's office to acquiesce in a taxpayer's petition for certiorari, or to accept a lower court's decision against the government.

Most of the firm's early tax cases came on referral from other lawyers or accountants. Few lawyers then would even look at a federal income tax case, as they considered these to be matters for accountants. In a sense the accountants had a monopoly on this work. A typical such situation for the firm came about when an accountant prepared an income tax return. If the revenue agent raised questions about the return, the taxpayer naturally referred the matter to his accountant, who undertook to handle the taxpayer's case through the administrative stage. If the accountant had been admitted to practice before the Board of Tax Appeals, he or she could take cases there. The more responsible and reputable accountants recognized that they would be at a disadvantage in settlement negotiations if they took cases there with the expectation of settling before trial. These accountants generally recommended that their taxpayer clients look to legal counsel in important matters that might get into litigation. Accountants who were familiar with the Sutherland firm's tax reputation would recommend the firm to their clients or to their clients' regular counsel. This was the source of some of the firm's important tax cases for many years.

OTHER FIRMS' CASES

The firm occasionally got involved in litigation in order to protect the interests of a client who was not himself a party to the lawsuit. In some such cases the firm volunteered its help to counsel of record, while in others it filed amicus briefs, participated as associate counsel, or even served as lead counsel. The following two cases were taken up by the firm in order to help the counsel of record.

The first case in which the firm filed a brief in the U.S. Supreme Court was *Old Colony Trust Co. v. Commissioner* (279 U.S. 712 (1929)). The Court had raised a question as to the jurisdiction of the circuit courts of appeals to review decisions of the Board of Tax Appeals. Both parties to the case supported jurisdiction, and the ABA's Committee on Federal Income Taxation filed an amicus brief in support of jurisdiction. The firm filed its brief against jurisdiction in the hope of getting its client, Richmond Hosiery Mills, a chance to re-litigate an issue that another lawyer had lost in the Board of Tax Appeals and in the Fifth Circuit.

Sutherland and Brennan finished the amicus brief in a drawing room on a train from Atlanta to Washington. Upon arriving in the early morning hours they gave the

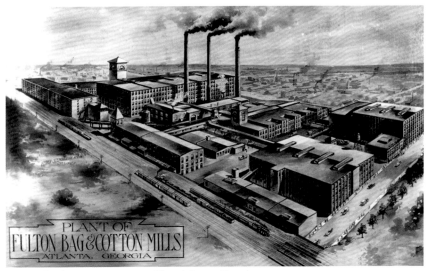

Plant of Fulton Bag & Cotton Mills – Atlanta, Georgia

manuscript to a print shop and received the printed copies just in time to file when the Court sat at noon for argument. Sutherland moved in open court for leave to file the brief, which was granted. He then moved to participate in the oral argument, which was denied by the genial chief justice and former president of the United States, William Howard Taft. The Court decided, eight to one, in favor of jurisdiction.

The case of *Maas & Waldstein v. United States* (283 U.S. 583 (1931)) was typical of those handled by the Sutherland firm for another firm's client, though its outcome was uncharacteristic. In order to protect a Sutherland client's case then pending in the court of claims (*Fulton Bag & Cotton Mills v. United States*, 57 F. 2d 914), the firm took over this case, in which the Supreme Court had just decided the same question against the taxpayer. With the consent of counsel in *Maas & Waldstein*, Sutherland filed a petition for rehearing, pointing out that original counsel had waived oral argument over the second counsel's "strenuous protest," and that if the case had been argued orally, "it is inconceivable that the Court would have fallen into the grievous error." Sutherland's petition showed that the firm's interest in the case was to see that its client, Fulton Bag, would not be "deprived of the right to have the questions properly argued before this Court." He pointed to a very early precedent in *Green v. Biddle* (1823), in which a motion for rehearing was filed by a man who was not attorney of record for any of the parties in the case. The man who had filed the motion for rehearing was, in Sutherland's words, among "other parties who were prejudiced by the lack of proper presentation of the question" there involved. But whereas the 1823 motion had been granted, Sutherland's 1931 motion was not.

STATUTE OF LIMITATIONS CASES

The firm filed many amicus briefs in the Supreme Court and other courts during these early years. While these were not always effective, the firm's partners felt this practice succeeded in building their reputation as a group of well-rounded lawyers who were better equipped to handle important tax cases than the so-called tax specialists to whom many of the large law firms had been referring their tax cases.

Much of the Sutherland clients' tax litigation during the firm's first two decades can be understood by reviewing two series of cases. One series, to be described in the next chapter, centered on the processing tax imposed by the Agricultural Adjustment Act of 1933. The other group, to be covered here, involved the statute of limitations.

In the late 1920s and early 1930s the statute of limitations in tax cases was the source of much litigation. A new revenue act had been passed on the average of every two years from 1916 through the 1930s, a time period which linked the Progressive reform era of Woodrow Wilson to the New Deal era of Franklin Delano Roosevelt. The revised acts spawned many successive changes in the limitation periods applicable to assessment and collection of tax and to claims and suits for refund. The resulting confusion created fertile ground for the kind of litigation in which the firm would regularly participate.

The firm litigated a variety of such cases. Some involved statutory construction, while others involved equitable relief against waivers on grounds of misrepresentation or mutual mistake (see, for example, *J.P. Stevens Engraving Co. v. U.S.*, 53 F. 2d 1 (5th Cir. 1931) and *Clifton Mfg. Co. v. U.S.*, 76 F. 2d 577 (4th Cir. 1935)). Several cases involved Section 611 of the Revenue Act of 1928, which protected the Treasury from having to refund millions of dollars in taxes that had been collected after the expiration of the limitation period that the courts had held to be applicable. But the most significant group of such Section 611 cases for the firm was decided by the Supreme Court in 1931 under the name *Graham & Foster v. Goodcell* (282 U.S. 409).

Graham & Foster v. Goodcell

Taxpayers had an established right to maintain an action for the recovery of income taxes on the grounds that they had been collected after the expiration of the statutory period. Many such claims were pending when the 1928 Revenue Act was signed into law. Section 611 of that act undertook to deny the right to refund in cases where there had been a timely assessment, followed by a claim in abatement, and delay in collection beyond the limitation period. A broad attack on Section 611 followed, in which the taxpayers either claimed that the section should not apply to their cases or argued that it was unconstitutional.

A group of these cases reached the Supreme Court in 1930, and although none of the Sutherland firm's cases had progressed far enough to be included, Bill Sutherland had a key role in presenting oral arguments for the taxpayers. Sutherland's involvement began when a Washington tax lawyer lost several cases in the court of claims. This lawyer was happy to let the Sutherland firm take over one of them for petition to the Supreme Court. Sutherland filed the petition for certiorari in that case on behalf of the Second National Bank of Saginaw. The petition was granted and this case was included in the group of nine cases that were set for argument in December 1930. The oral arguments extended over four days, and Sutherland was one of eight lawyers arguing for the taxpayers. He used the entire time allotted to him, and in the judgment of his associate, he made the most forceful and lucid presentation of the taxpayers' position. The lawyer in one of the cases to follow was so impressed that he asked Sutherland to argue his case as well.

Sutherland claimed that Section 611 was unconstitutional on the grounds that the taxpayer had a vested right of action to recover taxes illegally collected. Section 611 purported to destroy that right, contrary to the due process clause of the Fifth Amendment. In so arguing, Sutherland had to prepare for two possible defenses to his contention. One was a defense of sovereign immunity to suit: that the United States cannot be sued without its consent, and it can withdraw its consent for any reason. Sutherland's response was that Section 611 did not purport to assert sovereign immunity to suit. In some of the cases before the Court the taxpayer had sued the Collector of Internal Revenue, who had made the illegal collection, and that was not a suit against the United States. The Supreme Court ultimately refused to accept the defense of sovereign immunity.

The other avenue of defense for the government was based on the theory that Section 611 was curative legislation of a kind previously upheld, where government agents acting under a mistaken view of the law had made unauthorized collections that Congress later undertook to ratify. The firm tried unsuccessfully to distinguish those cases, and the Court, in a carefully prepared opinion by Chief Justice Hughes, upheld the validity of Section 611 on the theory of the early precedents. This decision in the *Graham* case came in January 1931.

Before the Supreme Court's decision, the firm succeeded in getting favorable settlements in some cases involving Section 611, and in at least one such suit for refund the government paid in full (*McEachern v. Rose*, 302 U.S. 56 (1937)). One of the firm's cases for the Clifton Manufacturing Company resulted in a similarly profitable outcome (*Clifton Mfg. Co. v. U.S., 293 U.S. 186 (1934)*).

From a financial standpoint, the firm's experience in the Section 611 cases was mixed. In these early years the firm usually took such tax cases for some fixed retainer plus a percentage of recovery or savings. Under the rules of the Bureau of Internal Revenue, such partially contingent fees were proper, provided that the retainer was substantial (meaning at least 10%) in relation to the total possible fee. Unless the firm won a case, it was usually underpaid for its time. However, when the Sutherland lawyers *did* win, they considered themselves very well paid, indeed.

BIOGRAPHIES

HERBERT R. ELSAS (1910-1995)

Like the Sutherland firm's founders, **Herbert Rothschild Elsas** proved himself a gifted student at a young age. At 13, he left Atlanta to attend Phillips Academy in Andover, Massachusetts. He later spent three years overseas as an intelligence officer in the 8th Air Force during World War II, work for which he earned the Legion of Merit award. Among his more notable contributions to the legal field, he was active in the ABA sections of Taxation and Real Property, Probate, and Trust, and he founded the Fiduciary Law Section of the Georgia Bar Association. He was for many years an adjunct professor of taxation at Emory Law School, and he served for several years on the board of directors of both Springs Mills and the Loxcreen Company. He was also active in Atlanta social service and cultural organizations, including a long stint as an officer in the Atlanta Symphony Guild and leadership positions in the Family Service Association of America, the Atlanta Community Chest, and the Lovett School. He and his wife, Edith Levy, had two children.[15]

Another of Elsas's more noteworthy roles was as a mentor to the younger lawyers in the firm. He helped many up-and-coming Sutherland lawyers improve their abilities at every level, from simple tasks to complex legal matters. Partner George Cohen said of Elsas, "When I was a young lawyer [he] thought my writing was a bit stilted, so he undertook the effort of polishing it a bit, and coached me in ways to sharpen my writing and argumentation." Cohen added, "Herbert was an amazingly accomplished lawyer." Elsas also led by example. Partner Pat Patterson called him "a superb businessman with a businessman's instincts and appreciation for legal problems. He certainly gave the firm a leadership position in the legal community in estate planning."

For many years Herbert and Edith Elsas went far out of their way to make the firm's younger lawyers feel at home in the firm and in Atlanta. Edith, said Sutherland partner Mike Egan, "was always one of the stars of the firm." The couple regularly held parties at their Paces Ferry Road home, to which all Sutherland lawyers and many unofficial "friends of the firm" were invited (the firm was much smaller then, of course). "She and Herbert did so much," said Patterson, "to make life in the law firm livable and lovable, if you will, for young lawyers. They entertained extensively. They went to great lengths to make the young people in the firm feel

The Ultimate Skins Game:
The IRS Takes On Golf Legend Bobby Jones

Atlanta native Robert Tyre "Bobby" Jones, Jr. was not only the greatest golfer of his time, but also a lawyer. Jones's father, Colonel Robert P. Jones, was a partner at Jones, Evins & Moore, and young Bobby managed to study and practice law while maintaining an unmatched record on the tournament circuit. Late in his life, the exceedingly modest Jones would indulge his acquaintances with stories about his toughest opponents on the golf course, but he never talked about the one opponent he could not beat: the tax man.[13]

In 1930, after winning all four of golf's grand slam tournaments, the 28-year-old Jones decided to take on some new challenges. Among his more ambitious plans was to design the nation's premier links at Augusta, Georgia, and to make a series of instructional movies titled "How I Play Golf." It was this latter venture that would get him into trouble. In November 1930 Warner Bros. agreed to pay Jones $120,000, plus 50% of the net receipts from distribution, for 12 films. This seemed a lucrative deal to Jones, who, as an amateur, had never accepted prize money for any of his numerous victories. He soon realized, however, that he would face a considerable federal tax on this income, and he decided to solicit help from the Sutherland firm.[14]

Bill Sutherland and Joe Brennan advised Jones to recast the transaction by a series of substitute contracts. Following their advice, Jones permitted his father, Colonel Jones, to take over the original contract and receive the proceeds. Jones would then appear in the films under a personal services contract with the Colonel. Since Warner had paid Bobby Jones $20,000 up front, the film studio would agree to pay the remaining $100,000 to the Colonel as trustee for Bobby's three children. The first 12 films were completed in 1931, and the following year the Colonel signed a $55,000 supplemental contract with Warner Bros. for a similar arrangement to make six new films entitled "How to Break 90."

The two film series were remarkably successful. An estimated 20 to 30 million moviegoers in 6,000 theaters saw the "How I Play Golf" series alone. They were so successful, in fact, that the local Internal Revenue agent in Atlanta could not help but wonder why Bobby Jones's 1931 and 1933 tax returns seemed so "light." After a brief investigation, the agency assessed additional income taxes of more than $50,000, which Jones paid under protest in 1936. The Sutherland firm then filed suit on behalf of Jones for a refund in U.S. District Court for the Middle District of Georgia, and the case was set for trial in Macon on February 3, 1938.

Although a simple affair, the trial took some interesting turns. Sutherland argued that the form of the transaction had been more important than the substance. He used two key witnesses – Bobby and the Colonel – to show the court that, because the Colonel had provided "moral and material assistance over a great number of years in the development of Plaintiff's ability as a golfer," it was "only fair that his father be given an opportunity to participate in whatever earning might accrue from these services."

Bobby Jones

The government, meanwhile, was represented by Mills Kitchens, a special assistant to Attorney General Homer S. Cummings. (Incidentally, future Sutherland firm partner Mac Asbill, Sr. was also serving as a special assistant to Cummings at this time.) Kitchens relied on the 1930 Supreme Court decision in *Charles A. Corliss v. Bowers*, in which the Court argued that income "subject to a man's unfettered command" is taxable to him "whether he sees fit to enjoy it or not." Kitchens argued that Jones's personal services contract to make the films was an agreement that the Colonel could not have fulfilled. The Colonel, he asserted, was only a conduit through which the income was passed to Bobby's children. Kitchens further insinuated, though he could not prove, that Bill Sutherland had organized the numerous contracts and trusts in a single scheme merely to duck the mandated taxes.

Then came an episode that ensured this case would leave a lasting mark in the annals of both law and sports. In a move that shows just how informal the law could be in Macon in the 1930s, Judge Bascom S. Deaver adjourned the court at the end of the first day and the group retired to the nearby Idle Hour Golf Course for a match. Prosecutor Kitchens and Judge Deaver took on Jones and "Uncle Joe" Neel, Deaver's 80-year-old weekly playing partner, in a best ball Nassau game. Jones sportingly agreed to spot his opponents one stroke per hole. He was, after all, going to have to face them in the courtroom the following morning. Jones was still one of the most popular celebrities of the day, so the unusual match drew a large crowd. When Judge Deaver won the first hole, a spectator called out, "Judge, if you enter an order declaring the match over right now, you'll always be able to say you beat Bobby Jones!" In the end, however, although Jones had not played for several months, he managed to win most of the holes on his way to shooting a two-over-par 72.

Unfortunately for Jones, he was not as lucky in the courtroom. Judge Deaver decided against him on June 15, 1938 (*Robert T. Jones, Jr. v. Page* (102 F. 2d 144)). The judge argued, "There could be no question as to the taxability of such income to the plaintiff" if Jones had, indeed, assigned his future income to his father. "This," continued Deaver, "is exactly what he did do, notwithstanding the circuitous and intervening devices" established by his tax attorneys. Was this Jones's punishment for having beaten Deaver on the golf course? Probably not, for irrespective of Deaver's motives, the Fifth Circuit Court of Appeals affirmed the ruling, and Bill Sutherland's certiorari petition to the U.S. Supreme Court was denied on October 30, 1939.

welcome." Herbert and Edith also taught those coming into the firm a great deal about professionalism. Patterson recalled, "They set an excellent example for young lawyers coming along, and for young partners, as to how they should comport themselves in terms of firm governance and firm participation."[16]

RANDOLPH W. THROWER (1913-)

It would be difficult to exaggerate the professional and personal accomplishments of **Randolph Thrower**. Like the firm's founders, Thrower had a long career that included an array of public and private services. He was renowned for his ingenuity and his diligence in pursuing cases, and he commanded the respect of his peers for his interpersonal skills and his knowledge of tax law.

The Tampa-born, Atlanta-reared Thrower graduated from Emory University and the Emory Law School (J.D., first honors, 1936) and joined the firm in 1936. Thereafter, his performance in the legal realm was exceptional. His most prestigious positions included his service as U.S. Commissioner of Internal Revenue under President Nixon from 1969 to 1971 and his stint as president of the American Bar Foundation. He also served for 17 years as a member of the ABA House of Delegates and was a trustee of the Lawyer's Committee for Civil Rights Under Law for three decades. He chaired the ABA's Section of Taxation and the Special Committee on Survey of Legal Needs, and he served as president of the Atlanta Bar Association, the Atlanta Lawyers Club, and the Atlanta Legal Aid Society.[17]

In addition to his service in the legal profession, Thrower sat on committees for the City of Atlanta and several universities. He chaired the Atlanta Ethics Committee, the Fulton County Advisory Board on Mental Health, and the Metropolitan Atlanta and Georgia Mental Health Associations. He served as trustee on the boards of Clark College and Reinhardt College, chair of the board of Wesleyan College in Macon, and emeritus trustee of Emory University.

Thrower also earned many professional and civic awards throughout his career. In 1984 his longtime association with Emory University led to the university's awarding of an honorary LL.D. In 1993 he received the American Bar Association Medal, the ABA's highest honor, for his extensive public, professional, and government service. (Warren Burger, Felix Frankfurter, Thurgood Marshall, and Oliver Wendell Holmes are

Randolph Thrower in Macon

Randolph Thrower liked to tell the story of an amusing incident that took place while he was with the Jones firm in Macon. The anecdote says much about the moral code of the time, the place, and the Jones firm:

Macon in the summer was hot, especially on the top floor of the building where the firm had its offices. The office of the principal partner with whom I worked had two attractions for me. First, being one of the more progressive partners, he had an oscillating electric fan. Second, he kept a clean desk, so I could easily move my law books and papers into his office for evening work. One such evening I was working at his desk, and as usual, had taken off my coat and tie…it was dreadfully hot, even with the windows open and the fan turned on. The cleaning crew had finished its chores so I felt safe in slipping off my pants.

Later my concentration was broken when I heard the front door of the office open. I looked longingly at my trousers, but they were too far away to be retrieved. A moment later one of the younger partners, a [Jones] family member, appeared at my door, and we exchanged greetings. All seemed well, but before I could stop him, he then turned and called, "Come here, dear. I want you to meet the young man in the office I've been telling you about." In response to his introduction, I half rose from my chair in recognition and then sat down. After we conversed briefly, he said to his wife and me, "Continue talking while I look at something on my desk."

She and I carried on an animated conversation to the point where I was inwardly congratulating myself on such sophistication. Then she said, "It looks like he's going to take all night. I think I'll sit down." She headed for a chair behind the line of sight of my desk. I could not think of any suitable way to divert her. All my feigned sophistication disappeared and I threw up my hands like a traffic officer and said, "Stop." She looked startled. Then I confessed, "I don't have my pants on." She recoiled to the door as if shot out of a cannon. We carried on a chilly conversation until, what seemed like ages later, her husband returned. Two days after this, the firm's very nice, but very proper, office and personnel manager asked me in hushed tones, "Is it true what I've heard?" I said, "Yes." Her only response was a deep sigh. That is all I ever heard from anybody about the incident.

Although Thrower soon left to join the Sutherland firm, he retained strong ties to both Macon and the Jones firm. In addition, he later recalled that the "pants" episode taught him an important lesson: "Keep your wits about you and don't be too casual in your dress."[22]

Edward R. Kane

Although Edward R. Kane (Vanderbilt LL.B. 1933) was only with the Sutherland firm for a decade and a half (1934-1948), he was a crucial member in the firm's early days. He proved himself a skilled debater and a quick study in tax and business law, and he gave valuable assistance to the partners in a variety of matters. He was wounded in action in World War II, and after the war he left the Sutherland firm to join the Atlanta firm of Jones, Bird & Howell.

Like Bill Sutherland, Ed Kane was known for his quick temper. Randolph Thrower once recounted an anecdote, told to him by an amused Elbert Tuttle, that illustrated Kane's preference for settling disagreements quickly, and sometimes painfully:

> On one occasion, Ed Kane was driving Elbert home. Now, Ed had a volatile temper, and he and Bill Sutherland [had been] arguing about legal matters. Driving home somebody offended Ed, or Ed offended someone else. At any rate, they came to a stop sign and Ed rolled down his window and he called over to the other fellow, did he want to make something out of it. The other gentleman said, "Yes," he would. So Ed said, "Follow me," and they drove over to Piedmont Park. They got out, Ed took off his coat and tie and handed them to Elbert to hold for him, and then the two went into a brief exchange of fisticuffs and wrestling, and ended up on the ground. Ed had the other fellow down and pretty well whipped. Ed then said, "Have you had enough?" The other fellow said, "Yes," so they got up, brushed themselves off, and shook hands. Ed took his coat and tie back. They returned to his car, he drove Elbert home, and never said one word about it to Elbert, as if this were just as casual as running into a grocery store to make a purchase.

Thrower added with greatly understated wit, "Ed was a remarkable, bright person, but a little volatile. I always liked Ed very much."[21]

among the past recipients of this award.) In 1995 he was given the Court of Federal Claims Special Service Award in recognition of his many contributions to the court. He received the 1998 Ben F. Johnson, Jr. Public Service Award from Georgia State University College of Law, and in 1999 he received the John Wesley Award from Reinhardt College. That same year he received the Lifetime Anti-Defamation League Achievement Award, as well as a special tribute from the Atlanta Legal Aid Society on the occasion of the society's 75th anniversary. At the 2003 11th Circuit Judicial Conference, Judge Susan Black presented him with the American Inns of Court Professionalism Award for the 11th Circuit in recognition of his lifelong professional, intellectual, and moral leadership.[18]

Thrower's superlative ethical standard was unmatched, as time and again he proved his ability to choose what was right over what may have been temporarily expedient. This was true in the 1950s when he unsuccessfully tried to end racial discrimination in Atlanta Bar Association membership. It was also true when, as IRS commissioner, he refused to allow White House officials to use the IRS to attack their political enemies (see Ch. 7). Thrower's reputation as an "untouchable" spread far and wide, and he was often called upon to mediate or investigate when ethical issues arose. As Atlanta Bar Association president he helped put in motion a far-reaching investigation of corruption in the administration of Governor Marvin Griffin. He also co-chaired a probe of cheating allegations in police promotion exams, a role that led to his appointment as chairman of the city's ethics committee.[19]

Any number of Sutherland lawyers could testify to Thrower's abundant legal talents and interpersonal skills. "You'd be hard-pressed," said one partner, "to find anyone who could say a bad word about Randolph Thrower." More than one has also marveled at Thrower's ability to push his younger colleagues almost as hard as he pushed himself. When Thrower invited a group of lawyers to his home on Sunday afternoons for a leisurely "swim," the invitees always knew that the gesture was really a thinly veiled enticement to getting work done. "He'd never ask the associates to work harder than he did," said former Atlanta managing partner Bill Bradley. "The problem was keeping up with him." Bradley spoke for many when he called Thrower "an extraordinarily bright lawyer. A brilliant lawyer. He's somebody who sees the whole field. He just sees it all." Incidentally, those who visited Thrower's home also marveled at his second-rate bartending skills. Said one anonymous partner, "He mixed light. He would have a gin and tonic and a scotch and soda on the tray, and you couldn't tell them apart!"

By all accounts, Thrower truly cared about the people he worked with, and he spent countless hours reviewing, reworking, and debating matters with the other lawyers on a case. "He'd go over a long document," said Bradley, "which I thought was perfect, and he'd say, 'I have a few comments I want to go over.' Well, he'd have more than a few comments. He would have already internalized the entire document. I couldn't have been luckier than to have somebody like that to work with."[20]

～

July 28, 1933: Postmaster J. J. Kiely holds NRA (National Recovery Administration) "We Do Our Part" posters.

While at first the NIRA seemed to foster harmony within industries, it soon began to look more like a hindrance to growth, and prospective court challenges mounted.

CHAPTER THREE

THE FIRM CHALLENGES THE NEW DEAL:
THE PROCESSING TAX CASES

P resident Roosevelt's New Deal led to an unprecedented expansion of the federal government, and this benefited the firm in unexpected ways. New Deal legislation created a barrage of bureaus and laws aimed at alleviating the misery of the Depression and rebuilding Americans' confidence in the financial structure. This federal expansion proved ripe for two major challenges: constitutional law and tax law.

Although the Atlanta lawyers were reluctant to uproot themselves and move north, Washington was too important to ignore. The impetus for opening the Washington office was the "processing tax" caseload of the New Deal 1930s. These cases were a tremendous boon to the fledgling firm and involved a great deal of profitable litigation for its cotton mill clients. Some of these cases also sent the Sutherland lawyers into the Supreme Court. Interestingly, although the processing tax cases involved millions of dollars, Sutherland was virtually the only Southern firm capable of handling them. Since these cases were so lucrative, and so critical to the firm's survival, it is worth telling their story in some detail.[1]

THE AAA

Processing taxes were imposed under the Agricultural Adjustment Act (AAA) of 1933, which was a product of President Roosevelt's famous first "Hundred Days" of legislation (also known as the "First New Deal"). In this First New Deal, the federal government sought to remedy the financial crisis and instill confidence in the financial system, while also providing immediate relief through agencies like the Public Works Administration (PWA) and acts like the AAA. The PWA provided public works employment for masses of unemployed men, but the AAA had a different mandate. It was designed to cut excess production of agricultural products and to provide increased income to farmers by granting them subsidies, which were financed by taxes on the processing of the same commodities. It was enacted in May 1933, and became effective as to cotton on August 1, 1933.

The AAA processing tax was imposed on the first domestic processing of cotton and certain other basic commodities, such as peanuts and hogs. But while the amounts charged to producers of other commodities were more or less manageable, the amounts payable by cotton mills were shockingly high. To wit, the tax on cotton averaged around 4 cents a pound at a time when cotton was selling at between 9 and 10 cents a pound. Cotton growers in the South commonly referred to the processing tax on cotton as the Cotton Farmer's Tariff. So while the firm represented only a handful of hog and peanut processors, it represented upwards of 30 textile mills. The firm attained good results when it litigated the few peanut cases, and it was able to get a satisfactory out-of-court settlement in the hog producers' cases. But the cotton cases were the ones in which the greatest amounts of money were at stake, and thus were the source of the most work.[2]

The amounts in question were enormous for their day. Between 1933 and 1935, the federal government collected around $600 million in processing taxes under the AAA. Furthermore, when the Supreme Court eventually ruled the act unconstitutional, Congress said reimbursement could only take place if it could be shown that the economic burden of the tax had been borne by the taxpayer. On those amounts that had been withheld, a windfall tax of 80% was imposed on the amount shifted by the taxpayer to others. These two economic issues – the AAA tax and the related windfall tax – involved hundreds of millions of dollars, and thus gave the firm several years of profitable work.[3]

There seemed to be a substantial basis for challenging the constitutionality of the tax when the AAA was passed in 1933, but few were in a rush to litigate the question. The Sutherland firm anticipated the probability of such litigation and accordingly undertook to advise its clients to preserve their rights by timely refund claims. The firm also suggested payment under protest, although this had not been necessary to sue for refund since the 1924 Revenue Act. As it turned out, though, payment under protest added strength to some of the firm's arguments on consti-tutional grounds during actual litigation.[4]

For the client Fulton Bag and Cotton Mills, the firm carefully prepared a written protest specifically detailing the constitutional defects in the AAA and the processing tax, and this was submitted alongside the first monthly payment of tax. The firm had for several years handled tax matters for other cotton mills in Georgia and South Carolina, and it also advised them at the outset of the AAA to take steps to preserve their rights to contest the validity of the processing tax. The firm filed timely claims for refund, with an eye toward filing suits at an appropriate time.

Before the Supreme Court decided any of the AAA processing tax cases, an interesting development arose from one of the Sutherland firm's injunction cases. The firm filed suit for Stonewall Cotton Mills in the district court in Mississippi in August 1935 seeking to enjoin collection of the tax, but the district judge denied the injunction and dismissed the complaint. The firm then appealed to the Fifth Circuit Court of Appeals. The judges there refused to stay collection of the processing taxes pending hearing on the merits. While the firm's case was pending in the Fifth Circuit, and before the hearing there, the firm planned to file a petition for certiorari with the U.S. Supreme Court and seek a stay from a Supreme Court justice. (The law at the time authorized certiorari to review cases pending in a court of appeals before or after rendition of judgment there.)

The Sutherland firm then had the clerk of the Fifth Circuit transmit the record to Bill Sutherland's friend, Supreme Court clerk Elmore Cropley. Sutherland and Brennan traveled to Washington and, with Cropley's help, did some quick research on procedures. Ordinarily the firm would have had to approach Justice Benjamin Cardozo, the circuit justice for the Fifth Circuit. But the Court was in recess and Justice Cardozo was in upstate New York. This gave Sutherland and Brennan a chance to try Justice McReynolds, a well-known opponent of the New Deal.[5]

Justice McReynolds

Sutherland arranged to see Justice McReynolds to sound him out before filing the petition. He found that McReynolds was willing, and the firm was thus able to file and present the formal papers to him the next day. Sutherland, Brennan, and their cohorts worked late into the night preparing their argument, but before they could proceed, the president of Stonewall called Sutherland and told him to drop the matter. As it turned out, Stonewall was owned by Crown Overall Company, and Crown's president said that, as suppliers to the American working man, they could not afford to take

Justice Cardozo

the lead in fighting the New Deal. Needless to say, Sutherland and Brennan were disappointed at losing their chance to get the first injunction case to the Supreme Court, but they heeded their client's wishes nevertheless.

In the end, the first court case in which the validity of the processing tax was challenged grew out of an equity receivership in the Massachusetts District Court. The receivers for Hoosac Mills asked the court to disallow the government's claim for unpaid processing taxes on cotton. In October 1934 the district court held the processing tax valid and allowed the government's claim. (8 F. Supp. 552). The receivers appealed to the First Circuit Court of Appeals, and that court held the AAA unconstitutional and the processing tax invalid on July 13, 1935 (*Butler et al., Receivers for Hoosac Mills v. United States*, 78 F. 2d 1). The Supreme Court affirmed on January 6, 1936 (297 U.S. 1). One week later the Court decided *Rickert Rice Mills v. Fontenot* (297 U.S. 110), holding that taxpayers were entitled to enjoin the collection of such taxes. The full implications of the Supreme Court's decision remained to be seen, but soon thereafter the funds that had been impounded in the district courts were returned to the firm's clients.[6]

THE REFUND CONTROVERSY

Well before the First Circuit's 1935 *Butler* decision, the Department of Agriculture had become concerned over the possibility that the AAA might be held unconstitutional.[7] The Treasury, meanwhile, had grown equally worried about the possibility of having to refund hundreds of millions of dollars of already-collected processing taxes. Congress therefore proposed a bill that would deny processing tax refunds unless the claimant could establish that he had neither included the amount of the tax in the price of the article nor passed on any part of the tax to his vendee. In other words, the law would restrict the refunds to only that amount which could be shown to have been a burden, and in which the economic burden of the tax was born by the taxpayer. Since there was simply no precedent for that kind of restriction upon a vested right of refund, the Sutherland firm decided to claim a vested right was being violated by the ruling, and thus challenge the constitutionality of the restrictions on the recovery.[8]

Up until the time this proposed amendment was offered in Congress, the firm was convinced that there would be no basis for enjoining the collection of the tax. Section 3224 of the Revised Statutes clearly provided that no suit should be maintained in any court to restrain the assessment or collection of any tax. Besides, the traditional method of testing the validity of a tax was to pay it and sue for refund. There was an adequate remedy at law, which made equitable relief inappropriate.

In June and July 1935 the firm brought suits against the Collectors of Internal Revenue in Georgia and South Carolina to enjoin any further collection of the processing tax. The firm also obtained temporary injunctions before the First Circuit decided the *Butler* case and before Congress finally passed the laws restricting the right to processing tax refunds. Other Southern law firms filed similar suits on behalf of their clients, and a number of other taxpayers brought their cases to the Sutherland firm.

The court ruled that the restriction was justifiable, provided it was possible to show the extent to which the economic burden was shifted or borne. As a condition to granting equitable relief in these cases the courts generally required the taxpayers to continue filing monthly processing tax returns and to pay the disputed amount of taxes, to be held pending the final determination of constitutionality.

Sutherland, Brennan, and Thrower took the reins for the Sutherland clients. For many months the work was a burden to the firm because the team only received small retainers, while their fees were contingent upon the eventual recovery. Recovery was often years away, but current expenses had to be met. So on payday Sutherland and Tuttle would go over the books to get a sense of the firm's immediate needs, then go to the bank and borrow enough money to meet the payroll.[9]

Once the taxes began to be refunded, the financial results of the injunction cases made 1936 a banner year for the firm, as indeed it was for the textile industry as a whole. In addition, the processing tax era continued, so to speak, because the firm still had the suits for refund to prosecute. These also proved very profitable.

The firm had filed its first suits for refund for Covington Mills, Canton Cotton Mills, and a few others in the Middle District of Georgia, the legal residence of the defendant Collector of Internal Revenue. Since the refund amounts claimed were large, newspapers widely reported on the filing of these suits. This publicity brought the firm a number of new cases and bolstered its stature in the Southeast.[10]

Other New Deal Tax Litigation: The Revenue Act

The firm's suits for refund of processing taxes were filed against the Collectors of Internal Revenue, and such suits were pending in the district courts when, in June 1936, Congress enacted the latest Revenue Act. This act was a follow-on to the 1935 Revenue Act, which was colloquially referred to as the "soak the rich" tax because it dramatically raised the tax rate on higher incomes. By this point the New Deal brain trust had concluded that economic recovery would be speeded by a dramatic increase in government spending and a concomitant rise in income tax rates.

The Sutherland firm's clients had a more specific set of interests with regard to the 1936 Act. Among other provisions, the act provided that no Collector of Internal Revenue should be liable for the collection of any tax under the AAA. It also established a Processing Tax Board of Review in the Treasury Department to hear cases where the commissioner of Internal Revenue had disallowed claims for refund of processing taxes, and it gave the Circuit Court of Appeals jurisdiction to review decisions of the Processing Tax Board of Review. The 1936 Revenue Act also rephrased and enlarged the restrictions on refunds that had been added to the AAA by amendment in August 1935. Most significantly for Sutherland's clients, the act provided that no processing tax refund should be allowed unless the claimant established to the satisfaction of the commissioner that he bore the burden of the amount. It also created a presumption for determining whether and to what extent the processor shifted the burden of the tax by comparing gross profit margins during the tax period with such margins for a specified period before and after the tax.

In the firm's refund suits it took the position that the plaintiffs had a vested right of action against the Collector to recover the full amount of processing taxes illegally collected, and that this right could not be impaired without violating the Fifth Amendment. The firm contended that the 1936 Act put an impossible burden of proof on the processors since there was no way of determining the extent to which the economic burden of the tax had been shifted. In the case of a cotton mill the question would be what price the mill would have paid for its cotton and what price it would have received for its goods if the processing tax had never been imposed. These were matters that were not susceptible of proof, and the provisions of the 1936 Act therefore operated to impair the taxpayer's right to a refund of the tax even to the extent that the taxpayer bore the burden of the tax.

Anniston Mfg. Co. v. Davis

The firm's most important Revenue Act case in these years was *Anniston Mfg. Co. v. Davis* (1937). The firm filed challenges to the 1936 Revenue Act in the district courts in South Carolina, Georgia, Alabama, Mississippi, and Louisiana. In the firm's suit for Anniston Manufacturing Company, the district court in Alabama sustained the Collector's general demurrer in July 1936 (15 F. Supp. 257), and the firm promptly appealed to the Fifth Circuit. This was to be the test case, and the courts in the other states withheld decision pending its outcome.

The Fifth Circuit decided against Anniston, holding that the suit against the Collector was a suit against the United States (87 F. 2d 773). The judge in the case ruled that in the 1936 Revenue Act the United States had withdrawn its consent to be sued for refund of processing taxes, so that the courts lacked jurisdiction. The firm then promptly filed a petition for certiorari. The court granted certiorari and the firm argued its case on April 2, 1937. Sutherland and Brennan shared the oral argument for the petitioner.

The Supreme Court affirmed the judgment of the Fifth Circuit, but not for the reasons given by the lower court (301 U.S. 337). Chief Justice Hughes, writing for the Court, recognized that the firm's action was brought against the Collector personally, and that this remedy could not be taken away without substituting some other remedy that would be "fair and adequate." He then said that it would be the taxpayer's duty to present fully all facts pertaining to the shifting of the burden of the tax, but if the question was not susceptible of proof the claimant could not be denied recovery. With reference to Sutherland, Tuttle & Brennan's argument on impossibility of proof, the Court said that "the provision should not be construed as demanding the performance of a task, if ultimately found to be inherently impossible, as a condition of relief." The board of review had to make findings of fact, and the Court ruled, "Findings that may properly be made on evidence must support a decision." Findings that were not supported by the evidence would be upset by the reviewing court. The court would then direct the board to enter "judgment to which the claimant is constitutionally entitled and the Commissioner must refund the amount determined to be due."

The Supreme Court's decision in the *Anniston* case was a mixed blessing in that it made it possible for the firm to get fair consideration in the bureau and the board of review on its claims for refund. These claims would not be allowable insofar as the evidence showed that the claimants had shifted the burden of the tax. Sutherland and Tuttle therefore set out to support their claims with statistical evidence as to the claimants' true burden. The firm succeeded in recovering substantial amounts by following this procedure (see sidebar: Denim Study).

The Revenue Act of 1936 provided further opportunities related to the invalidation of the processing tax. Title III of that act imposed the "unjust enrichment tax," an 80% windfall tax aimed at taxpayers like the firm's clients, who avoided paying the processing tax for many months as a result of injunctions obtained in the district courts. The firm litigated a few cases involving the windfall tax, and it was able to settle most of these cases on a favorable basis. Randolph Thrower was the firm's mainstay in the preparation and trial of processing tax cases in the board of review, where the firm tried cotton and peanut processing tax cases. Several of these cases were still pending when Thrower returned to the firm after World War II.[11]

SUING THE COLLECTOR

For years the firm's tax litigation was affected by the doctrine that a taxpayer could maintain a suit for refund against the Collector of Internal Revenue who collected a federal tax alleged to be illegal or excessive, and that this suit was against the Collector in his own person, and not against the United States. Although this doctrine rested upon somewhat shaky foundations, the Sutherland firm invoked it many times, often gaining some advantage that could not be had in a refund suit against the United States.[12]

The aforementioned *Graham* (1931) and *Anniston* (1937) cases are two examples in which the firm relied on the Collector's personal liability. In the former case the firm was unsuccessful in recovering taxes that had been collected after the expiration of the statute of limitations. However, the Court recognized the doctrine of the Collector's personal liability so that the challenged provision had to be justified as curative legislation, and the taxpayers' suits could not be summarily dismissed on grounds of sovereign immunity. The Court's recognition of the Collector's personal liability for collecting an illegal tax served the firm well in the latter case, in which Sutherland challenged the validity of retroactive restrictions on refunds of processing taxes. Since the firm sued the Collector, the Court recognized that the suit was not subject to the defense of sovereign immunity. The Court, therefore, had to strain to give the challenged provisions of the 1936 Act a construction that enabled the firm to obtain large refunds for its processing tax clients.

An important later case, *United States v. Nunnally Investment Company* (316 U.S. 258 (1942)), saw the firm successfully recover an additional refund of income taxes for the very same taxable year that had been the subject of a previous refund suit brought by the taxpayer against the Collector of Internal Revenue. The firm's suit against the United States in the court of claims was not subject to the defense of res judicata because the United States was not a party to the earlier suit against the Collector.

The firm made use of suits against the Collector to gain other advantages as well. A refund suit could be brought against the United States in the district of the taxpayer's residence, but the venue for a suit against the Collector was the district of the Collector's residence, which was often a more favorable forum. Federal taxes in Georgia were paid to the Collector of Internal Revenue at Atlanta, but for almost 20 years the job was held by political appointees who maintained their legal residence in the Middle District of Georgia. This accounts for the firm's many refund suits tried at Macon or Columbus.

On another interesting note, for many years a jury trial was not available in suits against the United States. The taxpayer could, however, get a jury trial by suing the Collector. A 1954 act authorized jury trials in refund suits against the United States, while legislation enacted in 1966 provided that refund suits could be maintained only against the United States, and not against the collecting officer. The firm chose to sue the Collector and demand a jury trial in a number of cases that the partners thought would appeal to the sympathy of a jury.

The firm's suits against Collectors led to some interesting situations. Since the Collector had collected the tax through his subordinates, the firm had to sue the individual who was the Collector at the time the challenged tax was paid. When a defendant Collector died after suit was filed, the firm had to revive the action against his personal representatives. Some of the firm's suits were thus brought against former Collectors and some against the executors of deceased Collectors. The executors of one deceased Collector were his son, who resided in the Middle District of Georgia, and the First National Bank of Atlanta. This gave the firm a choice of forums. The partners brought one case in the Northern District, making service on the bank in Atlanta, and having duplicate process served on the other co-executor by the Marshal for the Middle District. Tax cases were not particularly appealing to the lone judge of the Northern District, who suggested that he should disqualify himself because he had done his personal banking with First National for many years. The bank, as executor, had no financial stake in the outcome. The firm then took some of the burden off the judge by demanding a jury trial, through which it obtained a favorable verdict, which was sustained on appeal (*Page et al v. Howell*, 116 F. 2d 158).

The National Industrial Recovery Act (NIRA)

In addition to the AAA and the Revenue Act, interesting cases also grew out of the National Industrial Recovery Act (NIRA) of 1933. Like the AAA, the NIRA was an act of the First New Deal that was eventually held unconstitutional (*Schechter v. United States*, 295 U.S. 495). But before the Supreme Court struck down the NIRA, it was the source of considerable controversy and litigation.

The provisions of the NIRA were quite sweeping. Together with a multibillion-dollar public works program, it provided for a system of industrial self-regulation under federal supervision by the National Recovery Administration (NRA). The self-regulation portion of the act was aimed at reducing chaotic competition and stabilizing business through the implementation of codes that set wages and prices. It was also aimed at generating more purchasing power for consumers by defining labor standards, providing jobs, and raising wages. To this end, committees in each major industry drew up the codes of fair practice, regulating everything from plant expansion to operating hours and the length of the workweek. While at first the

NIRA seemed to foster harmony within industries, it soon began to look more like a hindrance to growth, and prospective court challenges mounted.

Richmond Hosiery Mills v. Camp

The Sutherland firm made one of the first attacks on the constitutionality of the NIRA on behalf of Richmond Hosiery Mills of Rossville, Georgia, for whom the firm had already handled a number of tax matters. Under the NIRA, a Code of Fair Competition was adopted for the hosiery industry. This code prohibited the operation of any productive machinery for more than two eight-hour shifts per day. The problem for Richmond Hosiery was that it had been operating its knitting machines for three shifts of eight hours each in order to enable its hosiery manufacturing facilities to operate on a two-shift basis. The company continued to do this after the code went into effect. Richmond's chairman was a justice of the Supreme Court of Tennessee, and the company's general counsel was a prominent Chattanooga lawyer. Both men believed that the code provision limiting machine hours was illegal and that the statute itself was unconstitutional.

The act provided that when any such Code of Fair Competition had been adopted by an industry group and approved by the president, any violation in a transaction affecting interstate commerce would be a misdemeanor, punishable by fine. When the U.S. Attorney for the Northern District of Georgia threatened prosecution of Richmond Hosiery and its officers for operating some of its machinery three shifts a day, the corporation asked the Sutherland firm to seek an injunction against the prosecution.

Elbert Tuttle and Joe Brennan filed Richmond's complaint against the U.S. Attorney in the district court at Atlanta in April 1934. Brennan also called on the services of Alton Hosch, who had been his classmate at Harvard Law School. (Hosch later became a renowned lawyer in his own right and served for many years as Dean of the Law School at the University of Georgia.) The firm sought to enjoin the U.S. Attorney from prosecuting Richmond for violation of the Hosiery Code, or otherwise attempting to enforce against it the provisions of the NIRA, insofar as the act and the code imposed a limitation on the operation of the complainant's machinery. The complaint charged that the act unconstitutionally delegated legislative power to industry groups and the president, and that the operation of the complainant's knitting machines was an intrastate activity beyond the power of Congress to regulate under the commerce clause. Equitable relief was sought on the grounds that criminal prosecution would result in irreparable injury to the complainant.

At a May 1934 hearing the district court denied the complainant's application for interlocutory injunction and granted the defendant's motion to dismiss the complaint. The district court recognized that if the act was unconstitutional as claimed in the complaint, an injunction should be granted. But in an elaborate opinion the court upheld the constitutionality of the act in all respects (7 F. Supp. 139). Federal District Judge E. Marvin Underwood, who handed down the ruling, argued that the NIRA's chief claim to constitutionality was that it had been passed in an emergency.

Immediately after this decision, the district attorney presented the matter to the grand jury, which indicted the corporation for violations of the Hosiery Code and the officers of the corporation for conspiracy to violate the code. Shortly thereafter the United States brought its suit against Richmond to enjoin further violations.[13]

As lead counsel for Richmond and its officers in all of these cases, Elbert Tuttle negotiated an agreement with government counsel to the effect that the firm would pursue as rapidly as possible its appeal in the suit against the United States attorney. Furthermore, it would seek an early hearing in the court of appeals before its regular fall term. Finally, the agreement stated that, whatever the decision of that court, both parties would join in a petition for certiorari to the United States Supreme Court. Government counsel agreed that this would be an ideal case to test the constitutionality of the NIRA, and in consideration of the firm's agreeing to expedite the proceedings in that case, government counsel agreed to keep the criminal cases and the government's own suit for injunction off the trial calendars.

After all this it appeared that the Richmond Hosiery Mills case would be the first challenge to the NIRA to reach the Supreme Court. But much to the firm's disappointment, it never got there. The appeal had been promptly filed, but the court of appeals took almost two months to decide the matter (*Richmond Hosiery Mills v. Camp*, 74 F. 2d 200 (5th Cir. 1934)). The court affirmed the decree of the district court without considering the constitutional issue. It took the position that there was no clear grounds for equitable relief since "it had been made to appear" that the district attorney intended to prosecute for only a single violation of the code that could result in a fine of only $500. The court concluded that this could not result in irreparable injury and that Richmond could protect its rights fully and completely in a criminal case. However, the court did not explain the source of their information as to the intention of the district attorney, and such information was inconsistent with the multiple counts of the indictments that had been obtained. In addition, the government had not urged, or even suggested, the grounds on which the court of appeals decided the case.

Meanwhile, Richmond Hosiery's business was suffering from a combination of the pending suits and the Depression. A new board of directors was elected, and they wanted this litigation terminated as soon as possible. Tuttle therefore discussed settlement possibilities with the U.S. Attorney, and just a week before the Fifth Circuit's decision he offered to settle the litigation by having the corporation plead guilty to two counts of violations that would carry a maximum fine of $1,000. All other counts on both indictments would be nol prosed, and the civil litigation dismissed.

A final settlement was reached, but it was not easy. Counsel for the NRA took a hard line, but eventually the Justice Department approved a disposition of the cases on the basis of the corporation's pleading guilty to six counts. Upon a showing of the corporation's distressing financial condition, the district judge imposed a fine of only $1,000. This was all accomplished within the time for filing a certiorari petition, which by agreement was abandoned upon the disposition of the rest of the litigation.

The Estates and Trusts Practice

Because the processing tax cases offered mainly future compensation, the partners had to find ventures that would be more immediately profitable. Herbert Elsas, Bill Sutherland, and Ed Kane thus turned much of their attention to building an estates and trusts practice. This practice area was quite undeveloped in the South, so Elsas took advantage of his New England and Harvard connections to travel north with Sutherland to study the most modern methods. The Sutherland firm soon became the first in the South to introduce these concepts into the handling of wills and trusts.[14]

The partners were persuaded to go into this area largely because of New Deal transfer taxes. These taxes forced many families to bring their businesses public, including Southeastern cotton mills, which were some of the firm's most important clients. The partners thus believed they had found an area in which they could kill many birds with one stone. They could become experts in an area of importance to their clients; they could grow by doing similar work for new clients; and they could expect little in the way of competition from other regional law firms.

In those days, the "rules" had it that lawyers drew wills as a service to their clients, while accountants handled taxes. Drafting a will was considered a fairly routine matter that any lawyer fresh out of law school could handle. The lawyer who prepared a will, or his firm, would be expected to probate it and look after the administration of the estate.

With its background in taxation, the Sutherland firm took a different approach. If a client had valuable properties to pass under his will, he needed guidance with respect to the tax effects of various plans for the disposition of his property. The partners impressed upon their clients the importance of what was later to be known as "estate planning," and the firm was able to make substantial charges, unusual in those days, for the work that preceded the actual drafting of a will.

Herbert Elsas and Bill Sutherland developed some interesting approaches to the preservation of businesses, such as the use of trustees and committees to maintain the preferred level of family control. In many cases the client adopted plans for the disposition of property by trusts, both inter vivos and testamentary, and the firm developed special skills in drafting wills and trusts that would provide tax savings for the client and his family over many years. The firm pioneered in devising flexible provisions for such long-term trusts, giving to the trustee broad discretion as to the distribution of income and principal to beneficiaries. Their provisions also established trust committees with powers to control the exercise of a trustee's discretion, and even power to remove a trustee, to substitute another, or to terminate a trust.

The practice developed rapidly, and the firm handled some big regional and national names. The partners drew former president Herbert Hoover's will, as well as the wills of many important families in the Southeast. Elsas and his colleagues' growing reputations were instrumental in attracting new business to other areas. The Sutherland firm was also somewhat unique in the region for its representation of individuals and families at a time when most firms represented banks. Its specialists

Alvin H. Hansen, 1945

in wills and trusts did a great deal of corporate work as well, as family representation often led into other profitable ventures, including mergers, acquisitions, and criminal fraud cases.

Elsas and Sutherland at one point actually considered starting a trust company, but they were unable to put all the pieces together. They did, however, act as trustees for many inter vivos and testamentary trusts, and they were named as committeemen for numerous trusts. Some early clients of the firm were reluctant to name any of the Atlanta banks as executor or trustee, even with a provision for supervision by a trust committee. These clients preferred individuals in whom they had confidence and who would be authorized to engage specialists for investment advice. In the late 1930s the firm's partners began acting as trustees under these circumstances.

As more and more trusteeships developed, the partners decided to hire an investment expert. In 1941 Henry Thielbar came to the firm in that capacity. He was a graduate of Princeton and the Harvard School of Business Administration, and he had been engaged in investment advisory work with a Baltimore firm for five years. He arranged for assistance from the New York investment counsel with whom he had been associated.

World War II interrupted the growth of the firm's "trust department." When Herbert Elsas joined the Air Force he resigned as trustee of some 25 trusts, and Bill Sutherland became his successor trustee. Thielbar continued with the firm until he joined the War Department in 1943. Meanwhile, Edith Elsas, Herbert's wife, joined the firm's own home-front war effort by helping to keep the trust books. The burden of administering so many trusts was acute during the remainder of the war, and at war's end it seemed advisable for the firm to arrange to be relieved of most of this work. Another Atlanta institution with a capable trust department took over most of the trusts with the approval of the various trust committees and interested parties.[15] Herbert Elsas remained at the helm of the estates and trusts practice in the postwar years, and he continued to act as trustee to various estates up to the 1990s (see Ch. 13). He took newly hired associate Michael J. Egan under his wing in the 1950s, and Egan went on to play an important role in this practice. Lloyd Leva Plaine, Larry White and Kent Frazier also became key players in estates and trusts in later years. Charlie Hurt eventually headed the practice after Egan's retirement. Even at the end of the 20th century some families were still benefiting from trusts established with the assistance of the Sutherland firm in the 1930s.[16]

The Denim Study

The Sutherland firm in the 1930s brought matters before some of the most important regulatory and legal bodies in Washington, including the Justice Department, the IRS (then known as the Bureau of Internal Revenue), and the Supreme Court. And while not all of these were tax matters, the processing tax cases became the firm's bread and butter in the nation's capital. One of the Sutherland partners' wisest decisions was to use the latest statistics from the Departments of Agriculture and Labor to get a grip on whether the burden of a tax was, in fact, shifted. Randolph Thrower and Bill Sutherland did some preliminary work in this vein and came to their own conclusions as to the exact figures, but they knew that having the backing of a team of nationally recognized experts would help their case immeasurably. As Thrower recalled, "Bill Sutherland concluded that we would need to get the outstanding people in the country to crack this nut. And so we prevailed upon a group of clients – mills – to finance a project."

This project, which became known as the "denim study," helped establish the firm's reputation as a serious, scholarly champion of its clients' rights. The study came into being when a group of eight cotton mills – producers of most of the denim in the country – asked the firm to represent them in connection with their claims for refund of the processing tax and their liability with reference to the unjust enrichment tax. Following the advice of Chief Justice Hughes in the *Anniston* case – that plaintiffs develop all of the facts pertaining to the shifting of the tax burden – the firm commissioned two of the country's most renowned economists, Professors Alvin Hansen and Edward Mason of Harvard University. (Hansen was best known for assisting in the establishment of the Social Security System and for having introduced Keynesian economics to the United States in the 1930s. Mason, meanwhile, wrote ground-breaking studies on the relationship between the free market and the state.)

Sutherland, Brennan, and Thrower worked closely with the professors because, according to Thrower, "Bill did not believe in turning someone loose with the possibility he might make a grave error." The group used new statistical techniques to reach what they believed to be an accurate determination, namely that in the denim industry approximately 23% of the processing tax was actually borne by the mills and not shifted to others. With this prestigious report Sutherland, Tuttle & Brennan was able to get a favorable reaction from the economists and statisticians in the Department of Agriculture, and as a result the firm obtained many satisfactory settlements in the Bureau of Internal Revenue. In Thrower's words, the study "broke the logjam for all of the cases, ours and others, in the textile industry."[17]

General Counsel for the Treasury Department Elbert P. Tuttle

*Judge John Minor Wisdom of the
Fifth Circuit Court of Appeals was to call it one
of the most important landmarks in American
legal history. By his estimation, it was "probably
the most cited case in constitutional law decided
in [the 20th] century."*

CHAPTER FOUR

ELBERT TUTTLE'S CIVIL LIBERTIES CASES

The firm's pro bono work in habeas corpus and civil liberties cases enhanced its reputation for excellence across a broad legal spectrum. Several of these cases in the 1930s went to the Supreme Court of Georgia and the U.S. Supreme Court, and one – *Johnson v. Zerbst* – became a landmark. All of the firm's lawyers were involved in one capacity or another, but Elbert Tuttle was the one most responsible for taking on these cases and spending countless hours on behalf of his clients' interests. Tuttle, it seems, was motivated as much by his sense of right and wrong as he was by Bill Sutherland's maxim of doing "whatever is necessary" to defend a client. Randolph Thrower later said of Tuttle's methodology, "Elbert in civil rights cases would not ask me to look up the law on a particular subject. He would tell me what the law should be and ask me to find precedence…to support that proposition." With Tuttle at the helm, the Sutherland firm was the only firm of note and stature in the Southeast that was prepared to take these very unpopular cases. It is also worth noting that, since Bill Sutherland and Elbert Tuttle were in high standing in Atlanta society, they had little to gain, and much to lose, by working on behalf of marginalized clients.[1]

These cases are also significant for having established a pro bono tradition at the Sutherland firm. For many years it was common for a young lawyer to get his first trial experience through a court appointment to represent an indigent defendant in a criminal prosecution. Senior partners have also made their contributions, in some cases upon request by public interest organizations and in some situations where they themselves became aware of the need to provide legal services. Elbert Tuttle, said one Sutherland partner, "instilled a spirit in all of us that continues to this day."

The firm made substantial contributions of time and effort in three notable cases in the 1930s. These deserve to be described in detail because they tell us much about the evolution of the law and the difficulties Elbert Tuttle faced in championing the rights of indigent clients. The first of these cases had a heartbreaking conclusion, but the second and third were great successes for both Tuttle and the firm. The third case also turned out to be one of the most cited landmarks in American legal history.

Downer v. Dunaway (1931-1933)

The firm was drawn into its first such public interest case in a rather unusual way. Midway through an otherwise ordinary day at the Sutherland office in Atlanta,

Elbert Tuttle received an emergency call from the Georgia adjunct general. The general told Tuttle that two black prisoners were being held in a county jail in Elberton, Georgia, about 100 miles from Atlanta. One of these prisoners, John Downer, had been identified by a white woman as the perpetrator of an alleged rape the night before, and a large mob was now trying to storm the jail. The judge, sheriff, and mayor called Governor Lamartine Hardman for assistance, and the governor issued a proclamation putting Elberton under martial law. The adjunct general then ordered two local National Guard companies to the town. The mob seemed to know that the guardsmen were unlikely to open fire on civilians, so the general asked Tuttle, who was an officer in the Georgia National Guard, to bring several cases of gas grenades to Elberton to help protect Downer. Tuttle set out for Elberton accompanied by his best friend, National Guard Captain Leckie Mattox, who also happened to be Sara and Bill Sutherland's cousin.[2]

When Tuttle and Mattox arrived in Elberton just after dark, they saw hundreds of people milling about the sheriff's house and jail (the jail was upstairs in the sheriff's house), as well as local National Guardsmen standing beside their machine guns. Tuttle decided to try to disperse the crowd with the gas grenades, and as he and Mattox pulled the pins out of their grenades, they heard the firing of a machine gun from within the sheriff's house. They then lobbed their gas grenades toward the front steps of the house in order to clear out the mob. Upon entering the house, Tuttle found it "filled with determined and angry men milling around from room to room." He then heard another burst of machine gun fire spattering down the steps, and he realized that the guardsman with the gun was the only thing keeping the mob from dashing up and seizing the prisoners. The gas grenades played havoc with the mob, and this confusion allowed Tuttle to join forces with the local company commander and a local Baptist preacher to gradually push the mob out of the sheriff's house. The guardsmen then held the mob at bay until additional National Guard companies arrived from Atlanta a few hours later.[3]

Although the mob had been forced out of the sheriff's house, the scene was anything but tranquil outside, as around 1,500 people continued trying to storm the jail while the guardsmen were waiting for the reinforcements. At a few points some members of the mob fired shots into the sheriff's house, which led the guardsmen to return fire. Tuttle recalled that when an Elberton man was injured in one of these brief exchanges, "this put the mob into a frenzy." Tuttle convinced the fire chief to disperse the crowd with a fire hose, but the mob took control of the hose and turned it onto the National Guard troops. The mob directed the hose at the jail as well, breaking the windows and soaking the prisoners inside. Some of the mob also threatened to destroy the building with dynamite if the prisoners were not turned over to them. They even set off a warning explosion, but they were unable to bring themselves to destroy the sheriff's house and the National Guard soldiers inside.[4]

When the additional National Guard troops arrived from Atlanta, Tuttle and the others succeeded in rescuing Downer and the other prisoner through an ingenious, improvised ruse. Just before midnight, with the jail lights turned off, they dressed the prisoners in National Guard uniforms and shepherded them out with a company of infantrymen. Two days later, the editors of the *Atlanta Constitution* wrote in praise of the men who held off the mob, "Too much honor cannot be accorded to all of those Elbert County and state officials, including the National Guard rank and file, who effectually defeated the mob and saved the state from the disgrace of another unwarranted lynching."[5]

After the National Guard spirited Downer out of Elberton, they brought him to Atlanta, where he was promptly indicted and brought back to Elberton to stand trial. Unsurprisingly, the trial was held in the same atmosphere of mob intimidation, as 500 spectators packed the courtroom and the courthouse. This time two National Guard infantry companies with fixed bayonets were lined up to keep the angry crowd from the courtroom. Everyone who entered the courtroom was searched for weapons, and the number of small arms that were confiscated could have constituted a minor arsenal.[6]

According to Tuttle, it was here that Downer's rights as a defendant were violated. Downer met his court-appointed counsel only an hour before he was put on trial, and despite the hostile environment in which the trial was conducted, no motion was made for a continuance or a change of venue. The trial commenced and was completed in one day. At the end of the day, it took the jury six minutes to return a verdict of guilty, after which the judge sentenced Downer to be electrocuted 20 days hence. "We [then] had to put him in the middle of a phalanx of soldiers after the judge passed sentence," Tuttle later wrote, "to get him safely to the train and back to Atlanta to await his execution." Downer's counsel made no motion for a new trial, and the special term of court was adjourned so that there could be no appeal under Georgia practice.[7]

Tuttle was not satisfied that justice had been served in the case. It was true, he wrote decades later, that the forms of justice had been followed. The defendant was indicted by a grand jury; had counsel to represent him; had faced his accuser in open court; had been tried by a jury of 12; and had been given a sentence within the provisions of the Georgia statute. But Downer's appointed counselors appeared more interested in saving their own necks amid the threats of the mob than in protecting Downer. Clearly he had not received a fair trial.[8]

Tuttle felt instinctively that a trial under such circumstances was not due process of law, for the judge and jury could not help but be intimidated by the mob. At the suggestion of Austin T. Walden, a black lawyer who later served as an Atlanta judge, Tuttle volunteered to bring a habeas corpus action to seek relief for Downer. He hoped to rely on a prior U.S. Supreme Court opinion in the infamous 1915 Leo Frank case, which had also taken place in Georgia. Frank, a Jewish businessman accused of murdering a 13-year-old girl, had also been convicted in an atmosphere of mob violence. In an eloquent opinion in *Frank v. Mangum* (237 U.S. 309), the Court held that in such circumstances, if a jury is intimidated and there is actual interference with the course of justice, then the state has deprived the defendant of due process:

We of course agree that if a trial is in fact dominated by a mob, so that the jury is intimidated and the trial judge yields, and so that there is an actual interference with the course of justice, there is in that court a departure from due process of law in the proper sense of that term. And if the state, supplying no corrective process, carries into execution a judgment of death or imprisonment based upon a verdict thus produced by mob domination, the state deprives the accused of his life or liberty without due process of law.

In view of Tuttle's direct participation in the military activities, he enlisted the aid of Bill Sutherland, Granger A. Hansell (founder of the Hansell Post law firm, now Jones Day), and Jerome Jones from the Macon firm of Jones, Johnson, Russell & Sparks to seek relief for Downer in the federal court. Austin Walden also joined the effort. They presented a petition for a writ of habeas corpus to District Judge Bascom S. Deaver in Macon two days before the execution date. Deaver denied the petition but certified that there was probable cause for allowance, thus staying execution pending appeal. The Court of Appeals for the Fifth Circuit reversed the decision of the district judge and held that the writ should issue (*Downer v. Dunaway*, 53 F. 2d 586 (1931)). Downer was given a new trial, and a public interest organization retained a competent lawyer to represent him.[9]

A change of venue was granted, but it was not enough to prevent another round of dangerous mob activity. Downer's defense lawyers were dismayed by the state's decision to retry Downer in Lexington, Georgia, the seat of an adjacent county. They soon found that their fears were justified, as a new mob formed and followed Downer to Lexington to demand the keys to the jail. The situation was so potentially explosive that the county police officers moved Downer to Athens overnight. They brought him back to Lexington the next day for the trial, and at this second trial he was again convicted and sentenced to death. The Georgia Supreme Court then dismissed his appeal and denied his motion for rehearing a month later (*Downer v. State*, 178 Ga. 185 (1933)).

An unsavory incident that took place amid these efforts in the Georgia state courts reinforced Elbert Tuttle's staunch beliefs about the problems of equality and the law. After an exhausting day of working to obtain a federal writ of habeas corpus for Downer in Macon, Tuttle drove back to Atlanta late at night with Austin Walden. A police officer in East Point, south of Atlanta, stopped the car because the presence of a black man "abroad" was a violation of the local curfew law that was in effect in and around the City of Atlanta. Tuttle, who was understandably embarrassed and appalled, explained to the officer that they should be exempted because they were returning from a federal court session. They were not arrested.[10]

As for Downer's predicament, Tuttle was not simply troubled by the mob atmosphere surrounding Downer's initial incarceration and both of his trials. He and the other members of the National Guard who were in the courtroom during the first trial also had serious doubts as to Downer's guilt, in part because they heard what they believed to be the true story. The parents of Downer's accuser,

> *Although Elbert Tuttle has received the lion's share of praise for his work in civil liberties cases, Bill Sutherland also did his part, often going far beyond what one might have expected from a well-educated, affluent lawyer in the Depression-era Deep South.*

they learned, had discovered that their daughter was sexually active with her male suitor. The young woman then chose Downer as a scapegoat in order to evade social ostracism and her parents' punishment. (Rather suspiciously, she married her paramour in the week between the alleged incident and Downer's first trial.) Tuttle's team thus went to Governor Eugene Talmadge seeking a stay of execution or commutation to a life sentence. Unfortunately their claim was difficult to prove, and at any rate it was unlikely that a politician in those days would make such an unpopular decision in a case involving a black defendant and a white plaintiff. The governor denied a stay, and Downer was executed.[11]

Despite the lamentable outcome, Tuttle learned many valuable lessons throughout this matter, and in later years he recalled just how important the case had been in edifying his already acute sense of right and wrong. From a legal standpoint, *Downer v. Dunaway* also had an impact on federal review of criminal trials in state courts. On this point Tuttle later wrote, "John Downer, just as did Leo Frank…made his contribution to the development of Constitutional Law for the protection of many others unknown to him."[12]

Herndon v. Lowry (1937)

The next of these cases was very arduous for the firm, but this time the outcome was a heartening victory. Five years after the Downer case, Bill Sutherland got a call from Whitney North Seymour, a colleague from Harvard Law School. Seymour, a New York lawyer who later headed the ABA, had become acquainted with Sutherland's firm while working in the office of the solicitor general of the United States under President Herbert Hoover. Ironically, he had been Sutherland's opponent in the oral argument of two cases in the Supreme Court. This time around, though, Seymour asked his former adversary for help in the case of Angelo Herndon.[13]

Herndon (no relation to the Alonzo F. Herndon family, founders of the Atlanta Life Insurance Company), a young black communist organizer, had been convicted of an "attempt to incite insurrection" in violation of a section of the Georgia Penal Code. He had attempted to pass out communist literature on the post office steps of Atlanta in an effort to persuade Southern blacks to join the American Communist Party.[14] He had not advocated open rebellion, but, said the state, as a communist he was theoretically championing a new form of government. Consequently, he was sentenced to 18 years on a chain gang for the simple act of

Federal judges Elbert P. Tuttle (right) and Lewis R. Morgan (center) followed by U.S. marshal go to lunch after hearing testimony in Americus, Georgia (October 1963)

passing out leaflets. The judgment of the trial court had been affirmed by the Georgia Supreme Court in 1934 (178 Ga. 832).[15]

Seymour needed a Georgia lawyer, and he knew that the high community standing of Bill Sutherland and Elbert Tuttle would add a degree of respectability that the case had not previously possessed. Indeed, Sutherland's involvement in this matter illustrates an important point. Although Elbert Tuttle has received the lion's share of praise for his work in civil liberties cases, Bill Sutherland also did his part, often going far beyond what one might have expected from a well-educated, affluent lawyer in the Depression-era Deep South. Sutherland may have been financially secure and highly regarded in his community, but he was also amenable to the free exchange of ideas. He had, after all, clerked at the Supreme Court for Justice Louis Brandeis, who was certainly one of the most progressive justices of his day. Many contemporary observers, including Will W. Alexander of the Commission on Interracial Cooperation and President Buell G. Gallagher of Talladega College, were impressed with Sutherland's tolerant attitude toward civil liberties. In fact, Gallagher once wrote Walter White of the NAACP that Sutherland exuded "a kind of fanatical passion for free speech."

Yet although Sutherland was clearly taken with the idea of defending the right to free expression, he was wholly uninterested in championing Angelo Herndon's vision of a socialist future. At one point early in the Herndon matter, a representative of the International Labor Defense organization (ILD) dismissed the notion that Sutherland should represent Herndon, chiefly because Sutherland "was not interested in the class struggle and wanted to take the case simply as a civil liberties case."[16] After consulting with Seymour, Sutherland agreed to take the case on civil libertarian grounds. Seymour explained that some faculty members of Columbia Law School wanted to get the case to the United States Supreme Court, but that they were faced with a procedural obstacle resulting from the failure of Herndon's counsel to raise constitutional questions at the trial or in the state supreme court. Walter Gellhorn of the Columbia Law faculty came to Atlanta to assist Sutherland in getting the Georgia Supreme Court to entertain a motion for a rehearing in which the crucial constitutional questions could be raised. Such a motion had been tendered, but the clerk of the supreme court and the chief justice had refused to allow it to be filed, on the grounds that it had not been presented within 10 days of the judgment.[17]

There was a question, however, as to the proper construction of the court's rules. Justice R.C. Bell had written the opinion of the court on the arguments' merits and had returned to his home in South Georgia. Sutherland and Gellhorn therefore traveled to Bell's hometown and convinced him that the court could properly entertain a motion for rehearing presented at the same term of court, which had not yet expired. Justice Bell wrote Chief Justice Russell to that effect, and Sutherland followed up by calling on the chief justice after returning to Atlanta. The court allowed the filing of the motion for rehearing and asked for the Sutherland firm's briefs.

Arrangements were then made for Whitney North Seymour to take over as Herndon's counsel in further proceedings. Briefs were filed on the constitutional questions, and after consideration, the Georgia Supreme Court denied the motion for rehearing. Justice Bell wrote another opinion for the court, refusing to rule on the constitutional questions (179 Ga. 597). Seymour appealed to the United States Supreme Court and argued the merits of the constitutional questions there. A divided court held that the constitutional questions had not been duly raised and dismissed the appeal (295 U.S. 441).

Seymour then joined with Sutherland to explore the possibility of a petition for a writ of habeas corpus in the Georgia courts. Herndon had been free on bond pending appeal, and after the decision of the U.S. Supreme Court arrangements were made to have him surrender to the sheriff of Fulton County. A petition for a writ of habeas corpus was promptly filed with Superior Court Judge Hugh M. Dorsey, and the writ was issued forthwith, returnable in 15 days.

Judge Dorsey was one of six superior court judges in the county, and the firm's New York friends questioned the wisdom of choosing him for this kind of case. Many years before, Judge Dorsey had been the active prosecutor in the aforementioned sensational case of Leo Frank. In the face of threats to his own life, Georgia Governor John M. Slaton had commuted Frank's death sentence to life imprisonment, but soon thereafter a mob lynched Frank in Marietta, Georgia. Slaton's political career floundered, but Hugh Dorsey was elected and served two terms as governor. He was later appointed to the bench.[18]

Despite the New Yorkers' reservations, the Sutherland partners had no qualms about presenting the Herndon petition to Dorsey. In fact, they felt he was the best choice precisely *because* of his involvement in the Frank case. As they saw it, since many observers thought Frank had not committed the crime of which he was

Angelo Herndon
– Atlanta, 1932

accused, Dorsey bore a certain stigma for having decided the case. Sutherland and Tuttle therefore believed Judge Dorsey might want to publicly show that he was not racially or religiously biased. Whether or not this "stigma" actually influenced Dorsey's decision, Sutherland and Tuttle were not to be disappointed in their choice of judge.[19]

At the hearing on the writ, Sutherland argued that the Herndon conviction under the terms of the vaguely worded sedition law "places Georgia in a ridiculous position before the people of this country and the world." The insurrection statute, he pointed out, was completely outdated, as it had been passed in 1866 to punish anyone who tried to incite the newly freed slaves to violence. Sutherland called the state's case against Herndon "flimsy" and "totally unbelievable," and he added, "The ruling on this case, no matter from whom it may come, will be a landmark in Constitutional law." After considering the matter for three weeks, Judge Dorsey held that the Georgia statute, as construed and applied in Herndon's case, was "too vague and indefinite to provide a sufficiently ascertainable standard of guilt," and was thus void under the due process clause of the 14th Amendment. Several Georgia lawyers expressed the view that no other trial judge in Georgia would have reached Judge Dorsey's decision, but Tuttle was still troubled that Dorsey had not called the Georgia sedition law unconstitutional on the grounds that it "prohibited free speech, free assembly, and free press."[20]

Dorsey's decision was then brought before the Georgia Supreme Court, where Bill Sutherland argued that limitations on freedom of expression encouraged violence.[21] Dorsey's decision was reversed by the Georgia Supreme Court, but six U.S. Supreme Court justices later affirmed that Dorsey, Sutherland, and Tuttle had been correct (*Herndon v. Lowry*, 301 U.S. 242). Justice Owen J. Roberts, speaking for the majority, wrote, "The statute, as construed and applied, amounts merely to a dragnet which may enmesh any one who agitates for a change of government…. So vague and indeterminate are the boundaries thus set to the freedom of speech and assembly that the law necessarily violates the guarantees of liberty embodied in the 14th Amendment." This was a great moral victory for the Sutherland firm.[22] One incident near the end of the case says a great deal about the more distasteful customs of the day. Judge Dorsey's order discharging the prisoner was stayed pending the state's appeal, but Herndon was released on a reduced bail. He was then free to return to New York, and his friends insisted that he be accompanied by a lawyer on the overnight trip from Atlanta in order to minimize the possibility of an incident. The most that could be done was to have the firm's young associate Ed Kane take the same train as Herndon, in separate but rather unequal accommodations. The "Jim Crow" car was not a sleeper, so Herndon passed an uncomfortable night on the northbound train before being welcomed back to New York as a hero by his radical supporters.[23]

Johnson v. Zerbst (1938)

The last of the firm's three great civil liberties cases of this period became a landmark. In *Johnson v. Zerbst* (304 U.S. 458) the Supreme Court held that the trial of an accused in a federal court without aid of counsel, unless assistance of counsel was intelligently waived, violated the Sixth Amendment to the Constitution. The decision established the right to counsel for every defendant charged with a federal crime, a right that was later extended to defendants in state courts. Until very late in the 20th century, it was the most often cited of any federal case in the history of the United States, which is all the more remarkable when we consider that Elbert Tuttle handled the matter pro bono.[24]

The origins of the case were rather unremarkable. Two Marines, Bridwell and Johnson (their first names have been lost to time), were arrested in Charleston, South Carolina, and charged with passing counterfeit $20 bills. They were indicted in the federal district court in that city, but they went to trial without counsel because the court had not informed them that they were entitled to appointed representation. Unsurprisingly, they were unable to defend themselves properly in court, and they were convicted and sentenced to four years and six months in the federal penitentiary in Atlanta.[25]

Bridwell and Johnson filed appeals from the district court at Charleston on the advice of their fellow prisoners, but their appeals were denied because they had missed the deadline. Then, with the help of these "jailhouse lawyers," the two men prepared and filed petitions for writ of habeas corpus with the district court at Atlanta. In these new petitions they claimed that they had been denied their constitutional rights in the trial at which they were convicted.

The district court held that it had no jurisdiction to order the release of the two prisoners, but the district judge found that the two men had been deprived of their constitutional rights in the federal trial in which they were convicted and sentenced (*Bridwell and Johnson v. Aderhold, Warden*, 13 F. Supp. 253 (N.D. Ga. 1935)). Elbert Tuttle was then asked by the ACLU, through a New York lawyer, to look into the case and take any available steps to remedy what seemed to be an unjust sentencing.

Almost a year after the district court held that habeas corpus was not an available remedy in this situation, Tuttle filed a second petition for habeas corpus and the same district judge again denied relief. On appeal, the Fifth Circuit Court of Appeals affirmed the lower court's decision (92 F. 2d 748 (1937)).

At this point the ACLU advised Tuttle that they could no longer defray expenses in the case. Yet Tuttle was so convinced that a trial without counsel violated either the Fifth Amendment's due process clause or the Sixth Amendment guarantee of the right to counsel, he personally paid the costs of the appeal to the Supreme Court. At the clients' request, he filed a petition for writ of certiorari, and the Supreme Court granted certiorari over the government's opposition (303 U.S. 629). On the merits, the petitioners' brief argued that the failure of the court to assign counsel for their trial deprived them of their rights under the Sixth Amendment. They further argued that their conviction in violation of such rights was a nullity, so that they were entitled to be released on writ of habeas corpus.[26]

The government filed an elaborate brief arguing vigorously that the Sixth Amendment imposes no duty on a trial court to appoint counsel in the absence of a request, and that the petitioners' failure to request the appointment of counsel amounted to a waiver of their constitutional right. Faced with the holding in *Powell v. Alabama* (287 U.S. 45), that the due process clause of the 14th Amendment required a state court to assign counsel where a defendant was not otherwise represented, the government argued that this holding was limited to capital felony cases involving special facts. The government argued further that even if the court erred in failing to provide counsel, such error did not divest the court's jurisdiction and could not be reached by habeas corpus.[27]

Tuttle argued the case orally before a Court of eight justices, with Justice Cardozo absent, and by a vote of six to two the Court reversed the lower court's decision. In view of its significance to American jurisprudence, the majority opinion is worth quoting:

> *A court's jurisdiction at the hearing of trial may be lost "in the course of the proceedings" due to failure to complete the court – as the 6th Amendment requires – by providing counsel for an accused who is unable to obtain counsel, who has not intelligently waived this constitutional guaranty, and whose life or liberty is at stake.*

Congress then passed a statute giving the Supreme Court the power to prescribe Rules of Criminal Procedure. The new set of rules included the following order:

> *If the defendant appears in court without counsel, the court shall advise him of his right to counsel and assign counsel to represent him at every stage of the proceeding unless he elects to proceed without counsel or is able to obtain counsel (Fed. R. Crim. P. 44).*[28]

Years later Tuttle said of this case, "It is hard to believe, in light of the developments that followed that decision, that it was decided by the Supreme Court [as late as 1938]." The eminent Judge John Minor Wisdom of the Fifth Circuit Court of Appeals was to call it one of the most important landmarks in American legal history. By his estimation, it was "probably the most cited case in constitutional law decided in [the 20th] century."[29]

Named for Tuttle in 1990 — Elbert Parr Tuttle U.S. Court of Appeals Building,
56 Forsythe Street, Altanta, Georgia (2005)

EPILOGUE

Two decades after Tuttle's three major civil liberties cases, he was asked to give the graduation commencement address at Emory University. He took the opportunity to put his earlier pro bono work into perspective while commenting on the difficulty of being an independent thinker in the modern world. He warned the students that they were graduating into a world in which "conformity is expedient and the trivial is safe…[and in which] originality is so impoverished that ideas are guarded as secrets lest they be stolen, rather than thrown out to be tested and tried, to inspire or to die in accordance with their worth." Tuttle closed this address with a rumination on the difficulties of standing up for clients like those whom he had defended in the 1930s:

> *Let us recall the stigma that attaches to the lawyer today who has the temerity to defend an unpopular client. How readily are we inclined to identify the lawyer with his client, to confuse a vigorous defense in behalf of justice with partisanship for the client's beliefs. The task is at hand! Who dares to be the hero? Who dares for the sake of justice in court to counsel an accused whose alleged conduct or circumstances makes him really untouchable? If **capable** counsel is denied by the pressure of popular opinion, then our trials are a mockery of justice.[30]*

Mac Asbill, Jr. (left), with General Smith and a fellow Marine

Virtually all of the firm's lawyers left to enter the armed services, with only Bill Sutherland and Joe Brennan remaining at home to man the business.

CHAPTER FIVE

WORLD WAR II AND THE SUTHERLAND FIRM

W orld War II touched every aspect of American life. Millions left their hometowns to join the military effort or to seek employment in the burgeoning defense industry. Men donned uniforms and were sent overseas, while untold numbers of women also left their homes to work heavy machinery for the war effort. New towns sprouted up around military bases and factories, and the mass movement of the population had significant social consequences.

Another important consequence of the war was that it got American industry humming at full capacity once again. The federal government oversaw a massive effort to build a formidable defense apparatus, leading the nation from the tail end of a decade-long depression to full employment virtually overnight (contrary to popular opinion, World War II – and *not* the New Deal – ended the Great Depression). Big business's adoption of a "plowshares into swords" policy spawned new prosperity, as automobile manufacturers converted their assembly lines for tank and jeep production, and aircraft manufacturers and shipbuilders began building bombers, fighter aircraft, and battleships.

But while America's biggest corporations prospered with the outbreak of war, many small enterprises were not so lucky. Not only did small businesses lose out in the conversion to a wartime economy of scale, but they also suffered from the loss of key employees who left to join the war effort. Sutherland, Tuttle & Brennan was one such enterprise. It had grown into a formidable Southeastern firm in the 1930s and was among the five largest in Atlanta when war was declared in 1941. Yet virtually all of the firm's lawyers left to enter the armed services, with only Bill Sutherland and Joe Brennan remaining at home to man the business. The others – Elbert Tuttle, Ed Kane, Herbert Elsas, Randolph Thrower, C. Norman Stallings, Ben F. Johnson, Jr., and Benjamin S. Horack – spent several years in the military.[1] Among the myriad "shortages" endured by Americans on the home front, then, we can include the human deficits endured by small businesses like the Sutherland firm.

This exodus of lawyers very nearly killed the firm. In the words of Randolph Thrower, because the key players left so quickly, "we had almost a wipeout overnight." The Washington office was essentially abandoned for the time being, while Sutherland and Brennan did their best to preserve the Atlanta practice. Even this pairing was uncertain, for Joe Brennan had had some military training at

Elbert P. Tuttle

Georgetown, and like most men of his generation he had the will to serve his country after Pearl Harbor. But Tuttle and Sutherland convinced him that he had a responsibility to the others to stay in Atlanta to keep the firm afloat. Besides, they argued, even if Brennan did enlist, his vision problems would likely prevent him from serving in combat.[2]

The loss of manpower meant that promising areas of the practice would have to be abandoned for the time being. For example, the firm's active participation in the processing tax cases of the 1930s could have led to a great deal of legal work in the textile industry. During World War II the cotton mills had excess profits tax and renegotiation cases that involved large amounts of money, and the firm would have been uniquely qualified to handle such matters. But despite the cotton mills' interest in seeking such legal services, the firm was too shorthanded to take them on.[3]

Sutherland and Brennan did enlist the services of a few outside specialists during the war. Pete Troy, an associate and CPA who had come to the firm in 1940 to do some specialty work in the processing tax cases, stayed until 1944. Henry Thielbar, an investment expert, was hired in 1941 to assist Herbert Elsas in the estates and trusts practice, and he remained with the firm until joining the War Department in 1943. The firm also got temporary help from Juliette Metcalf, who spent a year as an associate at the firm while her husband, an FBI employee, was stationed in Atlanta. Professor Charles Lowndes of Duke Law School also did some work for the firm, contributing invaluable help in the preparation of briefs in several tax cases, including the Charlotte Woolford Trust case in the court of claims (*Trust Company of Georgia et al v. United States*, 60 F. Supp. 470).[4]

The war had one bright spot for the firm in the area of personnel: It brought Madison Richardson into the fold. Richardson (Harvard LL.B. 1913) was a lawyer of the old school who had been a solo practitioner in Atlanta for many years. He came to the firm as special counsel in 1942, largely because he knew that his old friend, Bill Sutherland, was in dire need of help. Richardson considered this service a way to contribute to the war effort while also helping friends in need. In addition to Richardson's long record practicing law in Atlanta, he was a legal scholar who impressed the younger lawyers with his sound advice. During the war years he readily tackled novel questions and procedures for clients of the firm, as in the case of *National Labor Relations Board v. Montag Bros., Inc.* (51 NLRB 366, 140 F. 2d 730). Richardson's wit and chivalrous demeanor also left an impression on virtually everyone he came across. Herbert Elsas's wife, Edith, said of the diminutive, mildly eccentric Richardson, "He was like a character out of Dickens." Richardson left the firm in 1946 when the last of the prewar lawyers returned, but he was persuaded to come back to the firm as counsel in 1956. He remained active in that capacity until his death in 1971.[5]

SUTHERLAND LAWYERS' WAR EXPERIENCES

Given the significance of the war to the history of both the nation and the firm, the partners' war experiences are worth examining in some depth. The Sutherland lawyers who served during the war endured a variety of hardships and learned many valuable lessons. Fortunately they all returned alive, though two were wounded in action. Ed Kane received a bullet wound in his thigh, and Elbert Tuttle was nearly killed in hand-to-hand combat in the Pacific Theater.[6] Major Herbert Elsas of the Army Air Corps, Captain Randolph Thrower of the Marines, and Lieutenant Colonel C. Norman Stallings of the Army all returned unscathed from extended tours overseas. So also did the firm's summer law clerk, Lieutenant Jim Wilson, who served on a Navy destroyer in the Pacific. In addition, at least four more future partners – Mac Asbill, Jr., Pat Patterson, Baxter Jones, Jr., and Ed Schmuck – also served during the war.

Anyone who joined the military services during the war had to make personal sacrifices, of course, but we should keep in mind that the Sutherland lawyers were not desperate young men in search of adventure on the high seas. They were well educated, well employed, and living in relative comfort compared with much of the American workforce during the Depression. Furthermore, Tuttle was well into his forties, and even the associates were upwards of 10 years beyond the traditional enlistment age. These men had much to lose by joining the war effort, but like most Americans of their generation, they took everything in stride and made their sacrifices for the greater good.

ELBERT TUTTLE

When Congress declared war in 1941, Elbert Tuttle had the most military experience of any of the Sutherland lawyers. He had served in the Army in the First World War and as an officer in the Georgia National Guard between the wars. Upon returning to active duty after Pearl Harbor, the 45-year-old Tuttle declined a desk job, choosing instead to accept deployment as a lieutenant colonel to command the 304th Field Artillery Battalion, 77th Infantry Division, in the South Pacific. During this command he served at Guam, Leyte (Philippines), Kerama

ATLANTA DIRECTORY LISTING

1944 — Sutherland, Tuttle & Brennan

Retlo, and several other islands. He was severely wounded in hand-to-hand combat on Ie Shima, the Pacific island near Okinawa on which Ernie Pyle, the famed war correspondent, was killed.

Historian and journalist Jack Bass recounted the story of Tuttle's brush with death in his book *Unlikely Heroes*:

> *[Tuttle] was asleep in his tent when a Japanese suicide squad staged a surprise predawn raid attack on his unit…Tuttle suffered wounds in his neck, back, left hand, and both legs from a hand grenade that exploded beside his tent. Then, while he was subduing a Japanese soldier in hand-to-hand combat, another one clubbed him from behind and bloodied his bald head.*
>
> *When the battle ended, the attackers were all dead, and Tuttle's executive officer found him sitting on a tree stump, barefooted, clad in shorts and a shirt, and caked with blood still oozing from his wounds. With great concern, he asked, "How are you? How do you feel?" Someone had just handed Tuttle a cup of hot coffee, and at that moment the sun shot above the horizon across the ocean. Tuttle realized he was there to witness the nineteenth day of April, 1945. "Dan," he said, "I never felt better in my life."[7]*

Tuttle's injuries gave him the opportunity to return to Washington to work at a higher rank away from the action, but he refused. He remained in active service and was discharged at the end of the war as a colonel. He was highly decorated for his service, receiving the Legion of Merit, the Bronze Star, and the Purple Heart with Oak Leaf Cluster. In addition to Tuttle's personal citations, the 304th was cited in 1944 for "outstanding performance of duty in action against the enemy on the Island of Leyte." The citation noted "the extraordinary heroism and esprit de corps displayed by the 304th Field Artillery Battalion," which reflected "the highest credit to the organization and conforms to the very highest traditions of the military service." Tuttle reached the rank of brigadier general in 1947, and for three years he commanded the 108th Airborne Division, U.S. Army Reserve. Tuttle's son, Elbert, Jr., also served in the war, having enlisted in the Marines with his cousin Mac Asbill, Jr. (Elbert, Jr. once flew his Navy torpedo bomber two hours from Tinian Island to Guam to bring his father back to the Tinian base, where the two spent the weekend together.)[8]

While the war was still raging in the Pacific, Tuttle wrote a letter to the Georgia Bar Association to tell the folks on the home front to keep up their end of the fight. The following brief excerpt shows Tuttle's steadfastness in the face of difficult conditions, as well as his respect for the young men who were putting their lives on the line for the cause of victory:

> *As you read in the newspapers daily, our job of blasting [the enemy] out of the mass of caves and other subterranean works is a tough one, but everything is going along well and optimism still runs high, except when the clouds turn gray and the rain pelts down. Then my admiration for the doughboys boils*

*over the top, because they keep right on slugging it out… Don't let **any** stone remain unturned by the American people to make this sort of thing impossible for the future. Nothing else matters so much as that.*[9]

RANDOLPH THROWER

Of all the firm's lawyers who served during the war, Randolph Thrower's service was the most varied. When the war began, he applied for a commission in the Army and the Navy. But when he got wind of the important work being done by the understaffed FBI, he applied, was hired, and was well entrenched by the time he heard back from the services. He ended up serving as an FBI special agent from 1942 to 1943 and as a captain in the Marine Corps from 1944 to 1945.[10]

Thrower had some interesting experiences in the FBI, to say the least. Even before the United States was dragged into the conflict, the federal government had feared the organized activities of a variety of foreign interests, especially Nazi-sympathizing German-Americans, communist-sympathizing labor organizers, and Japanese resident aliens. Shortly before Pearl Harbor, when war was raging in Europe and Asia, the FBI was given jurisdiction over internal subversion, sabotage, and espionage.

Once the U.S. actually entered the war, the nation's defensive apparatus required both domestic vigilance and geopolitical acumen. This made for an interesting mix of work, with Thrower right at the center of things. The Soviets were now America's wartime allies, and they were threatening to withdraw from the war if the U.S. did not commit itself to a second front. The feeling in the State Department and Department of Justice was that communist agents and sympathizers in the U.S. might return to a program of espionage and sabotage if the Russians made such a separate peace. This was not totally out of the question, for not only had the Russians made such a peace with the Germans in the First World War, but Hitler and Stalin had joined together to carve up Poland at the war's outset. In the event of such a peace, the FBI had to be ready to pick up the leadership of these subversive cells.

After Thrower's FBI training, he was assigned to investigate alleged subversives in upstate New York. His group investigated the employees of defense plants in this area and uncovered a surprising amount of subversive activity. They found, for example, that the union at the 43,000-employee General Electric plant in Schenectady, New York, was being run by a small cadre of very dedicated communist party members. But since a separate Soviet-German peace was never made, the FBI did not receive the order to arrest these men. After the war, though, these labor leaders were quickly purged.

Thrower was also ordered to investigate applicants who were under consideration for the top secret Manhattan Project. His superiors assured him that it was a job to be taken seriously, and in retrospect we know that this was the case. By 1945 the

Manhattan Project had employed more than 130,000 people and had cost nearly $2 billion (more than $20 billion in 2004 dollars). We also know that when the Soviet Union detonated an atomic device of their own in 1949, it was widely suspected that spies in the Manhattan Project had passed secret information to the Soviets. This suspicion was later proved true. When Thrower began his investigations, the first name he received was a man who, only two weeks earlier, had been identified as the head of a spy cell at Rensselaer Polytechnic Institute. This candidate was being considered for employment as a mathematician, but he would not make the cut.

Thrower found the investigative work stimulating, but he had always intended to join the armed services. Midway through the war he tried to join the Marine Corps, but he found that it was much easier to get into the FBI than it was to get out. FBI director J. Edgar Hoover was quite jealous of his organization, and he had worked out something of a gentleman's arrangement with the armed services, whereby the latter agreed not to grant commissions to FBI men. But as Thrower's luck would have it, the day he visited the Marine Corps recruiting officer in Albany, New York, the recruiter had just received highly confidential word that the Marines were authorized to quietly enlist some FBI agents to work as air combat intelligence officers and ground control officers.

Despite the Marines' needs, an "unseen influence" seemed to be holding up Thrower's paperwork. Bill Sutherland then introduced Thrower to a friend, a Marine Corps general who was heading personnel affairs. Thrower and the general had dinner together and immediately developed a good rapport, which eventually led to the young man's admission into the Marines. Thrower's telling of the tale bears repeating:

> The general told me that he had recently remarried. His first wife had died, and his second wife was younger. He was in his early 50s, and she, I think, was in her late 20s. It worried him that he wanted to have children, and she wanted to have children, but he wondered about it, whether it was the right thing to do. So I told him about [my wife] Margaret's father, who had remarried at 52 and had eight more children. Hearing that story pleased him greatly, and he took care of me. Thereafter I was shortly in.[11]

As for Sutherland's act of kindness in introducing the young man to the general, Thrower described this as typical of Sutherland's ability to use his influence to help his friends and employees. In Thrower's words, "He did this sort of thing…and he would help anybody, too."

Once in the Marines, Thrower was deployed as an Air Intelligence officer, spending one month in the Philippines and eight months in Okinawa. In addition to his more formal intelligence duties, he was charged with reading, and sometimes censoring, letters written home by other Marines. He also had time to write letters of his own, and he is said to have sent his wife a letter a day while he was overseas. Given the time he spent at war, these must have totaled around 300. In one letter he called his accommodations at Okinawa "a comfortable foxhole with little chance of a direct hit." Fortunately he was right, and he returned to Atlanta after the war's end.

HERBERT ELSAS

Herbert Elsas served in the combat intelligence branch of the 8th Air Force in the European Theater. The massive, Britain-based 8th was at the center of allied air operations in Europe, and it paid a high price, suffering half of the U.S. Army's total air casualties during the war. Captain Elsas's most important role in the 8th was helping direct allied air raids over the European continent. He also oversaw an important study that led to improvements in the British wireless intercept system, a crucial part of the intelligence-gathering matrix. He had learned German and French as a child, and his facility in these languages led to some unusual – and sometimes dangerous – assignments. At least once, and perhaps several times, he had to go behind enemy lines in order to help direct allied aircraft on reconnaissance and bombing missions.

Elsas often sent letters home, but he never had a leave that was long enough to enable him to return to the U.S. And since the Army heavily censored letters in order to expurgate strategic information, Elsas's family had little information as to his activities or where-abouts. His wife, Edith, remembered some years later, "We didn't know where Herbert was, only that he was in the 8th Air Force in the European Theater." Even Elsas's homecoming after VE-Day was bittersweet, for he returned to the United States with standing orders to head to the Pacific. Everyone at this time expected an

Legion of Merit Award

invasion of Japan, which would surely have cost tens of thousands of American lives. Fortunately, the surprisingly quick Japanese surrender prevented Elsas and countless others from being put back in harm's way.[12]

Like many men of his generation, Elsas was always quite private about his war experiences. His son, Alan, said of his father's exploits, "Today he would be considered a war hero…but for all his accomplishments, he never talked about it." Although Herbert did not discuss his military service with his friends or family, he did find ways to quietly pay tribute to the men with whom he had served. Most notably, whenever he and Edith visited London in the years after the war, their first stop was always the airmen's chapel at St. Paul's Cathedral.[13]

General James Doolittle presented Elsas with the Legion of Merit. The accompanying text of the award, which hangs in the Elsas Room at the Emory University

Law Library, testifies to Elsas's admirable achievements:

> *For exceptionally meritorious conduct in the performance of outstanding services, while serving with the Intelligence Section, Headquarters VIII Fighter Command, from May 1943 to June 6 1944. When the exigencies of escort missions for heavy bombers required deep penetrations of Germany, it became necessary to devise some system for supplying information of the location of our planes and the location and intentions of the enemy. The British "Y" or wireless Interception System of German interphone communication was selected for development and Captain Elsas was charged with performing the needed research and study.*
>
> *The thorough knowledge and background acquired by him in a very short time resulted in many valuable modifications and changes being incorporated in this wireless interception system. Captain Elsas also instituted a system for making a pictorial representation of friendly and enemy actions so that Group Leaders might be as well posted as possible on what enemy action to expect. The ingenious, extreme devotion to duty, untiring effort, and keen insight displayed by Captain Elsas in the successful achievement of a difficult task, reflect the highest credit upon himself and the armed forces of the United States.*

FUTURE PARTNERS

A few of the Sutherland firm's later additions also served during the war. Jim Heffernan, for example, who went on to do acclaimed work in the Washington tax practice, joined the Navy. Owing to his youth, however, he could not enlist until late in the war, and by the time he finished his training the fighting was over. But several other future partners were trained and deployed early enough to be in the thick of things overseas. Ed Schmuck served as an intelligence officer in the European Theater and participated in the Battle of the Bulge. Baxter Jones, Jr. joined the Army as a private when the war broke out, and he was honorably discharged in 1946 at the rank of major. Three of the firm's other future partners – Jim Wilson, Mac Asbill, Jr., and Pat Patterson – also served for several years during the war, and their stories are told here.

JAMES H. "JIMMY" WILSON, JR.

Second-year law student Jim Wilson was studying in Harvard's Langdale Hall library when he heard about the bombing of Pearl Harbor. The next day, he and nearly everyone he knew at Harvard went to the local naval district headquarters to enlist. Since Wilson had a college degree, he was quickly commissioned as an ensign and sent to Key West, the base for anti-submarine warfare in the Gulf of Mexico, aka the "Gulf Sea Frontier." The location seemed a bit strange to Wilson, who expected an environment crawling with enemy combatants. He later recalled of his orders, "I said, 'What's going on here?' I thought we were going to invade Martinique or one of the other French-held islands. But it wasn't anything nearly that dramatic."[14]

The U.S. was losing the war in the Atlantic at the time because it lacked modern anti-submarine vessels. Wilson was assigned to the base communications department, where he got a firsthand glimpse of the Navy's limitations early in the war. One story from this communications post became legendary. "The Coast Guard had a cutter called the *Nike*," said Wilson. "One day this boat spotted a submarine, and it sent a message to the headquarters: '*Nike* chasing sub.' But after a short time the boat's commander sent a very different message: 'Sub chasing *Nike*.' That kind of thing was our problem then."

The Gulf headquarters were moved to Miami, and when a group of Waves (or Women Accepted for Volunteer Emergency Service, the acronym for the women's service of the Navy) started doing Wilson's job, he realized he should go elsewhere. He applied for destroyer duty, and in the meantime he was sent to Dartmouth and Princeton – what he called "the Ivy League tour of duty" – to study navigation and seamanship. Most of his class was slated for armed guard duty on convoys headed to Murmansk. This was considered a very dangerous assignment, as it consisted of little more than an ensign manning a three-inch gun. German U-boats regularly sunk such vessels.

Wilson avoided armed guard duty, but his Pacific destroyer assignment was no picnic. "As it turned out," he recalled, "the destroyer duty I got was a heck of a lot more dangerous than the armed guard duty. We were getting control of the Atlantic with subs, but all hell was breaking loose in the Pacific." Wilson began his campaign across the Central Pacific with the 1944 Kwajalein invasion, and he was involved in every invasion in that area until the end of the war. His service included Iwo Jima, the island that saw some of the fiercest fighting in the entire theater. Here he saw the flag being raised on Mt. Suribachi, the scene that became perhaps the most iconic image of the Pacific war.

At the end of the war, Wilson's commanding officer tried to convince him to reenlist, saying, "You'll never make more than $10,000 a year as a lawyer. You're better off in the Navy." The officer's estimate may not have been too far off at the time, but fortunately Wilson had other plans. He returned to law school and soon rejoined the Sutherland firm.

MAC ASBILL, JR.

Bill Sutherland's and Elbert Tuttle's nephew, Mac Asbill, Jr. ("Mackey"), was still a few years shy of joining the law firm, but in consideration of his lifelong service to the firm and his exceptional experience in the war, a few words on his military service are in order. Mac, Jr. served for two years as an aide to Marine Corps general Holland "Howlin' Mad" Smith, who commanded the Marines in the Central Pacific. Asbill accompanied the general on amphibious landings throughout the Pacific Theater, from Tarawa to Iwo Jima, and eventually earned the Bronze Star and an honorable discharge at the rank of captain.

Midway through the war, Asbill met his future law firm colleague Jim Wilson. Wilson had clerked at the firm before joining the Navy, and Sutherland and Tuttle had suggested that he try to meet up with Mackey, who was serving in Hawaii at the time. Wilson visited Asbill in General Smith's temporary Pearl Harbor headquarters, and the two hit it off immediately. As Wilson later recalled, the famously cantankerous general was, fortunately, "very fond of Mac, so he was very nice to me."[15]

General Smith acquired a reputation for toughness in the South Pacific campaigns. In his memoir, *Coral and Brass*, he relished reprinting Asbill's reflections on his leadership: "[Smith's] methods of controlling the division were skillfully varied to suit the personalities and situations involved. He used threats, exhortations, sound advice, sympathy: he cursed, demanded, cajoled, urged and praised. Invariably, his method was the right one." An excerpt from Smith's memoir also says much about the young Asbill's leadership qualities and his relationship with the general. Shortly after the bloody battle of Iwo Jima, Smith wanted to climb Mt. Suribachi to look over the island, but there was no road to take him to the top. The general therefore asked Asbill to go up and find a suitable route. When the young man came back, he shook his head and announced, "No, General, I can't let you climb that cliff. You're too old to make it." Smith went on to write, "I accepted his decision. I have commanded hundreds of thousands of men in my life, but for the first time I got ordered around by my aide."[16]

WILLIAM R. "PAT" PATTERSON

Another future partner's service also merits our attention. Pat Patterson served in the Navy in the Pacific Theater, and although in later years he insisted that his military service was "completely undistinguished," it is worth recounting nonetheless.[17]

Patterson was one of thousands of young men who joined the V-12 program, through which colleges trained students to be naval officers. After several months in such a program, a young recruit would apply for an officer's commission. Patterson left his hometown of Hickory, North Carolina, to join the V-12 program at Newberry College in South Carolina. An executive officer there was impressed with Patterson's ability to handle the work, and within three weeks the young man was transferred to the more rigorous program at the University of Rochester.

Patterson was immediately impressed with the difficulty and variety of naval-oriented math and science courses at Rochester. Another aspect of Rochester also

Elbert P. Tuttle, Mac Asbill, Jr., and Dr. Elbert P. Tuttle "Tut" – Elbert P. Tuttle's son and Mac, Jr.'s first cousin

made an impression. In Patterson's words, "One of the things that was particularly outstanding about Rochester was it was *cold*. I mean, it was *flat cold*. I arrived on November 4 and it was snowing. We didn't see the ground again until May." The harsh northern climate continued to dog him when he was later transferred to the University of Notre Dame's midshipman school.

Patterson and his cohorts were given three future duty choices while at Notre Dame, and all three of Patterson's choices were to transfer to "deck" – shorthand for "wherever the action is." This would be hard to pull off, because around this time he also learned that he had developed a form of astigmatism, which would likely mean an unappealing commission in the supply corps. Like most young men, though, Patterson wanted to be a line officer, "firing guns and that sort of thing." (Years later he was to say, "If I'd had any sense I would have been happy to have been a supply officer. But I had more youthful aspirations than that.")

Fortunately Patterson's commanding officer took a liking to him, and the young man was soon on his way to deck. This was two years into the war, however, by which time the Navy had nearly reached its deck officer quota. Notre Dame midshipmen were accordingly notified that they would be designated Seamen First Class and sent to Great Lakes Naval Training Station for reassignment. Patterson therefore asked to be transferred to the deck program. His request was granted, and he was commissioned as a deck officer at Cornell University two days before Christmas of 1943.

From that point on Patterson served in the Navy's amphibious program. He was sent to Coronado training base in California, where he was introduced to the world of landing craft and assault boats. This branch of the Navy was a crucial part of the war effort. The amphibious craft were the famous "Higgins boats," named after a Prohibition-era rumrunner who was able to evade authorities by landing his boats in the swamps of Louisiana. Many observers later argued that these won the war for the U.S. because they made possible the efficient landing of soldiers onto defended beachheads. Patterson was assigned to an assault transport ship, the USS *Mendocino*, which carried 1,500 assault troops and their supplies. He later recalled that, although this assignment "was not exactly battleship status," it was nonetheless "quite good service."

The *Mendocino* was deployed throughout the Pacific, which allowed the once-landlocked Tar Heel to live up to the old Navy slogan and "see the world." He was placed in few life-threatening situations, though he had a close call during an assignment toward the end of the war. "I was called on for one landing, and the ship I was assigned to was late leaving Pearl Harbor to get to the new assignment, so I didn't get it. Thank God for that. It was the Iwo Jima invasion. I saw the ship back in Pearl Harbor six months later, and it had lost all of its assault boats."

Patterson later said of his service, "I treasure the Navy experience I had. It was a very maturing experience. But," he added, "it also taught me I didn't have any desire to go on and be a naval officer."

WARTIME CASES

Despite the war's effect on the firm's personnel numbers, the remaining partners were able to handle a few important cases. For example, after the *Anniston* decision Sutherland and Brennan kept a close eye on developments in other lawyers' cases that might have a bearing on Sutherland clients' interests. One such case, *Webre Steib Co. v. Commissioner* (324 U.S. 164 (1945)), had gone up from the Processing Tax Board of

USS *Mendocino*

Review through the court of appeals to the Supreme Court. It involved the sugar processing tax and presented questions as to the board's application of the statutory presumption and burden of proof in the light of the Supreme Court's decision in *Anniston*. As with some important tax cases handled by other firms in the 1930s, Sutherland participated in the oral argument in the Supreme Court.

THE COXSON CASE

Randolph Thrower took on a pro bono case shortly before he left Atlanta to join the FBI, and in later years he often recalled just how much the case had influenced him.[18] He first learned of the matter when an outside lawyer with a good deal of experience in civil liberties cases paid the firm a small fee to assist with the case of a young man who had been convicted of rape. Elbert Tuttle encouraged Thrower to take over the case because he knew Thrower would learn a great deal from the older lawyer.

The case itself involved a black man in his late teens named Will Coxson. Coxson was in jail in Marietta, Georgia, after having been convicted and sentenced to death for the rape of a white woman. The incident had taken place one morning after the woman's husband, a migratory dairy worker, had gone off to work. There was very little doubt about the rape, but the identity of the actual assailant was uncertain. The victim described him as a light-skinned black man, and when the police arrested a man who seemed to fit the description, she identified him. The officers then told her he had a plausible alibi. Coxson was then brought in, and she identified him, even though, by all accounts, Coxson was quite dark-skinned. As it turned out, both Coxson and the first man had been in the area of the crime. Coxson had run home, and the police tracked him with dogs. The police then claimed to have gotten a "three-way confession" through a paid jailhouse stool pigeon.

According to Thrower, although the lawyer appointed to represent Coxson did an excellent job of showing that it could just as likely have been the other man, Coxson's chances were hurt because this lawyer had not fully prepared. Thrower and his colleague thus took the case on habeas corpus on the following grounds. They first argued that, although the original lawyer had been adequate in trial, he had not interviewed witnesses ahead of time or pursued any tests that might have helped his client's case. The other grounds were that the jury and the grand jury were unconstitutionally established by reason of the systematic exclusion of blacks. Needless to say, this last point was a provocative one, and it would prove difficult for the lawyers to manage.

Coxson had been taken to Fulton County to avoid the possibility of a lynch mob, so Thrower and the other attorney brought the petition in Fulton County. The state moved to dismiss the petition, and that was granted by the superior court. The two lawyers then appealed to the state supreme court, and the court ruled that if their allegations about the inadequacy of representation were upheld,

In later years Thrower would look back on this case as the one that tormented him more than any other.

the conviction should be invalidated. This was quite advanced for the time, and could have set up a landmark decision. But unfortunately for Coxson's team, they lost on the issue of the constituency of the jury and grand jury.

At this point an ugly behind-the-scenes incident colored Thrower's impression of the proceedings. The chief justice of the Supreme Court of Georgia, a good friend of both Bill Sutherland and Elbert Tuttle, spoke to Sutherland about Thrower's attempt to use the racial composition of the jury to his client's benefit. As Thrower later explained it, the chief justice "said he thought it was appropriate for me to raise the representation issue, but that he hated to see a fine young man like me getting into these racial issues. Well, the only thing I really ever held against Bill was that he didn't tell him to go to hell, which he did not do. But [Bill] did not press in any way to change our progress in the case."

Thrower then took the case back for trial on the issue of fair representation. One of the senior judges in Fulton County held against them, and they headed back to the appeals court with the expectation of having to go to the U.S. Supreme Court. It was then that the war forced Thrower to leave Atlanta and turn the case over to the other lawyer. The ACLU had been paying the other lawyer a small fee, and when their funds dried up he dropped the case. When this happened, Coxson's chances all but evaporated. He was eventually executed.

In later years Thrower would look back on this case as the one that tormented him more than any other. As he saw it, "both men knew about [the crime], and both ran, but there was no more reason to believe my client did it than the other man. It makes me madder than any case I've had." It was also painful on a professional level, for Thrower was not able to bring it to the Supreme Court. He later suggested that "on some of the issues it would have been a landmark case."

In a 2001 lecture, Thrower explained just how much the case had affected his life and his attitude toward the law:

> *A lawyer can have seared upon the mind the experience of having a client executed when, under law, the life should not have been taken. This happened to me...For the past 60 years, no case has kept me awake at night as much as this, wondering what else I might have done to save the life of this young man. These are not the sort of experiences that can be put on the scales and weighed against billable hours and the bottom line.*[19]

V-Day: The Firm Restored

Of the Sutherland lawyers who temporarily left the firm to join the war effort – Tuttle, Kane, Elsas, Thrower, Stallings, Ben F. Johnson, Jr., and Benjamin S. Horack – all but Johnson and Horack returned to the firm after the war. Johnson left to teach law and later became dean of the Emory University Law School, while Horack returned to his native North Carolina and went on to head a large firm in Charlotte. Stallings came back to the Atlanta office after the war but left for good in 1949 to practice law in his native Tampa. He later became a senior partner with a prominent firm in that city. And Jim Wilson, the summer law clerk who would go on to have a long, fruitful career with the firm, went back to Harvard Law School after leaving the Navy.[20]

The others came back to stay, and all were quite surprised that there was still so much work for them to do. Randolph Thrower, for one, fully expected to be unemployed after the war, as it seemed impossible that a law firm could survive the sudden return of so many lawyers after such a lengthy absence. He began to make plans to find work elsewhere, but when he spoke to Bill Sutherland about the matter, Sutherland told him that the firm needed him as soon as possible. Thrower later recalled of this good fortune, "I had no idea that the firm, with two lawyers, could absorb eight or ten more overnight." He added, "I had looked forward, wherever I went, to having a clean desk, because I'd had a big stack of cases [before the war]. But when I got back, I found that very few files, if any, had been moved off my desk."[21]

Ring Building — 18th Street, NW, north of L Street, Washington, DC

The partners were divided as to whether the firm should expand into new areas, and serious arguments took place before the "yes" vote eventually won the day.

~ CHAPTER SIX ~

POSTWAR EXPANSION

The immediate postwar years were a time of readjustment and major debates over future growth. The partners were divided as to whether the firm should expand into new areas, and serious arguments took place before the "yes" vote eventually won the day. Meanwhile, the founders and the "second generation" lawyers continued to build the firm's reputation, while talented new acquisitions also began to make their mark.[1]

NEW OFFICES, NEW TALENT

In the fall of 1946 the Washington office took on new significance when Bill Sutherland decided to move north once and for all. Sutherland had long tried to persuade the younger lawyers to take up residence in the capital, and he was able to get a few of them to go for short periods. But he decided to take the plunge himself because the other partners were less than enthusiastic about leaving Atlanta permanently. He was briefly joined by G. Maynard Smith, a Georgia lawyer who had been a special assistant to the attorney general in Washington. Smith left the office after one year. Although Sutherland's arrival in the capital anchored the long-term growth of the Washington practice, the number of lawyers increased slowly in the 1940s and 1950s. When Jim Heffernan was hired in 1952, the Washington office had only two partners and four associates, and when Jerome Libin came aboard in 1961, the total had only gone up to nine lawyers.

The firm made two additional moves forward in the year following Bill Sutherland's relocation. The Washington office was moved into the newly remodeled Ring Building at 1631 K Street, NW, and the firm was strengthened by the addition of Jim Wilson to the Atlanta office and his close friend from Harvard Law School, Mallory R. Smith, to Washington. Wilson had already earned the partners' respect when he served as their summer clerk in 1941, so they were happy to have him join on a full-time basis after the war. Likewise, Wilson was able to persuade Smith that the Sutherland firm had great potential for a young associate. The partners could also be quite sure that they had acquired two future legal heavyweights, for Wilson and Smith were number one and number three in their class at Harvard Law.

*The Asbills' addition also made the
Sutherland firm more of a family affair
than it already was, for both Mac, Sr.
and Elbert Tuttle had married
Bill Sutherland's sisters.*

But perhaps the most significant acquisition of this period came at the end of
the wartime decade. In 1949, as the firm celebrated its first quarter century, it was
fortunate enough to garner the services of two major players, including the co-
architect of the original founding plan. Mac Asbill, Sr. (Harvard LL.B. 1917) came
on as a partner in September of that year, joining his son Mac, Jr. (Princeton A.B.
1942; Harvard LL.B., magna cum laude, 1948), who had been hired as an associate
two months earlier. The hiring of the elder Asbill capped a decades-in-the-making
plan to unite the South Carolinian with his two old friends Elbert Tuttle and Bill
Sutherland. As for the talented younger Asbill, he would make a name for himself
in his own right during his long career with the firm.

The elder Asbill had, of course, discussed with Sutherland and Tuttle the advantages of settling in Atlanta to practice law as far back as the 1910s. Asbill was the first
of the trio to come to Atlanta to practice law shortly after serving in the Army during
World War I. But when Tuttle and Sutherland formed their partnership in 1924, Mac
decided that it was more professionally advantageous to remain with a different firm
for the time being. Over the course of the next few decades he built a strong
reputation in antitrust law and litigation. In 1934 he moved to Washington as a
special assistant to Attorney General Homer Cummings, and he remained in that
city for the rest of his career. He also served as a section chief in the Antitrust
Division of the U.S. Department of Justice under President Roosevelt. When
Cummings returned to private practice in 1942, he brought Asbill into his
Washington firm, Cummings & Stanley. Mac, Sr. continued with the Cummings firm
until Mac, Jr. finished law school. It was then that Sutherland and Tuttle decided the
time was right to bring the Asbills into the Sutherland fold.[2]

The realization of the original plan was a stroke of luck for the firm. Mac, Sr.
added much to the firm's stature, and he brought with him a wealth of experience
and contacts from up and down the East Coast. The Asbills' addition also made the
Sutherland firm more of a family affair than it already was, for both Mac, Sr. and
Elbert Tuttle had married Bill Sutherland's sisters. (This was before the firm established its nepotism policy, of course.) The younger lawyers also appreciated the
significance of these familial and friendly bonds. As Randolph Thrower later said,
"It was a meaningful thing to all of us that what [the original three] had planned
did eventually evolve." But although the firm's lawyers understood the significance
of the Asbills' hiring, not all of the firm's friends and clients were so well informed.
"I'm very much impressed with what you've done," wrote a colleague of Herbert

Elsas's in response to the hiring announcement. "I've never even heard of *one* Mac Asbill and you've added *two*."[3]

Mac, Jr. had already had some remarkable experiences by the time he came to the firm. During World War II he served as an aide to Marine Corps general Holland "Howlin' Mad" Smith in the Pacific Theater. He enrolled in Harvard Law School after the war, and after graduating in 1948 he spent a year as a law clerk to Supreme Court justice Stanley Reed. He was then torn between practicing law with his father and practicing with the Sutherland firm, but this Gordian knot was broken when Sutherland and Tuttle agreed to take on both Asbills.[4]

The Asbills and Jim Wilson were certainly valuable additions to the organization, but some key personnel were also lost in these postwar years. Most notably, founding partner Elbert Tuttle withdrew in January 1953 to become general counsel of the United States Treasury, after which the firm changed its name to Sutherland, Asbill & Brennan. The following year Tuttle was appointed to the United States Court of Appeals for the Fifth Circuit (see Ch. 7). In addition to Tuttle, Ed Kane and C. Norman Stallings left in 1948 and 1949, respectively, to join other firms.[5]

But the most tragic loss was that of the newcomer Mallory Smith. After joining the firm with Jim Wilson, Smith quickly established himself as a promising young lawyer. He was so good, in fact, that he traveled to Alexandria, Egypt, in 1950 to settle a claim for a Georgia client against an Egyptian cotton broker who had reneged on a deal. Smith closed the matter in Egypt, and on the return flight his plane crashed in the Libyan Desert, killing everyone aboard. "We lost a great young lawyer and a great potential partner," lamented Randolph Thrower. The Harvard Law School later

Mallory Smith

Jim Wilson met Mallory Smith on their first day at Harvard Law School. Smith, a South Carolina native, had gone to the registrar's office to see the list of new students, and when he saw that Wilson was a Georgian, he decided to introduce himself. The two became fast friends, and they went on to work together on the *Harvard Law Review*. They eventually graduated number one and number three in their class before joining the Sutherland firm.

Wilson marveled at Smith's operational abilities during their time at Harvard. In his words, "Mallory was always a step ahead of everyone else." One of Smith's greatest accomplishments before graduating from law school was tutoring the children of an old-money Boston Brahmin family. Smith taught the youths the important academic subjects, and he took special care in teaching them how to play poker ("at which," said Wilson, "he was very good"). Smith's legal abilities matched his dexterity in gaming, which perhaps proves beyond a reasonable doubt that the partners sought associates with multiple talents in these early years.[18]

The young Turks of the firm: Michael J. Egan, Jr., Willis B. Snell, and Randolph W. Thrower

named a room in their student center after Smith. Smith's legacy also lived on in his daughter, Margaret Warner, a journalist who regularly appeared on PBS's *The News Hour with Jim Lehrer*, among many other television news programs.[6]

The Washington office also suffered a temporary setback when Mac Asbill, Jr. returned to active military duty during the Korean War. When the war broke out, Asbill foresaw that he would be called back into the Marine Corps, so he decided to launch a preemptive strike and join the office of Secretary of the Army Frank Pace. Together with Frank Shackleford from the Sutherland firm's Atlanta office, Asbill organized the Army's Office of the General Counsel. He returned to the Sutherland firm's Washington office after the war. Jim Wilson spent one year in the Washington office to help fill the gap left by Asbill and Mallory Smith.

The firm's expansion in personnel was accompanied by new business practices, and one of the most significant additions to the firm's professional methods in the postwar years was the keeping of time records. The partners had avoided this move for nearly three decades out of a sense of tradition and a preference for informality, but the field of law was changing rapidly. Although many of the firm's early cases had helped build its reputation, they did not put food on the table, which led Herbert Elsas to joke, "When I came into the firm, I had to do a bit of research as to how we would eat." Elsas quite sensibly saw that a change in this culture of informality might go a long way toward shoring up the firm's financial situation. Inspired in part by Elsas's business sense, the partners eventually realized that they had to be more vigilant about time. In 1952 Sutherland, Tuttle & Brennan thus became the first Atlanta firm to make the move to time sheets. While many lawyers saw such records as an imposition on their freedom, the decision was a natural outcome of the firm's new priorities and changes in the legal field.[7]

This is not to say, however, that time records were never considered in earlier years. Bill Sutherland had a hard time overseeing his lawyers' work in Washington before he moved there himself, and Randolph Thrower later told of one occasion when Sutherland had made a rather "indecent" proposal regarding record keeping:

> *I enjoyed [the Washington job] so much that Bill Sutherland at one point asked me to keep time sheets so that he could get some concept as to what I was doing. Time records, well, I thought that was unprofessional. It offended my sense of dignity. I didn't have much, but whatever there was, it offended me. And besides, it was a big nuisance having to put down on paper exactly what I was doing because I was operating pretty much at will. If I wanted to be off an hour or so, I would, and if I wanted to work at night or on the weekend, I would. But I did for a while keep time records, all under protest, and they were, I have to admit, quite creative. After a while Bill gave up on it, and it was some years before we went back uniformly to time records.*[8]

The postwar years also saw the firm change at the planning level as the partners established the foundations of an administrative committee. The original plan called for a four-member committee with a partner and an associate from each office. The creators did not include Bill Sutherland, however, because he was the undisputed head of the firm. The first incarnation of this committee consisted of Laurens Williams, Mac Asbill, Sr., Herbert Elsas, and Jim Wilson. Jim Heffernan was also included as the unofficial secretary. Their first meeting took place in Ponte Vedra, Florida, where Tuttle, Sutherland, and Mac Asbill, Sr. had long taken their vacations.[9]

THE GROWTH DEBATE

Two of the most significant issues facing the firm in the decade or so after the war were expansion into newer areas of law and the rate at which the practice should grow. At this time, the young Turks of the firm began to urge the older partners to broaden the practice. There was something of a generation gap here as to whether the firm should continue to be primarily tax specialists. The older, more conservative leaders – excluding Mac Asbill, Sr. and Elbert Tuttle – were worried about stepping out into uncharted territory and encroaching on the work of firms that had, for many years, referred clients to Sutherland. It was more or less understood in those days that one firm did not "steal" clients from another.[10]

The young Turks eventually prevailed, and the 1950s was a period of considerable growth, both in the breadth of the practice and in the number of personnel. The growth of the Washington office had begun in earnest, of course, when Bill Sutherland decided to take up permanent residence in that city in 1946. And the addition of some key players in the late 1940s expanded the firm's expertise and reputation. The partners then began to add lawyers who would contribute to the development of new specialties. The Atlanta office, meanwhile, took on some very talented young lawyers. The decision to branch out into new areas was a difficult one, but fortunately the expansion was successful, and it continued through the 1950s and 1960s.

Several associates joined the firm in the 1950s, and those who ultimately became major players included Laurens "Laurie" Williams (Hastings A.B. 1928; Cornell LL.B. 1931), William R. "Pat" Patterson (Duke LL.B. 1950), C. Baxter Jones, Jr. (Emory J.D. 1948), Willis B. Snell (Michigan J.D. 1951), Kenneth H. Liles (Michigan J.D. 1947), James V. Heffernan (Cornell J.D. 1952), D. Robert Cumming, Jr. (Georgia LL.B. 1953), James P. Groton (Virginia LL.B. 1954), Michael J. Egan, Jr. (Harvard LL.B. 1955), and George L. Cohen (Virginia LL.B. 1956).

THE WASHINGTON AND ATLANTA OFFICES

Even before 1950 the firm was well on its way to putting together a nationally renowned tax practice. But the addition of Snell (1951), Liles (1952), Heffernan (1952), and Williams (1956) to the Washington office gave the firm more potential than ever in that direction. Liles and Williams were especially fortunate acquisitions because they were already well known in the field. Liles came to the firm after spending two years in the office of the chief counsel of the IRS, while Williams arrived after stints as assistant to the secretary of the Treasury and head of the Treasury's Legal Advisory Staff. Prior to Williams's Treasury assignment, he had been a senior partner in an Omaha law firm and president of the Nebraska State

Plaza Park, Atlanta, Georgia, 1949

Bar Association. He was well known to the Sutherland partners through his activities in the Taxation Section of the ABA, and in his prior endeavors he had developed many contacts in Washington and the Midwest. After Liles and Williams came aboard, more and more lawyers from across the country referred their tax cases to Sutherland. Williams was so knowledgeable on the tax law that the Senate Finance Committee asked him to do a presentation when the 1959 Revenue Act was under debate.[11]

James V. Heffernan

Williams was also the figure most responsible for the launching of the insurance practice out of the Washington office. Many of the firm's early insurance clients, including Mutual of Omaha, were a product of his insurance industry contacts from his time at the Treasury. Soon after he arrived, the firm began to work on insurance industry tax regulations, and the insurance tax practice eventually expanded to include legislation in the variable annuity field. Later the firm also registered a few of the early variable annuity products, which proved to be a complicated process because it involved both tax and securities regulations. The tax representation of insurance companies eventually spawned the firm's securities practice, and insurance entities remained important to this practice (see Ch. 12).[12]

Jim Heffernan was another great addition. He was a rare find in the 1950s, not only because of his tax expertise, but also because he was a Washington, DC, native. At the suggestion of fellow Cornell graduate Elbert Tuttle, Heffernan arrived unannounced at the Washington office in 1951. He was lucky enough to meet the visiting Joe Brennan, and the result of their meeting was a chair in the library in which Heffernan would work as a summer clerk. When Heffernan came aboard permanently the following year, he was joining a modestly sized Washington office comprised of two partners (Bill Sutherland and Mac Asbill, Sr.) and four associates (Willis Snell, Ken Liles, Mac Asbill, Jr., and Jim Wilson, who was only in Washington temporarily).

Law firms were much smaller in those days, and many did not have a tax practitioner. Consequently, the Sutherland firm continued to get tax work from other law firms. Some were one-off jobs, but many were from long relationships. The Washington tax lawyers developed ties to the Delaware-based firm of Richard, Layton & Finger through Mac Asbill, Jr.'s contacts, and this firm regularly farmed its tax work to Sutherland. Over time the Sutherland firm built up a more permanent client base. Antitrust law was another area of expansion. Mac Asbill, Sr. had been known for his antitrust work long before he came to Sutherland, so the firm got into that area through his skills and connections. Willis Snell also got involved and later headed this practice.

The Washington office remained predominantly a tax practice, and many of this office's tax cases had political connections. Among the firm's more prominent clients was Fred Saigh, owner of the St. Louis Cardinals. Saigh is perhaps best remembered by baseball fans for placing a blank contract in front of future Hall of Famer Stan Musial and telling him to fill in the amount he thought he deserved. But it was an altogether different challenge that brought Saigh to the Sutherland firm. Due in part to Saigh's affiliation with the Democratic Party, he was targeted for underpayment of income taxes after Dwight Eisenhower's 1952 presidential election victory, and his company brought some of these tax issues to Sutherland. At around the same time, Jim Heffernan handled a similar case for a prominent Democratic politician who was under investigation by the IRS. Heffernan continued to work for this politician's family for many years.[13]

The new Atlanta office associates, meanwhile, helped to extend the practice to areas other than taxation. Baxter Jones (1951) handled a variety of litigation matters unrelated to taxation; both Bob Cumming (1953) and Jim Groton (1954) were essentially in general practice for several years. Cumming eventually took the lead in litigation following Jones's untimely 1962 death, and Groton developed several new specialties. The Atlanta additions of note were rounded out by Pat Patterson (1950), Mike Egan (1955), and George Cohen (1956), all of whom acquired solid backgrounds in federal taxation, though none were limited to that field. Patterson eventually single-handedly built up the firm's real estate practice, Egan specialized in fiduciary law matters, and Cohen handled securities regulation and other corporate matters.

Personnel and Office Expansion in the 1960s

The Atlanta office grew a great deal in the 1950s, but it was not until the 1960s that the Washington office extended its practice into broader fields. This move was aided by the addition of two experienced lawyers who joined the firm as partners. Edward J. Schmuck (Fordham LL.B. 1932) came aboard in 1963 after serving as vice president and general counsel of Acacia Mutual Life Insurance Company. Edward J. Grenier (Harvard LL.B. 1959), meanwhile, had acquired a specialized background in communications and other administrative law matters with another Washington firm before coming to Sutherland in 1968. He would go on to spearhead the phenomenally successful energy practice (see Ch. 9).

Schmuck was an important element in the development of the firm's insurance tax practice. He brought a number of insurance clients to the firm through his reputation, his knowledge of insurance laws, and his notable ability to explain the most complicated matters in simple terms. In addition to the Travelers Insurance Company, one of his most important contacts from his time at Acacia was Great West Life Insurance Company of Canada. The Sutherland firm began a long relationship with Great West, initially on tax matters and later by registering the company's variable annuity products.[14]

In addition to the fortunate acquisition of Grenier and Schmuck, 11 new associates came to the Washington office in the 1960s, five of whom eventually

The First Woman Associate

The firm hired its first woman associate in 1962. When talented Yale Law School graduate Paula Lawton Bevington caught the attention of some Sutherland partners, these men knew that Bill Sutherland had to be the one to okay her as a hire. They therefore decided to use Mike Egan to broach the subject with Sutherland at the annual partners meeting. As Egan later recalled, "The others said, 'Mike, Bill likes you, so you've got to be the one to bring this up with him.' Now, Bill didn't really like the idea of hiring a woman, but he was a smart guy. He could see the direction things were heading [in the field of law], so he didn't fight it."[22] Bevington proved to be more than competent for the job. After her time at Sutherland, she went on to a number of leadership positions in business, law, and international development, including a stint in the Peace Corps.

became partners: Jerome B. Libin (Michigan J.D. 1959), Frank J. Martin, Jr. (Harvard LL.B. 1963), James F. Jorden (George Washington LL.B. 1966), Francis M. Gregory, Jr. (Notre Dame J.D. 1966), and Donald V. Moorehead (George Washington J.D. 1968).

During this decade the Atlanta office also saw unprecedented growth, as the partners sought fresh talent to develop the new practice areas. This expansion mirrored the growth of Atlanta, which was beginning to look like the rising star of the New South. And in a nod to changes in the profession and in the nation as a whole, the firm hired its first female associate. All told, 27 new associates joined the Atlanta office in the 1960s, of whom 16 remained to become partners. Two of these partners left in the early 1970s, and the remaining 14 included N. Jerold Cohen (Harvard LL.B. 1961), J.D. Fleming, Jr. (Georgia Tech Ph.D. 1959, Emory J.D. 1967), Carey P. DeDeyn (Emory J.D. 1969), Barrett K. Hawks (Emory LL.B. 1963, Harvard LL.M. 1964), Robert M. Royalty (Harvard LL.B. 1959), Jim Paulk (Virginia J.D. 1964), Walter W. Wingfield (Virginia LL.B. 1964), Bennett L. Kight (Emory LL.B. 1966), J. P. Hyman (Florida J.D. 1968), and C. Christopher Hagy (Harvard J.D. 1967).[15]

With the growth in personnel, both offices saw a corresponding expansion of office space. Atlanta took on extra space in the First National Bank Building several times before eventually moving into the First National Bank Tower when this structure was completed in 1967. In 1991 the office moved to 999 Peachtree Street. The Washington office, meanwhile, moved from the 10th floor of the Ring Building at 18th and M Street to enlarged quarters on the sixth floor in 1952. Eleven years later the office was moved to the newly constructed Farragut Building on Farragut Square. When the Washington practice outgrew the Farragut Building in 1973, it moved to 1666 K Street, just across the square. Eventually even this office proved too small, and in 1987 the firm moved to 1275 Pennsylvania Avenue.

The dual office system engendered a unique professional environment. The offices were quite small, of course, and travel between them was limited by financial considerations. The lawyers made efforts, however, to visit each other's cities, and they also got to know each other at the annual meeting. In later years, when the firm's size prevented younger lawyers from being sent to the other office for informal visits, the partners continued to encourage the younger lawyers to plan their own trips. "At that time, you definitely felt like you were part of one firm," said Washington partner Jerry Libin, "and everybody knew each other from the firm meetings, and from working together as well." An effort was also made to get the lawyers to work together across offices on a regular basis. Cross-office work became more frequent as the firm grew, but that growth also made it harder for the lawyers to get to know each other.[16]

The Cooperatives Practice

Another area of growth in the postwar years was agricultural cooperatives. As with the firm's other avenues of expansion, the lawyers helped develop this practice by taking advantage of their personal contacts, becoming experts in the area in question, and watching the work snowball into a lucrative practice. The cooperatives area came to the partners' attention in the late 1940s when Elbert Tuttle was serving on the Cornell Board of Trustees. While acting in this capacity, he became acquainted with George Pfann, general counsel of the Ithaca, New York-based Grange League Federation (GLF). Pfann, who was a football legend at Cornell while Tuttle was a law student there, thought highly of Tuttle and explained to him the ins and outs of the cooperatives' legal needs. Farm cooperatives were in a state of flux at the time and were considering whether to give up some of the benefits of nontaxable status. Tuttle and Herbert Elsas got a handle on this area and soon built up enough expertise to keep the cooperatives clients coming.[17]

Tuttle and Elsas tried to run the co-op practice out of Atlanta, but most of their clients were in the North. Mac Asbill, Jr. and Bill Sutherland therefore took it over as a Washington office operation, after which it blossomed. Asbill became particularly adept at representing farmers' interests. He handled several major cases in the circuit courts, and, as Herbert Elsas later mused, "he must have done well because they kept coming back." The firm continued this relationship even after the GLF became Agway, the largest farm cooperative in the country. The co-op practice expanded into profitable tax and legislative work for national associations like the National Council of Farm Cooperatives, farm banks, federal land banks, and federal intermediate credit banks.

Baxter Jones and the Orly Plane Crash

One notable postwar hire became the second of the firm's lawyers to die tragically in an airplane crash. In 1962 C. Baxter Jones, Jr. and his wife, Julia, joined all 106 members of the Atlanta Art Association on a tour of European art museums. On June 3 their plane crashed while taking off from Orly Airport in Paris, killing all the Atlantans aboard. Of the 132 people on the flight, only two survived. It was at the time the highest death toll on record for a disaster involving a single aircraft. The tragedy dealt a serious blow to both the Sutherland firm and the City of Atlanta. *Atlanta Constitution* editor Eugene Patterson, an acquaintance of the Joneses, was inspired to write of those who had perished, "It is doubtful that any American city has ever lost, at a single stroke, so much of its fineness…. [This was] a terribly large cross section of the most sensitive and truly civilized of our people." More than 20 Atlanta law firms handled the litigation and settlements that followed, with Bates Block (Jones's brother-in-law and the guardian of his children) the lead plaintiff in a suit representing 62 families. It took seven years to reach a settlement, and the sum of $5.2 million was the largest amount paid out for a plane crash up to that time.[26]

On a more uplifting note, the tragedy led the Atlanta arts community to throw its support behind a fitting tribute to those lost in the crash. Six years later, after some fundraising and zoning difficulties, the Memorial Arts Center opened as a living memorial. The facility included the now familiar Atlanta cultural institutions of the High Museum, the Atlanta Symphony Orchestra, and the Atlanta College of Art. The government of France donated Rodin's statue *The Shade* as a monument to the crash victims. This statue, placed within a stone semicircle that includes the names of all the art association victims, has remained on the High's lawn fronting Peachtree Street ever since.[27]

Although Baxter Jones died prematurely, he accomplished great things in his two decades of practicing law. His father was the lead lawyer in the Macon firm of Jones, Johnson, Russell & Sparks, the firm in which Randolph Thrower first began practicing in the 1930s. Young Baxter decided to follow in the family footsteps in Atlanta by attending Emory Law School. When World War II broke out he joined the Army as a private and eventually reached the rank of major before being honorably discharged at the end of the war. He then finished law school and joined the Atlanta firm of Powell, Goldstein, eventually gaining a great deal of experience in litigation. Jones seemed a natural fit when, in 1951, the Sutherland firm was looking for an experienced trial lawyer. Owing to his prior experience and his formidable talent, he became a Sutherland partner within two years. While at Sutherland he did groundbreaking work in the area of education representation (see Ch. 8), and he became the Atlanta office's chief litigator before his life was tragically cut short.[28]

BIOGRAPHIES

James H. "Jimmy" Wilson, Jr. (1920-)

Another of the firm's many strokes of luck in the early decades was the acquisition of **Jim Wilson**. The son of an Oliver, Georgia, Methodist minister, Wilson proved himself a quick study at an early age. He stayed in Georgia for college and graduated with honors from Emory University in 1940. After his first year at Harvard Law School, where his cohort included future presidential adviser William Bundy, he spent the summer of 1941 with the Sutherland firm as its summer clerk. During the war he served in the Navy on a destroyer in the Pacific, and in 1947 he graduated summa cum laude from Harvard Law and joined the firm on a full-time basis.

Jim Wilson not only was first in his class at Harvard Law, but he also had the second-highest grades ever recorded at the school. The only debate was as to whether he had been bettered by Louis Brandeis or Felix Frankfurter. Wilson was so well regarded when he finished that the dean of the law school asked him to join the faculty. Wilson seriously considered taking the offer, but as he later recalled, "I was 27 years old by then, and I thought of myself as sort of being middle-aged, and that I needed to get on with a law practice." He also had offers from other firms up and down the East Coast, but he chose the Sutherland firm largely because of the relationships he had already established there.[19]

Countless Sutherland lawyers attested that, in addition to being an excellent lawyer, Wilson was a superlative teacher. Pat Patterson, one of Wilson's first protégés at the firm, explained that Wilson "always had an immense grasp of the knowledge necessary to be an excellent lawyer. He has been an excellent guide for young lawyers as to how they should conduct themselves, what they should do, and how they should behave." Carey DeDeyn was one of these young lawyers, and like many others he was anxious at the prospect of working with the man who had gotten the second-highest grades ever at Harvard. "You can imagine how it was," said DeDeyn, "for a young lawyer to go into an office with this man who was so bright. It was intimidating." He soon found Wilson "a great man – absolutely brilliant." DeDeyn became acquainted with Wilson when the pair worked together on employment cases for Wilson's client, Southern Railway Company. They once worked on an appeal while taking a train to New Orleans for a conference of attorneys. DeDeyn marveled at Wilson's writing ability ("always with a pencil, because it had an eraser!"), but he was even more impressed that the elder partner's writing was so strong even after the obligatory New Orleans-bound martinis. "Jimmy was still able to write excellent passages for the brief. He's a lot of fun, just a great person."[20]

Despite Wilson's remarkable record, he almost slipped through the firm's fingers. The story of how Wilson, the untested law student, originally came to the firm was a favorite of Randolph Thrower's, and it bears repeating here. During Wilson's first year at Harvard he wrote to fellow Emory alumnus Thrower and asked if he might find a place with the firm that summer. Thrower, who was still an associate, knew that Wilson had been a talented undergraduate and a campus leader at Emory, so he assured the partners that the latter's attributes were legion. The partners in turn assured Thrower that all the Harvard freshmen were surely similarly talented.

Thrower eventually told the partners that the processing tax cases were overwhelming him with paper and that he needed some help to move the boxes. "So," said Thrower, "Jim Wilson was attached on that basis." With Wilson's foot in the door, it was only a matter of time before his talents caught the partners' eyes. Said Thrower:

> As soon as he arrived I began to ask Jimmy what kind of grades he had gotten [after his first year]. He kept telling me that he hadn't heard, until it was beginning to arouse some concern in me as to what was happening. Finally one morning at the lunch recess, I asked him again and he pulled out of his pocket this dog-eared penny postal card addressed to him. And on the back, the dean of admissions was congratulating him on successfully completing his first year. Well, I sighed with relief at that.
>
> A student's position in the class was a number, and in the blank space they just had a careless strike through there, and I asked Jimmy, "What is this, a one?" He said, "It is." I said, "Is that a category or is that a position in the class?" And he said, "No, that's my position in class." I said, "You mean you were number one in your class?!" He said, "Yes." I said, "Excuse me, I've got to call Bill Sutherland."
>
> So I went to the nearest telephone to call Bill to crow a little bit, and I said to Bill, "Well, that young fellow that's been sitting in my office the last few weeks finally got his grades." And Bill said, "You don't have to tell me that they're good, because I got caught this past weekend – you and Joe were tied up with your case – and I asked him to help me. Well, that boy is a real lawyer. He is just outstanding." Well, I've never used profanity with any of the partners before or since, but I did on that occasion say, "Bill, you are the luckiest SOB I ever heard of! He was number one in his class!"[21]

From that point on Wilson was in good stead with the partners, and his legal reputation grew with each passing year. Randolph Thrower later said that his role in bringing Wilson into the fold was "the greatest contribution I ever made to Sutherland, Tuttle & Brennan."

BURDETT MCKENDRIE (MAC) ASBILL, SR. (1893-1992) AND MAC ("MACKEY") ASBILL, JR. (1922-1992)

The hiring of **Mac Asbill, Sr. and Mac, Jr.** in 1949 was the culmination of the longstanding plan to team the elder Asbill with his two old friends, Bill Sutherland and Elbert Tuttle. Mac, Sr. played a major part in planning the Sutherland firm, but professional circumstances prevented him from joining when it was founded in 1924 (see Ch. 1). In the ensuing years he established a reputation in antitrust law and litigation, first in Georgia and then in Washington, DC. He moved to Washington permanently in 1934 to serve as a special assistant to Attorney General Homer Cummings, and he later joined the firm of Cummings & Stanley.[23]

When Mac, Sr. finally came to the Sutherland firm, his professional abilities and temperament complemented those of Sutherland and Tuttle. Jim Wilson worked for a short time with Mac, Sr. in Washington, and he described Asbill's professional style as "quite different from Bill Sutherland and Elbert Tuttle. Bill and Elbert were both very scholarly. Mac was more practical: smart, but very wise in the ways of the world. It was a great opportunity to practice law with all three of them and learn different things from each of them."

The younger Asbill also used his early experiences as a springboard to a fine career with the Sutherland firm. With the exception of the year he worked in the Office of the General Counsel of the Army during the Korean War, he spent his entire professional career with Sutherland. Throughout the years he held many positions of professional leadership, including chairman of the ABA's Section on Taxation in 1970-1971, chairman of the Washington chapter of the Fellows of the American Bar Foundation, and co-chairman of the National Conference of Lawyers and Public Accountants. He had four children with Jane Winchester, his wife of 50 years.

Mac Asbill, Jr. and Mac Asbill, Sr.

Both Asbills were favorite mentors of the younger partners and associates. Washington partner Nick Christakos called Mac, Jr. "a real joy to be around and to work with – a gentleman, a class act, and a very fine lawyer." Atlanta partner Carey DeDeyn seconded these sentiments, calling the Asbills "a remarkable family." Every lawyer in the Washington office marveled at Mac, Sr.'s longevity and his penchant for flouting convention by smoking and walking to the office from his Connecticut Avenue home well into his 90s.

The Asbills' sense of humor also became the stuff of legend in the Washington office. In the 1970s and 1980s a small group of Sutherland lawyers began putting humorous after-dinner entertainment into the firm's annual banquet. This group naturally thought it would be a good idea to have Mac, Jr. give his okay to the scripts in advance to ensure that the affair would remain "family friendly." Washington partner Steuart Thomsen recalled of this plan:

> *We always thought we were getting some cover by getting Mac involved and by giving him the scripts to look at in advance, to make sure that none of the material was too over the top. It took me a number of years to realize that Mac was exercising absolutely no restraint at all when it came to reviewing our material. In fact, when we wrote Mac's introduction of the program each year, if anything, it became a little raunchier by the time he delivered it.*

Another story about Mac, Jr. demonstrates how his quick wit often served him well in his legal work. In the 1980s Mac and a team from the Washington office were working for the Farm Credit System in an effort to forge agreements between financial institutions. At one point the general counsel of Farm Credit began raising questions about one aspect of a proposed agreement. Asbill confronted the man at an industry meeting

Mac Asbill, Jr. and Justice Stanley Reed

When Mac Asbill, Jr. finished law school he applied to Justice Stanley Reed for a clerkship on the Supreme Court. Reed had known Mac, Sr. from the Cummings firm, and he saw promise in the younger Asbill's record in law school and the Marines. Mac was hired, and he soon found himself doing certiorari memos through his initial summer while the Court was on recess. Asbill marveled at the informal yet intellectually rigorous environment of Reed's office. Not only did Reed respect the honest opinions of his clerks, but he was also one of the few justices to allow his clerks to draft opinions. Reed

Justice Reed

was willing to give his young clerks this leeway in part because, in Mac, Jr.'s words, "He had no vanity. He was the least vain man I think I've ever seen in my life."[24]

One humorous anecdote from Mac, Jr.'s year with Justice Reed shows Mac's forthrightness, Reed's open attitude toward his clerks, and Reed's steadfast moral principles:

*We had a case before the Court during that term involving **The Memoirs of Heckety County**, which is a book that Henry Miller had written, and it had been banned as being obscene by, I believe, the state of New York. I didn't think the book was very bad and that it should have been banned, and I happened to be the one that was working on this with [Reed], and he thought it should be. I tried to persuade him that the book was not obscene. It had, maybe, one passage in it that was pretty lurid, but the rest of it was not. And at that time I was young enough to be enamored with the idea of freedom of the press and anybody ought to be able to say what he wanted to, so I undertook to persuade him that this thing was not obscene.*

*I sent up to the Supreme Court library and got them to get me some obscene books, including **Ulysses** and a few other things, that I happened to know about and that I thought maybe would make the point. I got them all down there and I marked the passages and showed them to Reed. I remember him standing in my office looking at these things, and he'd read them, and he'd sort of whistle like, "Whew," you know, "that's bad. That's pretty bad." I was trying to show him that there were a lot of things worse than **The Memoirs of Heckety County**. Well, he went on and voted the way he was going to vote from the beginning. I never did persuade him. I think that decision was affirmed four to four because Frankfurter was a friend of Henry Miller's and recused himself! The Court split, but I was not successful in persuading Reed that he ought to change his view.[25]*

and asked him why he opposed the arrangement. The Farm Credit man responded by saying that, although he had an open mind about the matter, he was "not going to sprinkle holy water on it in advance." This prompted Mac to reply, "I'm not asking you to sprinkle holy water on it, I just want you to stop pissing on it!"

Father and son were very close, and they relished working together in the same office for so many years. The fact that they both passed away within months of each other is perhaps a fitting testament to just how close they were. Shortly after Mac, Jr.'s death, partner Glen S. Howard wrote in a eulogy:

> *He was a friend, a teacher, a colleague, a genuine hero to so many of us – a man we wanted to be like. To watch Mac attack a problem, with enthusiasm for the intrinsic challenge and yet with calm practicality – and then explain it all with clear simplicity – was to be inspired to try to achieve and maintain the same in our own work and in our lives. To observe Mac's ability to find the wry side of so many things – and to share his humor with the easy timing of a standup comic – was to be inspired to remember not to take ourselves or what we do too seriously.*
>
> *Sure, the notion of anyone being a "hero" or an "inspiration" seems hyperbolic (if not corny) in these cynical times, and Mac would certainly have dismissed with embarrassed humor any effort to hang those labels on **him**. But Mac Asbill, Jr. really was such an individual.*

Washington partner Frank Gregory wrote a letter to Mac Asbill, Jr. just days before Asbill's death. It reads as a testimonial to the high regard in which Asbill was held by the younger Sutherland partners:

> *I want you to know how much I appreciate all that you have taught me over the years, and also want you to know that I will do all within my power to perpetuate within the firm the standards and goals that you stand for. I will not accept a diminution in the standards or the standing of the profession and will not accept any role for our firm that does not embrace the highest qualities of lawyering and public service.*

Supreme Court Building – Washington, DC

From 1924 to 1962 the firm participated in the oral argument in 15 cases in the United States Supreme Court.

CHAPTER SEVEN

POSTWAR CASES AND PERSONALITIES

A CLOSE CALL IN THE SUPREME COURT: *Flora v. U.S.*

A s demonstrated in previous chapters, the early years saw the Sutherland lawyers do a great deal of pro bono work as a means of building the firm's reputation and serving the greater good. But even in the 1950s and 1960s, when the practice was firmly established, lawyers at Sutherland handled cases that demanded hundreds of hours of work with little immediate compensation. The 1958 case of *Flora v. U.S.* (357 U.S. 63; 1960 rehearing 362 U.S. 145) was perhaps the most noteworthy, not only because it was a significant moment in the interpretation of American tax law, but also because the firm's involvement aptly reflected Bill Sutherland's founding philosophy: When you get into a matter, you do the very best work, no matter how long it takes and whatever the financial reward.

The firm first became involved when Wyoming lawyer A.G. McClintock contacted his old acquaintance, Sutherland firm partner Laurens Williams, and informed him that his client could not pay to argue a tax case before the Supreme Court. Williams ran the matter by the partners, and they all agreed that the case would be worth taking on because many Sutherland clients would be influenced by its outcome. Randolph Thrower took the lead. They estimated that the case would take about two weeks of their time, but when it was finally resolved the firm had spent hundreds of hours on the matter and had twice appeared before the Supreme Court.[1]

The issue in the case was whether a taxpayer had to pay the full amount of an income tax deficiency before he could challenge its correctness by a suit for refund under 28 U.S.C. 1346(a)(1). A deficiency in income tax had been assessed against Flora, the taxpayer, and he had paid part of the assessment and sued for refund in the federal district court in Wyoming. The government moved to dismiss on the grounds that the court had no jurisdiction to entertain a refund suit where the taxpayer failed to pay the full amount of the assessment, even though the taxpayer claimed that the amount collected from him was excessive and illegal and constituted an overpayment. The federal district court disallowed the claim for refund, ruling that Flora "should not maintain" the action because he had not paid the full amount of tax levied by the IRS. The 10th Circuit Court of Appeals upheld the government's position (246 F.2d 949 (1957)). Flora then filed a certiorari petition, which was granted.

Thrower argued Flora's case on May 20, 1958, with assistance on the brief from Bill Sutherland, Mac Asbill, Jr. and McClintock. The Court decided eight to one against the petitioner (Justice Whittaker offered the single dissent), and Chief Justice Warren, speaking for the majority, relied upon a representation by the government that the procedural practice followed had been accepted by the courts generally. Thrower had challenged that argument in the first trial, but there had been no demonstration by the government. The Sutherland team then sought by petition for rehearing to show the error of that decision. They pointed out that the Court's decision in the first instance was based upon a mistaken assumption of fact – namely, that the requirement of full payment as a condition to suit had long been recognized in actual practice by taxpayers, the Treasury, and the Department of Justice. The Court granted the petition (360 U.S. 922).

It was then that, as Thrower later recalled, "we and the Government really went at each other." The firm spent hundreds of hours preparing for the June 1959 rehearing, and by the time the rehearing took place Thrower and the others thought they had it won. Thrower reargued the case with assistance from Sutherland, McClintock, and the young Sutherland lawyer George Cohen. They were very happy with their argument, but while the Court was deciding the matter, Thrower's team heard through cloakroom gossip that the chief justice was trying to trade them off. That is to say, Earl Warren wanted to change his decision, and he was looking for a way to do so without having to write an entirely new opinion. In the final analysis it appears that this is exactly what happened. The five to four majority opinion was, in Thrower's words, "a rambling, apologetic dissent," while the dissenting opinion was "a straightforward, winning opinion." So it seemed that Chief Justice Warren had traded off at the last minute, turning an otherwise consenting opinion into a dissent by rewriting the first paragraph. Meanwhile, Justice Frankfurter, the author of the majority opinion, apparently changed the first paragraph of his dissent in order to make it a consenting decision.[2]

The Court's *Flora* decision was an important milestone in 20th century tax law in that it helped establish the full payment requirement under the existing codes. In the words of the majority decision, "If we were to accept petitioner's argument, we would sacrifice the harmony of our carefully structured twentieth century system of tax litigation." On another interesting note, one of the Court's turns of phrase inadvertently gave fodder to income tax opponents in the ensuing decades. When Justice Warren wrote that "our tax system is based upon voluntary assessment and payment and not on distraint," he could not have known that this would help make the *Flora* decision a rallying cry for antitax advocates in the years to come.

THE PERCENTAGE DEPLETION CASES

The percentage depletion cases of the 1950s and 1960s were yet another example of the fortuitous discovery of a new practice that soon became an area of the firm's expertise. These cases were very significant for the firm in this period. Not only were they important to the growth of the tax practice, but they also necessitated effective cross-office teamwork at a time when the Washington and Atlanta offices were still learning how to work together. Litigation of the percentage depletion cases was also highly profitable and led the firm into other depletion and tax matters.[3]

These cases involved the percentage depletion allowance for taxpayers engaged in mining hard minerals. Under the 1939 Revenue Code a mining company was allowed a deduction equal to a specified percentage of "gross income from mining." The code defined "mining" as including not only the extraction of ores or minerals from the ground, but also the treatment processes normally applied in order to obtain the commercially marketable mineral product.

The law put brick makers in a peculiar position. There was no market for brick and tile clay until it was made into burnt brick and tile. Brick makers therefore claimed that all of the processes required to produce their finished products were mining processes, and that their "gross income from mining" was the amount realized from the sale of their brick and tile. (This is what later became known as the "Cherokee principle.") However, the Revenue Act of 1951 added "brick and tile clay" to the list of minerals subject to percentage depletion. The Treasury's proposed regulations would have limited allowable processes to only a few preliminary processing steps.[4]

The firm's involvement in these cases came about rather auspiciously. The firm had handled some minor tax matters for a Macon brick company before the depletion issue arose, and in 1953 Kenneth Dunwody, president of Cherokee Brick and Tile Company, was referred to Sutherland on the more serious matter of the new tax requirements. He asked the firm to review the Treasury's proposed regulations to see if his taxes could be reduced.

The lawyers looked into the matter and decided to mount a protest. Most of the preparatory work was done in the Washington office, principally by Bill Sutherland and Willis Snell. Sutherland felt that a literal reading of the statutory provisions would justify the claim of the brick makers that the depletion rate should be applied to the selling price of bricks. He further suggested filing a protest against the proposed regulations. Dunwody arranged for the trade association, Structural Clay Products Institute (SCPI), to retain the firm for this purpose. The regulations were finally adopted in the form originally proposed, and SCIPI retained the firm to litigate the issue in a test case. Cherokee Brick and Tile was selected for that purpose.

Sutherland arranged to have Cherokee file suit for refund in the United States District Court for the Middle District of Georgia, and he also convinced the IRS and the Justice Department to expedite this litigation. In that connection Mac Asbill, Sr. arranged with the Justice Department to have the firm's complaint drawn in such a way that the government would admit that there was no market for Cherokee's clay before it was put in the form of brick and tile. Asbill also argued that only a negligible quantity of the brick clay mined in the U.S. could be sold before it was put in that form. The firm was then in a position where it could move

The Early Sutherland Firm and the Supreme Court

From 1924 to 1962 the firm participated in the oral argument in 15 cases in the United States Supreme Court. In many more cases the firm's partners filed or opposed petitions for certiorari, or filed amicus briefs in other cases in the Supreme Court. In some that the firm won there was very little if any financial award, and in some cases where the decision was against the firm, the reasoning in the Court's opinion enabled the firm to win substantial recoveries in other cases. The firm's experience in arguing all of these cases, including the "losers," gave it a certain prestige that brought in more profitable cases. In addition to those already described, the following were Supreme Court cases in which the firm's lawyers participated in the oral argument up to 1962: *Woolford Realty v. Rose* (1932), *Fox Film v. Doyal* (1932), *Planters Cotton Oil Co. v. Hopkins* (1932), *Virginian Hotel v. Helvering* (1943), *Webre Steib v. Commissioner* (1945), *Norton Co. v. Illinois* (1951), *Premier Oil Refining v. U.S.* (1955), *Sampson v. U.S.* (1962).[33]

for judgment on the pleadings, and if its motion was granted it would establish the "Cherokee principle." The judge granted the motion, the government appealed, and the Fifth Circuit affirmed (218 F. 2d. 424 1/21/55).

The partners then tried to get the IRS to accept the principle of the Cherokee case. The IRS commissioner, T. Coleman Andrews, refused to do so, but he told the leaders of the brick industry that if another court of appeals should reach the same result he would bow to the decision. The Sutherland partners then did a careful study to find favorable forums at the district and circuit levels for additional test cases that might be brought by members of SCIPI. One of these cases was *Haviland Clay Works Company v. U.S.* in the Northern District of Ohio. The firm got a favorable decision in the district court (169 F. Supp. 61 12/12/55), but the government was dissatisfied with the record and refused to appeal to the Sixth Circuit.

The firm also brought suit for Sapulpa Brick and Tile Company in the Northern District of Oklahoma. The government refused to accept the admissions made in the Cherokee case as to the lack of a market for brick and tile clay, so the firm had to try the case. Brennan and Snell traveled to Tulsa for the trial, and they got a favorable ruling in the district court (56-2 USTC 9709 – 5/8/56). The government then appealed the case to the Court of Appeals for the 10th Circuit, and once again the decision was favorable (239 F. 2d 694 – 12/20/56).

In the meantime the government had won the *Dragon Cement Company* case in the district court in Maine (144 F. Supp. 188 – 8/24/56). The taxpayer there had sought to apply the Cherokee principle to cement rock used to make Portland cement. The district judge repudiated the principle of the *Cherokee* case, which led the taxpayer to appeal to the First Circuit. The government had high hopes of getting the First Circuit to affirm and thus create a conflict with the Fifth Circuit so that the issue could be brought to the Supreme Court on certiorari.

The New York and Boston lawyers representing Dragon Cement Company went to Denver to hear the Sutherland firm's argument in the Sapulpa case, and after the decision in that case they enlisted Sutherland to handle the *Dragon* appeal. The two firms' lawyers collaborated in the preparation of briefs for the First Circuit, and the Sutherland firm made the oral argument. The First Circuit followed the Fifth and 10th Circuits in the *Cherokee* and *Sapulpa* cases and decided the case in favor of the taxpayer (244 F. 2d 513 – 5/14/57).

The government refused to apply the Cherokee principle to other taxpayers located within the Fifth Circuit, and Sutherland had to litigate two more cases for Cherokee involving later taxable years. The government appealed one of those cases to the Fifth Circuit, along with a number of other cases involving the same question. Two of these cases, *Merry Brothers Brick and Tile Company* and *Reliance Clay Products*, were set for argument in the Fifth Circuit in early 1957. General counsel for both of those companies asked the Sutherland firm to present the taxpayers' cases to the Fifth Circuit.

The Fifth Circuit refused to overrule the first Cherokee case and decided these cases in favor of the taxpayers (242 F. 2d 708 – 3/27/57). The government filed petitions for certiorari in both the *Merry Brothers* and the *Dragon Cement* cases, but the Supreme Court denied them (355 U.S. 824, 833). A few days later the IRS announced that it would follow these decisions in cases involving brick and tile clay and cement rock. The IRS took the position, however, that the principle of these cases was not applicable to cases involving any cement-making materials other than cement rock.

In all of these cases the firm was working under its arrangement with SCIPI, and this connection led to further work for individual companies. With SCIPI's consent the firm was retained separately by Acme Brick Company to handle its suit for a refund that involved refractory clay ("fire clay") as well as brick and tile clay. Brennan and Snell tried that case in the District Court for the Northern District of Texas and got a favorable decision in 1956 (167 F. Supp. 911). Largely on the basis of expert testimony from the Sutherland firm, the district court there held that the principle of the Cherokee case was applicable to both Acme's fire clay and its brick and tile clay. The case was affirmed in the Fifth Circuit and was one of the cases included in the government's petition for certiorari under the name of *Merry Brothers Brick and Tile Company* (355 U.S. 824). The firm also participated to a limited extent in a number of other Cherokee principle cases in which primary responsibility was in the hands of the taxpayer's regular counsel. These cases arose in district courts in North Carolina, Texas, Arizona, and California.

Lehigh Portland Cement Co. v. U.S.A.
After denial of certiorari in the *Dragon Cement Company* case, the Lehigh Portland Cement Company retained the firm to handle its multimillion-dollar suit for refund involving the percentage depletion allowance on material it quarried or

The Fifth Circuit amassed an impressive record with their cutting-edge decisions. Their landmark rulings struck down discrimination in voting, jury selection, and employment.

mined in various parts of the country. The firm brought suit in the Eastern District Court of Pennsylvania, and the case was tried at Easton for two months in 1959-1960. The *Lehigh* case involved 12 quarries in 10 states and required extensive study of the market for limestone in those areas. The government took more than 100 depositions in the general areas of the Lehigh quarries for use at the trial.[5]

The firm's goal in this case was to get the court to extend the Cherokee principle to all limestone quarried by the company. Brennan, Wilson, and Snell took the lead on preparation for the trial, first by fanning out across the country to interview the Government's witnesses in advance of the depositions, then by participating in the hearings. Snell also recruited a corps of expert witnesses, including geologists and engineers, to testify at the trial. Throughout this period the Sutherland lawyers had to develop a sense of humor about spending so much time away from home in a town with so few amenities. They did much of their work in their Allentown hotel rooms, and they spent what little free time they had drinking whisky and reading the "funny papers" – their term for the trial transcripts.[6]

It is perhaps also worth noting that Willis Snell's thorough research methods and Joe Brennan's tough cross-examination abilities made at least one government witness quake on the stand. Snell had spent a considerable amount of time researching the opinions of this expert witness, and with this information in hand, Brennan was able to point out numerous inconsistencies in the witness's opinions. According to Jim Wilson, at the end of the day "one of the government lawyers said to me, 'Do y'all have a tail on my client? He's scared to death of what you know about him!'" Wilson replied in the negative.[7]

In the middle of the trial, the Supreme Court granted certiorari in the *Cannelton Sewer Pipe* case, in which the Court of Appeals for the Seventh Circuit had applied the Cherokee principle to fire clay mined in Indiana. After the *Lehigh* case was tried and briefs were filed, the district judge announced that he would withhold his decision pending disposition of the *Cannelton* case by the Supreme Court.[8]

The Supreme Court decided the *Cannelton* case in June 1960 (364 U.S. 76), after which the firm had to abandon the main issue involved in the *Lehigh* case. So although the three Sutherland lawyers were sure they had the case won, *Cannelton* made it certain they would lose. A minor issue remained, and the firm got a favorable decision from the district court. However, the Third Circuit reversed it (334 F. 2d 469 (1964)). Nevertheless, the Sutherland team's expertise was widely recognized, and they continued to handle related matters for many more years.[9]

IN THE "EYE OF THE STORM": ELBERT TUTTLE AND THE CIVIL RIGHTS MOVEMENT

The 1954 Supreme Court decision in *Brown v. Board of Education of Topeka, KS* is familiar to any student of modern American history as the Rosetta stone for the dismantling of the Jim Crow system in the South. Less well known, however, is the role played by the Fifth Circuit Court of Appeals in the desegregation process, and particularly the pivotal role of one of its most respected judges, Elbert P. Tuttle, Sr. The Fifth Circuit Court of Appeals covered six Southern states and was at the heart of the controversy over school desegregation in the decade after the *Brown* decision. While serving as a judge on the Fifth Circuit bench, Tuttle worked to bring about sweeping decisions that helped undermine the legal foundations of Jim Crow. Tuttle and this court were so important that in the late 1960s Chief Justice Earl Warren said, "Since the day [Tuttle] assumed office, the Fifth Circuit has been in the very eye of the storm."[10]

Judge Ben F. Cameron, Fifth U.S. Circuit Court of Appeals

The 1955 Supreme Court decision in *Brown II* effectively placed enforcement of school desegregation in the hands of federal judges in the South. The vagueness of the decision left open the question of compliance and implementation, meaning that the Fifth Circuit judges had many decisions to make. Tuttle and the other justices – John Minor Wisdom, Richard T. Rives, and John R. Brown, collectively known as "the four" (so named by Mississippi's member of the Fifth Circuit court, Ben F. Cameron, who condemned their attempts to dismantle the Jim Crow system) – shared a desire to translate the school desegregation decision into a broad mandate for equality under the law.[11]

Beginning in the late 1950s, the Fifth Circuit effectively hammered away at the Jim Crow regime through a broad interpretation of *Brown* and its follow-ups. For

Judge Richard Rives, Fifth U.S. Circuit Court of Appeals

example, by issuing an order striking down segregated seating on city buses in Montgomery, Alabama, in 1956, they extended *Brown* into areas beyond education. (This was the final chapter in the famed bus boycott spawned by Rosa Parks's refusal to give up her seat, a boycott that also began Martin Luther King, Jr.'s civil rights career.)

This was, of course, a tumultuous period in the South. The *Brown* decision sparked a call for "massive resistance" to desegregation plans on the part of Southern whites, and many political leaders created further discontent by publicly lambasting *Brown*. Owing to this climate of hostility, Tuttle and the other judges

Elbert P. Tuttle (far right) and his wife, Sara

had to live under the constant threat of violence. They were criticized as "outsiders" (though only Tuttle was not a native Southerner) and, perhaps worse, as representatives of federal power. A rather typical 1963 editorial from a North Florida newspaper subtly denigrated Tuttle's motivations and pedigree by describing him as "born in California, a former newspaperman and transplanted Yankee."[12] Elbert and his wife, Sara, regularly received threatening phone calls, though they refused to get an unlisted number. Instead, they simply took the receiver off the hook each night at 11 o'clock.[13]

Yet hostility to the Court's decisions was not restricted to White Citizens' Councils and late-night telephone pranksters. Lower court judges also tried to stall the judicial process. According to historian and journalist Jack Bass, "Delay was the principal tool by which recalcitrant southerners were fighting the progress of desegregation." These intransigent judges purposely slowed the judicial process to discourage plaintiffs, delayed orders granting relief indefinitely, and stayed orders and delayed preparing records for appeal.[14]

Tuttle and his cohorts devised a few methods for taking on this system. They used existing laws in innovative ways and issued direct orders to grant relief, thus bypassing intransigent lower courts altogether. They also made unprecedented use of both the All Writs Statute and Rule 62 of the Federal Rules of Civil Procedure. This combination gave the Fifth Circuit court the ability to rule based on the belief that discrimination was causing "irreparable injury" to a plaintiff. For the cases in question, Tuttle argued that the denial of constitutional rights was injurious, even though, in his words, "[the injury] cannot be measured by any known scale of value." The Supreme Court gave its tacit approval to these methods by refusing to accept certiorari in these cases.[15]

Jack Bass has described how the Fifth Circuit turned the injunction into a powerful tool for legal implementation:

Beginning with school desegregation cases, the Fifth Circuit developed the civil rights injunction into a new force in the American legal system.... Early in the twentieth century, injunctions were used to kill Progressive

"...Bootle to Tuttle to Black!" Atlanta Constitution, *Jan. 11, 1961*
(Clifford Baldowski Editorial Cartoon Collection)

> *legislation.... But in the school cases, judges used the injunction to transform*
> *a "dual school system" into a "unitary, nonracial school system."*[16]

The Fifth Circuit amassed an impressive record with their cutting-edge decisions. Their landmark rulings struck down discrimination in voting, jury selection, and employment. They developed the doctrine of "affirmative duties," which shifted the burden from black plaintiffs to school boards to establish unified, integrated school systems. The Fifth Circuit court also helped eliminate Louisiana's pupil placement law, and they opened the Universities of Mississippi, Georgia, and Alabama to black students. They also decided reapportionment cases that restructured state legislatures, congressional districts, and local governments, including Georgia's reapportionment and county unit cases (*Toombs v. Fortson* and *Sanders v. Gray*, respectively).[17]

These decisions had far-reaching consequences. In legal terms, the Fifth Circuit judges helped the Supreme Court enter the political fray, while in social and cultural terms, one could argue that the changes they mandated helped transfer Southern power from rural elites to the industrialists, merchants, and others who spearheaded the region's modernization. As Jack Bass stated, "[Tuttle's] legacy is one of leadership

Birmingham, 1963

Elbert Tuttle's judgments during the Birmingham student protests of 1963 are a magnificent example of the ways in which his judicial philosophy positively affected the lives of thousands of citizens.[30] Birmingham was at the time the focal point of the civil rights movement in the South. Efforts to force desegregation through protests and boycotts were met with a now infamous crackdown by the city's police, who turned police dogs and fire hoses on peaceful protestors. After almost a month of fruitless demonstrations, black leaders turned to high school students to try to increase the size and impact of the demonstrations. The police were ready, however, and on the first day they arrested hundreds of teenagers. The Birmingham school board then suspended or expelled several hundred of these young protestors. The board set a hearing for the suspensions and expulsions for June, by which time the school term would have ended. This would prevent all of these students from either advancing or graduating. The NAACP was unsuccessful in its efforts to seek an injunction from the district court in Birmingham to send the young men and women back to school.

Constance Baker Motley, representing the NAACP, contacted Judge Tuttle and asked for an immediate appeal. It was late in the afternoon, however, before the district court order was prepared, and Ms. Motley called Tuttle to reschedule the hearing. Fortunately the quick-thinking judge had already checked the flight schedule from Birmingham to Atlanta. He told Motley that as long as she could make the late afternoon flight, he would set the hearing for seven o'clock that evening.

Federal appeals courts in those days heard cases as three-judge panels, but Tuttle sat alone that night because he thought it imperative that the court act quickly. Tuttle also felt that the two other available justices, Griffin Bell and Walter Gewin, were as yet untested in civil rights matters. Therefore the only people present at the hearing were the lawyers for the school board, the NAACP, and the Justice Department, and *New York Times* correspondent Claude Sitton. Tuttle heard arguments and acted on his authority as chief judge to issue an injunction ordering the children back to school the next morning. In his judgment that the students had been arrested illegally, he cited a recent Supreme Court ruling, and he broke precedent by adding a personal comment to his decision: "It appears shocking that a board of education, interested in the education of the children committed to its care, should thus in effect destroy the value of one term of school for many children at a time…when [the board members] are bending their efforts toward emphasizing the need for continuing education." Tuttle clearly felt this to be an important case, for as Sitton reported the next morning, the judge's "expression and tone

Civil rights demonstration in Birmingham, Alabama

reflected anger and distress over the treatment of the students." When the school board's lawyer argued that the injunction could not be carried out in time, Tuttle demanded that the lawyer and his colleagues personally contact the television stations and newspapers in Birmingham to inform parents that their children could return to school in the morning.[31]

The reaction to Tuttle's decision was predictable: It was lauded by civil rights advocates and harshly criticized by segregationists. Yet even the opponents benefited from the tenuous peace engendered by the decision. As Sitton wrote at the time, Tuttle's order "removed the threat that Negroes would resume mass protests such as those that brought a racial crisis marked by two riots and the bombings of a Negro home and a motel." Tuttle knew that the expulsion of the students was a last-ditch effort on the part of Birmingham segregationists to undermine the truce that Martin Luther King, Jr. had brokered, and with this behind them, peace settled in Birmingham. Soon thereafter, the Fifth Circuit upheld the power of a single appellate judge to issue such an injunction, and this court eventually affirmed the substance of Judge Tuttle's order (*Woods v. Wright*, 334 F. 2d 369 (1964)).[32] Sometime later Tuttle offered a succinct justification for his decision: "If those children had missed graduation, many of them never would have returned to school and their lives would have been permanently affected."

in transforming the American South, the federal courts interacting with the thrust of the civil rights movement to make real the promise of legal equality through a process that history may come to view as Judicial Reconstruction."[17]

Tuttle's formative years offer some clues to his iconoclastic attitude toward civil rights. One childhood story from his family's brief time in Washington is particularly illuminating. One day he was sitting with his mother on the front porch of their home, and across the street they saw a streetcar pass by a waiting black woman. After a second streetcar passed the woman, Mrs. Tuttle stepped inside the house, put on her hat, and walked across the street to stand beside her. The next streetcar stopped and the waiting woman boarded. Mrs. Tuttle then returned to the front porch and did not say another word about the incident. Tuttle later said that this was the finest lesson he ever had in responding to injustice.[18]

Sutherland partner Randolph Thrower pointed out that Tuttle's work for the Republican Party was also quite significant in the area of civil rights. As Thrower put it:

> *One of the most forward-looking things Elbert did in the civil rights area was to become an active Republican. The Democratic Party at that time was all white, and the county unit system put the control of the state into small counties outside of the metropolitan areas. As a...Republican leader, [Tuttle] invited in and participated with the blacks that constituted a substantial part of the party at that time. And [it was] probably the only organization that, locally and statewide, had meetings where black and white mingled and worked together in an atmosphere where they appreciated each other.[20]*

Yet despite the lasting significance of Tuttle's decisions, he clearly recognized that the judges did not bring the cases they heard. To Tuttle, the civil rights advocates themselves wrought the real transformations. As he said in his later years, "We became what I consider a great constitutional court, and I think we largely have to thank the black plaintiffs for that."[21]

Years after the movement's aims had been codified into law, prominent civil rights advocates and firsthand witnesses to the drama lined up to applaud the work of Tuttle and his colleagues. Nicholas Katzenbach, deputy attorney general in the Kennedy and Johnson administrations, said, "If you hadn't had those judges on the Fifth Circuit...you would have had much more in the way of demonstrations, violence, repression, revolutions – that may be too strong a word, but it was moving in that direction." Claude Sitton, former Southern correspondent for the *New York Times*, voiced similar sentiments when he said, "Those who think Martin Luther King desegregated the South don't know Elbert Tuttle and the record of the Fifth Circuit Court of Appeals." Former Atlanta mayor Maynard Jackson joined the chorus at Tuttle's 1996 funeral, saying the justice had the "courage to stand, alone sometimes, with complete confidence in the correctness of his position." Georgia Representative John Lewis concurred with Mayor Jackson, saying, "Jurist Tuttle did more than any lawyer, any member of the bar...to usher in a New South. This man must be seen as one of the founding fathers of the New America."[22]

But perhaps the most fitting epitaph comes from Tuttle himself. Looking back on his years on the Fifth Circuit court, he recalled, "There was no limit to the point to which we would make an effort to find some means within the law to correct what we saw clearly had been an injustice."[23]

THE FERGUSON HABEAS CORPUS CASE

In the late 1960s the Sutherland firm got involved in another seemingly "impossible" pro bono habeas corpus case. As in any case involving the death penalty, this one had its share of drama, but it also had a few unpredictable twists that set it apart from most capital cases.[24]

Billy Homer Ferguson was convicted of murder in Georgia and sentenced to death in 1958. After appeals to the Georgia and U.S. Supreme Courts, two new trials, two new convictions, and two new death sentences, Ferguson filed petitions for habeas corpus in state and federal courts. These petitions were pending in the United States District Court at Atlanta in 1967 when Ferguson dismissed his last court-appointed counsel. The court then appointed the Sutherland firm's C. Ronald Ellington and Walter Wingfield to handle the habeas matter.

Ellington and Wingfield had a lot of catching up to do, for Ferguson had been on death row for almost 10 years when they first visited him at the state penitentiary at Reidsville. The young associates also had to quickly master the capital offense learning curve. These were, after all, the days before public defenders had become a fixture of the legal landscape, so Ellington and Wingfield were in the rather unenviable position of having to learn the proper procedures on the fly. As with many such appointed counselors, they were only a few years out of law school, and they were relatively recent hires at the Sutherland firm. After consulting with their colleagues at Sutherland, the pair decided that their best first course of action was to amend the petition by adding new grounds. They could then introduce additional evidence at a further hearing.

The district judge, Sidney Smith, was sympathetic to Ferguson's cause. Although the evidence seemed to show that Ferguson had indeed committed the murder, the death sentence seemed unduly harsh. Ferguson was only 19 when he attempted to rob a television repairman's store to get money to support his new wife. One thing led to another, and Ferguson ended up killing the shop owner. Although the crime was loathsome, Smith thought the death penalty was excessive because of Ferguson's youth and the unpremeditated nature of the murder.

Smith had the matter under consideration when the U.S. Supreme Court held that the death sentence could not be imposed on the basis of a jury's verdict where, under state law, prospective jurors who were conscientiously opposed to capital punishment were excluded (*Witherspoon v. Illinois*, 391 U.S. 510 (1968)). In view of a Georgia statute that disqualified such jurors in a case involving a capital offense, Judge Smith concluded that under *Witherspoon*, the death sentence could not stand. Smith remanded Ferguson to the superior court for a limited period for compliance with the *Witherspoon* holding. Wingfield arranged to have Ferguson's original counsel appear with him in the superior court, where Ferguson was resentenced to life imprisonment. The habeas corpus proceeding was then reinstated in the federal court. There were two remaining grounds in support of the petition that the district court had not passed upon.

Wingfield was now required to advise his client of his right to press for a decision in the habeas corpus case. (Ron Ellington had by this time left the Sutherland firm to teach law at the University of Georgia. He later became dean of the university's law school.) Wingfield told Ferguson that there was a substantial chance of prevailing there and having his third conviction set aside. If this should happen, Ferguson could then be tried for the fourth time for the same murder, and he might then be convicted by a properly qualified jury and sentenced to death. Wingfield pointed out that this possibility could be avoided by dismissing the habeas corpus petition. Although the life sentence would stand, Ferguson would be eligible for parole within a few years in consideration of the time he had already served in prison.

But to Wingfield's astonishment, Ferguson was determined to pursue the habeas corpus matter with the prospect of getting a new trial at which he could, perhaps, be convicted and properly sentenced to death! Ferguson had apparently found religion while in prison, and his newfound contrition fostered a demand for harsh punishment. On Wingfield's motion, Judge Smith of the district court entered an order requesting the State Board of Corrections to submit Ferguson to the State Board of Psychiatry to investigate his mental capacity. After an investigation at the state mental hospital in Milledgeville, the state board reported that Ferguson was mentally competent, and the habeas corpus matter proceeded in the district court.

The district court dismissed the petition for habeas corpus in 1971, and on appeal the Court of Appeals for the Fifth Circuit found possible merit in one of the remaining grounds, namely whether the systematic exclusion of blacks from the grand and petit juries operated to deprive Ferguson, a white man, of his constitutional rights (*Ferguson v. Dutton, Warden*, 477 F. 2d 121 (1973)). The petitioner's position was supported by the holding in the case of *Peters v. Kiff* (407 U.S. 493 (1972)). The Fifth Circuit's order required the filing of a petition in the state court with reference to the systematic exclusion of blacks from juries, while also providing for a stay of proceedings in the district court pending such state court proceeding.

Wingfield then filed a new petition for habeas corpus in the Superior Court of Tatnall County, in which the state prison was located. The trial court denied relief, and the decision was affirmed (*Ferguson v. Caldwell*, 233 Ga. 887 (1975)). The Georgia court held that Ferguson had waived any constitutional objection to the composition of juries, and that in any event the decision in the *Peters* case should not be applied retrospectively.

In the meantime, Ferguson was released on parole in May 1974. He had learned a few trades in prison and had become engaged to marry a high school classmate. He soon announced the start of his practice as a handwriting analyst and examiner of questioned documents. His interest in the habeas corpus case began to wane, and after the last decision of the Georgia Supreme Court, he finally consented to dismiss his federal petition "without prejudice." Wingfield later recalled that Ferguson must have had mixed feelings about being freed, for he never thanked his counselors for keeping him alive. Ferguson's mother, however, was extremely grateful to the lawyers for performing their services over so many years. Billy Homer Ferguson moved to California, and Wingfield never heard from him again.

RANDOLPH THROWER AT THE IRS

When Richard Nixon appointed Randolph Thrower commissioner of the IRS in 1969, Thrower's colleagues knew that his work in Washington would bring great prestige to the Sutherland firm. On this count they were correct. But few would have guessed that Thrower's time at the IRS would also contribute to his reputation for maintaining absolute integrity in the field of law. For whereas many other Nixon administration officials ended up with prison sentences or lucrative book deals – and very often both – Randolph Thrower came through with his reputation intact. He stood up to the unscrupulous whims of the president's advisers and later refused to make a spectacle of his performance when the Watergate conspiracies captured the public's attention.[25]

Thrower's arrival in Washington was something of a homecoming, for he had spent part of the 1930s there while working on the processing tax cases. But although life in the nation's capital had its appeal, the politics of the new position soon took their toll. Presidential counselor John Dean began to seek tax information on various administration "enemies," and on several occasions he sent to the IRS lists of those he wanted examined. Later the White House even requested audits of their opponents and certain tax-exempt organizations. Thrower returned these requests with a notification that such matters must be run through a regular process, but, in his words, he "never got a response."

In 1970 Thrower received word that the president wanted him to appoint G. Gordon Liddy and John Caulfield to head the alcohol, tobacco, and firearms division of the IRS. Thrower thought these men were too inexperienced, and he and the deputy secretary of the IRS soon settled on a different appointee. The White House then added that they wanted this person to report to Thrower rather than through official channels. Thrower had no time for this, and in any event he was reluctant to be tied to the unscrupulous White House inner circle. He therefore declined. John Dean later wrote that when Thrower thwarted Caulfield's appointment, the White House decided to sever ties. Thrower recalled that the feeling was quite mutual, as it seemed the president's aides were doing Nixon a disservice. "I went home that night," said Thrower, "and told Margaret not to make any long-term plans. My resignation was requested and given."[26]

Confidential documents uncovered during the Watergate investigation showed that President Nixon was aware that Thrower was causing trouble for the White House. The president therefore declared in no uncertain terms that he wanted him out of the IRS. In January of 1971 Nixon signed a memo to Treasury Secretary-Designate John Connally saying:

In order to remove any possible confusion, may I simply reiterate for the record that I wish Randolph Thrower, Commissioner of the Internal Revenue Service, removed at the earliest feasible opportunity and replaced with someone mutually acceptable to you and me.[27]

Thrower later gave an affidavit to the Watergate special prosecuting committee in which he recounted that, following his resignation, he had requested a meeting with the president to discuss his concern about White House attitudes toward the IRS. As a result, he said:

[Secretary of the Treasury David Kennedy] told me that as a presidential appointee I had that privilege and said he would arrange the conference. He later advised that he had been unable to…and said Mr. [White House Chief of Staff H.R.] Haldeman had told him that the president did not like such conferences.[28]

Johnnie M. Walters, Thrower's successor at the IRS, also received White House investigation lists, including requests for IRS audits of Democratic National Chairman Lawrence O'Brien and Democratic presidential candidate George McGovern's campaign contributors. Walters, too, resisted this pressure and even sent copies of the lists to the secretary of the Treasury. This information came out during the Watergate investigations, and although Walters was commended for his propriety, he was also nearly indicted.[29]

Thrower's instincts about Caulfield and Liddy could not have been more acute, for both men's reputations were tainted by their connection to Watergate. Caulfield, a former New York City policeman, was appointed assistant director for enforcement in the Treasury Department's Bureau of Alcohol, Tobacco and Firearms in July 1972, a year after Thrower's resignation. By Caulfield's estimation, only his cautious nature and a bit of "Irish luck" kept him out of prison. Liddy, meanwhile, had the dubious distinction of having been at the center of the actual Watergate break-in. He served a term in prison and later "redeemed" himself as an author and talk radio icon.

∾

THE WHITE HOUSE

WASHINGTON

MEMORANDUM FOR

    SECRETARY-DESIGNATE
    JOHN CONNALLY

In order to remove any possible confusion, may I simply
reiterate for the record that I wish Randolph Thrower,
Commissioner of the Internal Revenue Service, removed
at the earliest feasible opportunity and replaced with
someone mutually acceptable to you and me.

President Richard Nixon's letter, re: Randolph Thrower's firing

Courtroom scene

*Once the firm began to take on more
litigators in the 1970s, the practice
grew in several directions.*

CHAPTER EIGHT

LITIGATION

OVERVIEW

Litigation was an important part of the firm's services from the very start. The original partners litigated tax cases beginning in the 1920s, with Elbert Tuttle also handling litigation unrelated to tax law. In the ensuing decades nearly all of the firm's first- and second-generation lawyers had a hand in tax litigation. Litigation was not the kind of practice area that the firm planned to grow into, in part because it was not traditionally a very high-paying endeavor. It was, in fact, a secondary concern up to the 1950s and 1960s. Nevertheless, owing to the Sutherland litigators' strong reputation in the postwar years, they rarely had to drum up business. They tried almost every viable matter that came along, and this attitude snowballed into new practice areas. Although the litigation practice grew slowly, by 2000 it had become the firm's largest.

Baxter Jones became the lead litigator soon after joining the firm in 1951. Together with Bob Cumming and Jim Groton, Jones was able to build up a respected litigation practice, including representation of the Fulton County School System. Cumming took the lead on litigation after Jones's untimely death in 1962, while Groton took over the education work and later developed a substantial architectural and construction law practice.

By the late 1960s the Sutherland partners were looking to take litigation to the next level. Cumming was the firm's only full-time litigator, with Groton and J.D. Fleming also handling a fair amount of litigation. The partners therefore decided to bring Frank Gregory into the Washington office to join Willis Snell, who had been doing some litigation work. Carey DeDeyn, too, became a key link in this chain. When he joined the Atlanta office in 1969 he quickly found a role as the litigation team's full-time associate.

Going into the 1970s, the litigation practice was still quite modest, as the firm was still largely built around its more traditional mainstays of tax, corporate, and real estate law. These were proven, profitable areas in which the firm had developed a substantial reputation. Furthermore, tax and corporate work could be developed or solicited, but litigation was more a matter of handling, in Bob Cumming's words, "whatever washed up on the beach." So as the practice grew in the 1970s, the litigation team worked cases big and small, often falling back on the old standby, tax litigation. The major figures involved in the litigation practice in the 1970s were the Atlanta-based team of Bob Cumming (head), Jim Groton (education, architectural and construction), J.D. Fleming (scientific, IP), John Chandler (1972), Charlie Lester (1972), John Bonds (1973), Al Lindseth (1973), John Fleming (1976; no relation to J.D. Fleming), Tom Byrne, Tom Cox, and Judy O'Brien. Carey DeDeyn became a full-time litigation partner in 1975. Meanwhile, Frank Gregory and Willis Snell continued to do litigation work out of the Washington office.[1]

Once the firm began to take on more litigators in the 1970s, the practice grew in several directions. Toward the end of the decade, these lawyers got into some substantial cases. The most notable of these were matters handled for Ford Motor Company and Mutual of Omaha. In fact, most Sutherland insiders later suggested that the firm's litigation practice became truly national during the Mutual of Omaha cases of the late 1980s and early 1990s.

Other aspects of the practice brought a great deal of work and added considerably to the firm's prestige. Education litigation is a good example. Jim Groton helped steer several school boards through challenges to their desegregation plans from the 1960s to the 1980s, after which Al Lindseth and the firm's other education litigators began to take on very high profile public school funding cases. Other litigation practice areas were added in the ensuing years. The 1990s and 2000s saw tremendous growth in the area of intellectual property and insurance litigation, and Terry Weiss jumpstarted a broker/dealer arbitration practice out of the Atlanta office.

Securities and professional liability also came into their own in the 1990s, when the hard work of Sutherland partners John Chandler and Beth Tanis began to pay off. This practice was born in the early 1980s, when KPMG tapped Randolph Thrower to handle a tax shelter liability issue. Thrower had earlier used KPMG as experts in a separate tax case, so it was only natural that they would hire the Sutherland firm to handle the tax shelter matter. Chandler took over the case, and the work grew into a lucrative practice. When some KPMG in-house lawyers moved to other accounting firms, they kept Sutherland's number on their rolodexes, and eventually the firm's securities and professional liabilities practice group expanded its representation to all of the "Big Four" accounting firms.

The work in securities and professional liability was multifaceted, and many lawyers got involved over the years, including Chandler and Tanis, Amy Rudolph, Patti Gorham, Tom Curvin, and Rocco Testani, each of whom brought a different set of talents and contacts. Chandler was particularly valuable for having brought prestigious insurance clients like State Farm – a longstanding tax client of Jim Heffernan and Jerry Libin – into the litigation orbit. The addition of Peter Anderson as a lateral in the 1990s further augmented the group's abilities, as he went on to develop a strong securities enforcement practice. Meanwhile, Washington office lawyers like Brian Rubin and Neil Lang handled numerous SEC and NASD matters. In 2005-2006 the Washington office lawyers also represented State Farm in some of the liability cases that followed Hurricane Katrina.

The architectural and construction litigation practice also brought in a number of important clients. This practice grew directly out of the Atlanta building boom of the 1960s, when many new buildings were constructed and the rapid rise in inflation caused a great deal of tension in the construction industry. At this time the Georgia chapter of the American Institute of Architects hired the firm to help them negotiate some important contracts with the state. Jim Groton took the lead in the matter, and his experience broadened to construction cases in virtually every major building project in Atlanta from the 1950s through the 1970s. Atlanta was ahead of the national building boom, so when other cities experienced similar growth and construction problems, it was easier for their builders

D. Robert Cumming, Jr.

to hire an experienced construction lawyer from Atlanta than to train a local lawyer. Consequently, the lawyers who had been doing this work in Georgia were routinely hired for national and international projects. In this way, Groton's local experience quickly brought him into contact with new clients across the country. In addition to Groton, just about everyone in the firm did some construction litigation work at one time or another, particularly Al Lindseth and Charlie Lester in the 1970s and 1980s, followed by Bill Wildman, Tony Smith, Paul Killian, and Judy O'Brien in the 1990s and 2000s.

So the litigation practice grew from "whatever washed up on the beach" to a very client-driven set of major representations. By 2006 this work was being carried out by upwards of 130 litigation lawyers working for clients across the U.S. Although it is difficult to market litigation – in the sense that it is difficult to "cause someone to be sued" – it is easier to market expertise. The firm built up its abilities in these areas through lateral additions and homegrown cultivation, and the litigation group was not afraid to market its abilities. John Fleming put this practice into the perspective of the firm's culture when he said, "We really are at the top of the stack [nationally] in terms of our capabilities, though we still have something of a small firm mentality in terms of the camaraderie and the fact that the partners still enjoy working with new associates."[2]

BOOM, BUST, AND BOOM AGAIN
OF LITIGATION IN WASHINGTON

The Washington litigation practice has its own interesting history, which can be read against the backdrop of both the litigation practice as a whole and the changing fortunes of the entire firm. Except for tax and antitrust cases, the Washington litigation practice was virtually nonexistent until the 1970s. It began to grow beyond tax and antitrust when Frank Gregory and Willis Snell did some litigation for insurance companies in the 1970s and early 1980s. Meanwhile, Don

John A. Chandler

Baker, former assistant attorney general for antitrust under President Ford, joined the firm to anchor the antitrust practice originally begun by Mac Asbill, Sr. In addition, Steuart Thomsen came to Washington in 1980 and later became a significant member of the litigation team. Despite these important moves, at the turn of the 1980s litigation remained a limited endeavor in Washington.

Yet only a decade later litigation was near the center of the Washington practice. At the height of the Mutual of Omaha cases (c. 1990), the Washington office was operating with between 100 and 150 lawyers, with the litigation group flying particularly high as a result of the Mutual cases and Baker's antitrust cases. The group was also handling many major FDA cases brought in by Joel Hoffman. The Washington office augmented its capabilities in the antitrust area and became a major player in the area of FTC "second requests" for information on planned mergers. The firm, and the Washington office in particular, got to be one of the major players in that area in the 1980s.

Unfortunately, the next few years turned out to be a tough time for the Washington office, and especially for the litigation group. A number of factors added up to a perfect storm of misfortune, with the bottom falling out of the market, as it did for many Washington firms, around 1991-1992. To begin with, the regulatory environment changed, so there were far fewer FTC second requests. Furthermore, the firm as a whole had not effectively coordinated its planning, as evidenced in the loose leadership structure that was in place until 1995. Individual lawyers had more freedom to work under this system, but some opportunities were not exploited. Don Baker was a respected antitrust lawyer, but the firm did not pursue some potentially large matters. Meanwhile, the Mutual cases wound down, and the firm's merger with a litigation-based New York practice failed. Another key factor was Frank Gregory's untimely death, which put a dent in morale and left a sizable leadership vacuum. There had been talk of building a reinsurance practice when the Mutual cases tapered off, but enthusiasm for this idea waned after Gregory's death.

The net effect of these troubles was a diminished workload and the departure of some very promising lawyers, including Don Baker, Sheila Carpenter, and Mike Denger. Denger's exit was especially unfortunate for the antitrust practice, for he was a homegrown partner who had become the head of the antitrust section of the ABA. Frank Gregory was heard to say that Denger's departure was "like building a new house and watching someone else move into it." Over a three-year period in the early 1990s the Washington office dropped to around 110 lawyers. The antitrust practice was particularly hurt.[3]

Fortunately the group was able to mount a turnaround later in the 1990s. This turnaround began in large part because the Washington litigation group pounded the pavement to drum up more business. Other litigation work came from within the firm, and some of the litigation lawyers' niche practices started to pay off. After the firm changed its management arrangement, the group gravitated toward a broader approach to litigation management. This helped make litigation a truly firm-wide practice, after which things improved tremendously. The group became more methodical in its planning, eventually creating 10 formal subgroups, each with their own leaders. Personnel changes were also a key factor in the rejuvenation of the practice, as Rick Murphy moved to Washington from the Atlanta office and the group took on some talented laterals. Big cases came in with regularity, and the level of satisfaction within the group grew exponentially.

AUTOMOTIVE LITIGATION

Washington partner Nick Christakos has explained that there are essentially two ways to plan a litigation practice. A firm can either develop an institutional client, or it can develop expertise in a particular area and in this way make the short list whenever related cases arise. With its automotive franchise practice the Sutherland litigation group managed to do both. This practice began in Atlanta through representation of the Ford Motor Company, and it eventually became firm-wide. By 2005 the firm was regional counsel for Ford, handling all of the company's dealer litigation in 23 states.[4]

The work for Ford originated when Joe Brennan handled a case in the 1950s for the company at the behest of a former classmate. Brennan repeated the task a few more times over the years, and this got the firm marginally involved in automakers' issues. Bob Cumming succeeded to this relationship in the 1970s. The first major matter of this period came in 1982, when the firm became heavily involved in a case in which an Atlanta dealer sued Ford and Ford Credit for a billion dollars. John Fleming, a new partner at the time, handled this case with Tom Byrne, who was then an associate. Fleming went on to oversee more of Ford's dealer litigation in the 1980s.

Then, in 1992, the firm was presented with an extraordinary opportunity. Ford was using around 100 law firms to handle their dealer and employment work at the time, and the company decided to streamline their operation by consolidating their legal representation. They wanted to reduce the number to about three, so they sent out a request for proposals to have a single firm represent them in each region. The Sutherland firm made the first cut and was one of 10 firms selected to make a final presentation to the company's executives in Dearborn. The team, comprised of Frank Gregory, Carey DeDeyn, John Fleming, and Tom Byrne, presented an impressive case, and in the end Sutherland was chosen to handle Ford's dealer franchise and employment litigation in the South. This arrangement grew dramatically when, in 1996, the enormous Mayer, Brown law firm got into a quarrel with Ford and pulled out of the Northeast. The Sutherland firm added these states to the list. In the 1990s, then, Ford became a multimillion-dollar client served by both offices, and these profits helped leverage some of the firm's work with other auto manufacturers. In addition, Tom Byrne developed Ford Credit into a very substantial litigation client in its own right by handling high exposure consumer class actions around the country.

The firm opened a Tallahassee office in 1994 in the person of Dean Bunch, Florida's leading lawyer on the manufacturer side of dealer disputes. The partners knew Bunch from the occasions in which he had worked with them on Ford matters. When they hired him, he brought along all the other automobile manufacturers, several of whom the firm went on to represent in other states.

EDUCATION LITIGATION

The Sutherland education litigation practice is almost as old as the firm itself. It began in the 1920s when the Fulton County Board of Education called on Elbert Tuttle and Joe Brennan to handle some legal matters. The Fulton board then became the firm's first retainer client when it named Tuttle its general attorney in the 1930s. The relationship between the Fulton board and the Sutherland firm would last until 2004, and in the meantime Sutherland would represent major school systems throughout the U.S., first in desegregation cases (especially from the 1960s to the 1980s) and then in litigation over the constitutionality of their education finance systems.

Tuttle continued to take the lead on the board's general legal work until he left the firm in 1953. The torch was then passed to Baxter Jones, who headed the practice until his death in the 1962 Orly plane crash. Several of the firm's lawyers worked with Jones on education matters, but the Virginia-born and New York-reared Jim Groton handled more than anyone else. Groton began apprenticing with Jones soon after coming to the firm in 1954. Upon Jones's death, the board decided to continue with the young Groton, who would head this practice through the 1980s. It was then taken over by Judy O'Brien in the 1990s, with further assistance from many other Sutherland lawyers over the years.

Groton was at the forefront of the 1960s and 1970s school desegregation process in Georgia. He was instrumental in helping the Fulton County Public Schools desegregate peacefully at a time when many other Southern cities and school systems were experiencing boycotts, violence, and other forms of "massive resistance." "Jim Groton steered Fulton County through the area of desegregation with very little turmoil or trouble," recalled Al Lindseth. "The county desegregated its schools without riots or violence, as occurred in many parts of the South. I give Jim a lot of credit for his sound advice."

The firm's education lawyers got into desegregation law after handling more mundane legal matters. Throughout the 1950s, for example, the Sutherland lawyers' chief education activities included overseeing the Fulton board's property transactions and construction contracts as Atlanta expanded. But by the late 1950s desegregation had become a major issue. Baxter Jones deserves special mention in this regard, for he had drafted a racially neutral pupil assignment plan for the ultimate desegregation of the Fulton County system even before the 1954 *Brown v. Board of Education* decision. Needless to say, this was a bold move for its day.[5]

James P. Groton

Jones, Groton, and the others had their work cut out for them in desegregation cases, for the Fulton board in those days was a bit of an old boys' network. It was chosen by the county grand jury, a special advisory board of "propertied citizens" that was, unsurprisingly, quite conservative. The Atlanta board, by contrast, was elected. Jim Groton later recalled a conversation he had in this period in which a lawyer for the Atlanta board contrasted his clients with Groton's: "This lawyer said, 'Jim, your board is very monolithic – they look alike and they think alike.' And I said, 'Monolithic, hell. They're Paleolithic!'"

The Fulton board's traditionalism limited its imagination as Southern communities began to address desegregation. Groton, therefore, inspired by Baxter Jones's tutoring, tried to counsel the board to observe the law. According to Groton, even though he and his clients "could all read what was happening in the federal courts," he still had to spend much of his time convincing the board. Constant changes in the law made this even more difficult. Although this was stimulating work on the cutting edge of the biggest issue of the day, it was also frustrating. "There were some pretty intelligent people on the board," said Groton, "but they'd been brought up with a certain way of life, and it was interesting to get them to change their approach to things."

As desegregation continued and the education litigation field developed, the courts began to use more sophisticated techniques to deal with strategies of resistance throughout the South. Groton did what he could to keep the board ahead of the curve and out of the courts, and over the years the Sutherland education team worked out various processes for desegregating the school system. They took Baxter Jones's original pupil assignment plan and modified it to fit the current circumstances with the aim of developing a racially neutral process for assigning students to schools. This task became even more complicated as racial housing patterns developed.

Whenever Atlanta expanded, the city normally took over a piece of Fulton County's territory with high property tax values but few students. That growth created predictable financial strains for the county school system. In the 1960s some Atlantans felt that the solution to the city's education problems would be to force the county and city school systems to merge. These people used school financing as a vehicle to weaken the county school system. During the 1960s the Fulton board was faced with a long series of school funding cases. If the board had lost any of them, the school system likely would have gone into bankruptcy. Fortunately for the board and the firm, Groton and a team of Sutherland lawyers managed to win them all.

Hightower v. West

Through Groton, the board worked out desegregation compromises from time to time with leaders in the black community. In 1972, however, the NAACP filed a lawsuit against the Fulton County Board of Education to hasten the desegregation process. The NAACP was critical of a pupil assignment agreement between the board and the local NAACP chapter, so they decided to revoke the local chapter's charter. They further contended that the plan should include more student busing.

Groton had studied this subject for years, so he was well aware of the usual routine of these cases: Typically a favorable federal judge, often a native of the area in question, would let a Southern school board off easy on desegregation compliance. The NAACP would then appeal to the Fifth Circuit Court of Appeals, which would invariably overrule the local judge. The Sutherland lawyers were determined not to let this happen in the Fulton County case.

Because the typical favorable federal judge would usually rule on some point of law in a school board's favor, Groton insisted that the Fulton board try the case on the merits. He and his colleagues put before the district judge an elaborate, factual timeline, starting with Jones's 1953 pupil assignment plan and running through the various steps in their efforts to comply with the *Brown* ruling. After a full trial the district judge approved of the board's desegregation plan. Predictably, the NAACP appealed to the Fifth Circuit Court of Appeals, but for the first time this court actually ruled in favor of a local board of education's desegregation plan. Like the boards of many Southern school systems, the Fulton board continued under court order until 2004, when an effort led by Rocco Testani and Judy O'Brien succeeded in getting it released from court supervision.

Armour v. Nix

The most controversial and public of this era's cases was the eight-year school litigation case of *Armour v. Nix* (U.S. District Court for the Northern District of Georgia, C.A. No. 16708; affirmed by Supreme Court, 446 U.S. 931 (1980)). In 1972 Atlanta lawyer Margie Pitts Hames – ironically the wife of Sutherland partner Bill Hames – brought an ACLU suit on behalf of a group of Atlanta parents. She argued that, although the local boards of education had all met current court requirements within their school systems, there were still grave problems. She contended that racially segregated housing patterns, and thus segregated schools, had resulted from years of official actions by local governments. Her lawsuit thus aimed to invalidate school district boundaries and to treat the 10 districts in the Atlanta metro area as a single school system. This would have required a massive busing plan for a new "super district" stretching over an area the size of the state of Delaware.[6]

Under existing jurisprudence, courts honored school district boundaries unless they saw an "interdistrict violation" in the form of segregation between school systems. The test in the *Armour* case, then, was not the history of school segregation, but the cause of housing patterns. In other words, the parties asked why Atlanta was so black and suburban areas were so white.

Groton took the lead in the case with Al Lindseth along as lead associate. Groton had previously represented the Dekalb County board in another federal desegregation case, so the defendants naturally sought his expertise. Lawyers for the other defendant school districts assisted the Sutherland team.

Hames petitioned to place the suit on hold until the U.S. Supreme Court ruled in a different suit seeking cross-boundary school desegregation in Detroit. In 1974 the Court ruled in *Milliken v. Bradley* that federal courts only have the power to order cross-boundary busing in exceptional circumstances. Over the course of the next three years, Hames amended the original complaint to reflect the new jurisprudence. In the meantime, six of the 10 school systems named as defendants were dismissed from the suit, leaving the state, Atlanta, Dekalb, and Fulton systems. For 16 months in 1978-1979 lawyers for both sides presented their case to a three-judge panel of the U.S. district court.[7]

Groton's team decided to employ social scientists to ascertain the cause of housing patterns. They had a hard time finding objective academics because social scientists in those days tended to think Southern school districts were manned by ignorant bigots. Nevertheless, Groton and Lindseth were able to put together a team of demographers, urban geographers, and economists. They asked the specialists one fundamental question: Was government action a cause of racial housing patterns, or did those patterns occur through nongovernmental forces?

The result was truly a landmark study. The team of experts found that very little, if any, government action had led to racial segregation. Although they recognized that personal prejudice had a role, other factors predominated, including real estate practices, geography, transportation distances, and personal living choices. With this study in hand, Groton made a very convincing case to the court that the housing patterns in question were largely due to nongovernmental factors. Success in the case was not assured, though, because the plaintiffs' lawyers had also worked extensively with experts of their own. Groton and Lindseth eventually shot many holes in these experts' arguments.

After 16 months of consideration, and seven years after the original suit was filed, the court passed a comprehensive judgment. They ruled that, while the government had acted to cause segregated housing as late as the mid-1960s, "governmental discrimination has long since ended and the Fair Housing Act passed in 1968 is now alleviating the effects of private discrimination." They went on to conclude, "To the extent that racial patterns persist, they are currently in existence because of personal preference and economic constraints."[8] In those days a three-judge ruling automatically went to the Supreme Court. Groton's team sent a brief to Capitol Hill, and in May 1980 the Court issued a five-to-three, four-word opinion: "The judgment is affirmed."[9]

The Supreme Court's decision was widely applauded. Dr. Benjamin Mays, famed civil rights advocate and then-president of the Atlanta Board of Education, praised the ruling as "a wise thing." He went on to assert, "There is no guarantee that because you are shuttling kids over several counties that you will have a better school system. I think we are pretty much stabilized here in Atlanta." Even the editors of the *Atlanta Constitution* concurred, saying "such a busing plan would not have worked and perhaps would have resulted in crippling the public education system throughout the Atlanta region."[10]

Desegregation Plans

Groton's team continued to monitor the desegregation process for many years. Under the jurisprudence of the time, school systems had to operate under a constant desegregation order, and these orders only began to fall from the radar screen in the 1990s. Years later Groton summarized both the legacy and the difficulty of this work: "I think we did a lot of good with the Fulton schools. I had to fight harder with my board than I did with the NAACP to get them to do the right thing." After Groton's success with the Atlanta metro school case, he did similar work in other states.

Other players also did important work in the education litigation practice. Al Lindseth took to this area in the mid-1970s and headed it beginning in the early 1980s. Lindseth had long since learned how to perform in a stressful environment, having cut his teeth as an infantry officer in Vietnam with the Army's 173rd Airborne Brigade. The West Point graduate went on to receive his J.D., cum laude, from Harvard Law School before coming to Sutherland. He was later joined in the practice by John Munich and Rocco Testani. Munich, former deputy attorney general in charge of litigation in Missouri, returned to the firm after winning the landmark Supreme Court case of *Missouri v. Jenkins* (515 U.S. 70 (1995)). His victory in that case resulted in an immediate savings of more than $90 million per year to the state of Missouri.

Lindseth's team built up a national reputation in complex school finance and desegregation cases. School boards had an affirmative duty to desegregate their schools in such a way that "vestiges" of the old system were removed. Such vestiges included transportation, the ways in which students and faculty were assigned, and the layout of buildings. Districts thus had to devise plans to ensure that faculties and students were integrated. The Sutherland team helped several districts get their desegregation plans approved, including Savannah (Chatham County), for whom they won approval of the country's first "voluntary desegregation plan." They also represented Knox County, Tennessee, in a massive reorganization of their school district through the closing of 23 urban schools. Although this was a

---

Georgia's First Desegregation Case

The difficulties of the desegregation process were exacerbated by the largely segregationist character of the Georgia state government of the 1950s and 1960s. The state had passed a law decades earlier mandating a cutoff of funds to any district that desegregated its schools, and everyone thought the Atlanta district would be first to be closed because the Atlanta desegregation case was the first to be filed. But the first desegregation order actually involved the University of Georgia. Because this was the "beloved" state university, the state politicians could not afford to close it, and almost overnight the legislature repealed nearly all of the segregation laws they had passed decades before. Jim Groton called this "an amazing series of events," during which "Atlanta dodged the bullet."[16]

---

highly controversial plan, it was necessary to put the schools on the track to the 21st century.

In another interesting assignment, the team got the state government of Missouri out of the Kansas City and St. Louis suits, which were the two most expensive desegregation cases in U.S. history. Missouri was ordered to pay for enormously expensive programs in those two cities, above and beyond the regular funding of the school districts. For a time, Kansas City was spending more than any school district in the country and building magnificent facilities for their public schools that would make most universities jealous (for example, swimming pools with underwater cameras). Some at the time called this the biggest waste of education money in American history. All told, the state paid more than $2.6 billion for these additions, which the Missouri attorney general believed more than qualified the state for compliance with the Constitution's requirements. The Sutherland team was able to resolve the cases through a combination of litigation and negotiations to get the settlements approved by the courts. It then got involved with the state legislature to implement the settlements.[11]

In the Washington, DC, suburb of Prince George's County, Maryland, the Sutherland team found another interesting scenario when black leaders asked the firm to help free the school system from a court busing order. The county was one of the nation's largest school districts, and it had a wide disparity in household incomes. The original court order was aimed at integrating predominantly white schools, as the county had been predominantly white when the order was written in the 1970s. By the turn of the 21st century, however, the racial composition of the county had changed completely, and an absurd situation existed whereby black students were bused to faraway schools that were predominantly black. Ironically, the firm's opponent in this case was the NAACP. After a six-week trial in 1998, Al Lindseth and Washington partner Lovida Coleman ended up resolving the case on a win-win basis. The busing stopped and the state chipped in $250 million to build a dozen new schools, predominantly in the urban, lower-income part of the county, where schools had been closed during the age of busing.

JIMMY CARTER'S GEORGIA LEGACY

The Dekalb and Chatham County (Savannah) school cases were, by many accounts, the firm's most unique education cases. The Sutherland team represented the two counties in suing the state to require it to pay part of the cost of desegregating those districts. Savannah successfully recovered money, while the Dekalb case was dismissed on technical grounds.

But the interesting aspect of the case was the process, not the result. The Sutherland firm argued that the state of Georgia had been responsible for much of the

---

Liberty Lobby Libel Suit

One rather unusual case handled by the litigation group in the early 1980s showed both the possibilities of strong cross-office cooperation and the extent of Bill Sutherland's connections. The firm's work on this matter began when a leader of the conservative organization Liberty Lobby asked Bill Sutherland if the firm could handle the appeal of a libel verdict. Although the firm was involved only in the appeal and not in the original trial or retrial, the connection to well-known figures makes it worth recounting.[17]

In 1976 the Liberty Lobby's newspaper, *The Spotlight*, printed an article about the upcoming congressional hearings on the assassination of President Kennedy. The author of the article suggested that at the hearings the CIA would frame ex-CIA operative and convicted Watergate conspirator E. Howard Hunt, Jr. for involvement in the assassination. In the process, the author described a supposed CIA memo that seemed to implicate Hunt and purportedly said that Hunt was in Dallas on the day of the assassination. Hunt decided to sue for libel.

In 1981, using defense counsel from a different firm, Liberty Lobby went to trial in a federal district court in Florida, and the case was tried as a public figure case under the *New York Times* actual malice standard. By this standard, when a public figure is attacked in the media, he cannot win a libel judgment merely by showing that the attack is untrue and unfair. Under the 1964 Supreme Court decision in *New York Times v. Sullivan*, the plaintiff must show "actual malice" on the part of the defendant. Hunt conceded that he was a public figure for this purpose. At this first trial, Liberty Lobby admitted that Hunt was not in Dallas on

segregation in these districts, not only because the laws of the state had once required separate schools, but because in the period following *Brown v. Board* the state had acted to prevent school desegregation. As part of the case, Al Lindseth took depositions from four former governors of the state – Lester Maddox, Ernest Vandiver, Carl Sanders, and Jimmy Carter (who had only recently been turned out of the White House) – as well as several lieutenant governors and state superintendents. Lindseth was the first person to cross-examine those men on all their actions in the integration period. And since he was trying to prove that they had resisted desegregation, they were rather unhappy with the nature of the examinations.

Lester Maddox, said Lindseth, was far and away the most unrepentant of the ex-governors. "He wasn't apologizing for anything, unlike the others, who'd all become much more liberal as the decades went by." Lindseth got Maddox on record explaining the reasoning behind all of his decisions as governor.

Jimmy Carter's deposition was the most compelling because, said Lindseth, "even the minor things take on significance when you're getting a deposition from an ex-

---

the day of the assassination, and the organization argued instead that *The Spotlight*'s editors did not display a reckless disregard for the truth. The jury disagreed, and they rendered a $650,000 judgment in favor of Hunt.

It was then that the Sutherland firm took over. Frank Gregory and Carey DeDeyn took the lead on the appeal before the 11th Circuit Court of Appeals, with backup from Steuart Thomsen. Both Gregory and DeDeyn thought it was a great First Amendment case. They argued that Hunt as a public figure did not meet his burden of showing actual malice. The court found that the evidence was adequate to support actual malice, but it reversed and remanded the case because the trial court had given a faulty instruction on the required showing for actual malice (improperly based on a "responsible publisher" standard), as well as a faulty instruction on punitive damages under Florida law. Although the court found that Liberty Lobby had not properly objected to the incorrect actual malice instruction, the majority found the error to warrant a new trial because it was "so fundamental that the failure to recognize it will result in a miscarriage of justice."

After the court overturned the original judgment, Liberty Lobby handed the retrial to celebrity lawyer Mark Lane, author of the JFK assassination study *Rush to Judgment*. Lane's defense strategy included making an issue of where Hunt had been on the day of the JFK assassination. The argument was anything but flawless, but it was enough to exonerate the Liberty Lobby a second time. Lane later wrote a sensational book about the CIA's alleged involvement in the assassination plot called *Plausible Denial*.[18]

president." The interview took place in a Carter Center conference room that is a replica of the Oval Office, and in Lindseth's words, "it was not a friendly deposition." Lindseth was trying to prove that Carter had opposed desegregation plans and busing while he was the governor. In the event that the president demurred, the well-prepared lawyer had dozens of newspaper clippings to prove his point. He eventually got Carter to admit the truth after showing him these documents, just as in a trial cross-examination. Lindseth said of the conclusion of the deposition:

> *In the end I had to ask, "Mr. President, isn't it true that you were actually very much opposed to busing?" And he gave me the perfect line for my case. He said, "Yes. Wrong though it was!" So in one fell swoop I got him to admit, yes, he had done it, and second, he thought it was wrong.*

Years later Lindseth bumped into Carter again, and the former president asked how the case had come out. Lindseth replied positively, and Carter said, "I'm glad. I thought that was a good case."

THE NEW YORK PUBLIC SCHOOLS CASE

When school busing cases decreased in the 1980s and 1990s, the Sutherland education litigation team moved into multibillion-dollar education adequacy cases, in which plaintiffs typically argued that not enough was being done to meet state constitutional requirements for an adequate education. The firm defended several states in such cases. Unfortunately, the most notable of these cases was a loss. Lindseth's team, along with lawyers from the office of New York attorney general Eliot Spitzer, represented the state of New York in a seven-month trial in 1999-2000 challenging the adequacy of the New York City public schools and the constitutionality of the state's $12 billion annual education budget. The Sutherland lawyers handled most of the trial work. The length of the trial and the amount of money involved made this the largest single case ever handled by the Sutherland firm.[12]

The case began when a New York City plaintiffs' group, Campaign for Fiscal Equality (CFE), alleged that the state of New York was not providing enough money for an adequate education. The state sought the Sutherland firm's team of Lindseth, John Bonds, John Munich, Rocco Testani, Lovida Coleman, Dan Schlueter, and several associates because they had established a strong reputation doing similar work in other states. As Bonds explained it, "We knew more than anyone else, and we knew the experts." The group went on to show that New York City was first in the nation in funding among large urban school districts, at more than $10,000 per student per year. They argued that this was "adequate" based on the state constitution, which called for a sound, basic education consisting of minimally adequate resources. The team pinned its hopes on the combination of the low standard and high spending, but at the same time they were realistic about their chances of winning such a politically charged case.

Their suspicions about the politics of the matter were eventually confirmed. The state did not win at trial, largely because the case was of the "New York City vs. Upstate" variety, with a hometown judge presiding (*Campaign for Fiscal Equality v. New York* (719 N.Y.S.2d 475, 2001)). The appellate division subsequently reversed the judge's opinion on the law and the factual record developed at trial, but unfortunately the court's opinion was rather impolitic, and the New York Court of Appeals reinstated the case. The question then became, how much would the state have to pay? The court ordered the state to pay an extra $24 billion over five years, and the state appealed.[13] As of 2006, then, the question of payment remained unanswered. At any rate, a potential constitutional crisis loomed in New York's future, for $24 billion was a huge amount by any standard.

The case was grueling for the Sutherland team because they had to spend two years working in a very hostile environment, including the arduous seven months of the trial. And since they were representing the state in a case against the city, the city press treated them as Southern interlopers right from the start. (The news media commonly referred to the Sutherland lawyers as "Dixie Solicitors.") It did not help that Sutherland was named counsel by a Republican attorney general who promptly lost his reelection and was replaced by New York City native Eliot Spitzer. Despite Spitzer's ties to the city, he chose to stick with the Sutherland team. "We did a great job," concluded John Bonds, "but the outcome was preordained." Bonds and Lindseth later agreed that the New York case was one of the most unpleasant experiences of their lives, which was saying a great deal considering both men had endured boot camp, military academies, and tours of duty in Vietnam.[14]

CONCLUSION

A great deal was at stake in these funding cases, and many questions lay at the center of the controversies. What level of education should a state provide? How much money was enough, and should it come from state or local sources? What forms of education reform were likely to have the most success at improving achievement, particularly among poor and minority students? Many solutions were proposed – vouchers, school choice, magnet schools, increased funding, teacher testing, etc. – but there was no empirical evidence that any of these was the right one. Budget deficits and huge court orders kept these questions on the table. Because education funding was such a large part of state budgets, the experts suggested that virtually every state would eventually have to address adequacy cases.[15]

The beginning of the Alaska Pipeline that runs from Prudhoe Bay to Valdez.

The Alaska Pipeline proposal (1974-1979) was the biggest case ever handled by the energy group and one of the biggest ever handled by the firm.

CHAPTER NINE

THE ENERGY PRACTICE

The energy practice was at the center of the most dramatic growth spurt in the firm's history. Ed Grenier and his Washington team took an obscure legal field and turned it into a nationally renowned practice in just a few short years. In the process they worked on some of the most cutting-edge issues of the 1970s and 1980s, when the nation was meeting the challenge of reinventing its energy markets. The oil shocks and "stagflation" of the period fostered an unprecedented slew of energy regulations and proposals. It took sharp sleuthing to stay on top of it all, and Grenier's group proved more than capable. The practice then became more multifaceted in the 1990s and 2000s as the group began to handle a greater variety of matters.

The roots of the energy practice lay in the soil of central Georgia. The firm had a long relationship with Georgia companies who mined kaolin, a form of china clay with many industrial uses. The kaolin deposits were mined through arrangements with the landowners, and these two sides rarely saw eye to eye. Nevertheless, mining companies and landowners had to provide mutual assistance in the development of economic information because they were trying to get the highest possible percentage depletion. That is, since the material had to be processed after it was taken out of the ground, they tried to get the highest possible state of clay refinement (see Ch. 7). Since these companies did not trust each other, they asked Joe Brennan to handle their taxes. Brennan, Willis Snell, and Jim Wilson worked out percentage depletion with the IRS, and they soon gained the confidence of the entire group of miners.[1]

The next important step in the development of the practice came with the hiring of Ed Grenier in 1968. Grenier had been a communications lawyer with the Washington firm of Covington and Burling, but he thought better of his long-term prospects at the Sutherland firm. The Sutherland partners considered him a great steal, so they took him on as a communications specialist. Grenier was likewise very impressed with the talent at Sutherland, and he was equally pleased that a senior partner, Herbert Elsas, actually met him at the airport when he came to Atlanta for the interview.

Grenier's great innovation in what was soon to become a powerful Sutherland energy practice was realizing that industrial gas *users*, as opposed to energy producers and distributors, generally lacked legal representation.[2] In 1971 no law

Edward J. Grenier, Jr.

firm with any energy expertise would represent energy consumers because of conflict-of-interest problems with pipeline or distributor clients. The Sutherland energy group would break precedent and make a name for itself by taking on the pipeline and distribution companies.[3]

A few years after Grenier joined Sutherland, Willis Snell informed him that the kaolin group had been having problems with Atlanta Gas Light and the Federal Power Commission (FPC). The gas company had raised the natural gas price 25% through a purchased gas adjustment clause. Grenier, an FCC specialist, essentially said, "FCC, FPC…what's the difference?" and took the job. He quickly learned that the pipeline interests were to blame for the price hike. Atlanta Gas Light had passed the pipeline's increase to their consumers, creating an enormous increase in price without any hearing as to its appropriateness. When Grenier explained this to the kaolin group, he found that a large group of industrialists was also interested in the gas price issue.[4]

Before long these parties – producers of a variety of materials – formed the Georgia Industrial Group to combat the price increase. Grenier asserted that because the problem was coming from Washington, the group should organize to pool its resources and intervene in pipeline rate cases, particularly those involving the suppliers of Atlanta Gas Light. When the group first entered the fray in these cases, the other lawyers said to Grenier, "You don't belong here," to which Grenier confidently replied, "Yes, we do, because we pay all your bills." This early move into federal regulatory cases and hearings essentially established the right of end users to participate at the Federal Energy Regulatory Commission (FERC). The electric group formed a few years later for similar reasons.

Much of the wrangling over energy took place at the federal level. When

Ed Grenier

Ed Grenier's knack for envisioning new opportunities while dealing with obstinate gas suppliers may have stemmed from his upbringing in the Bronx. Growing up in one of New York's toughest neighborhoods (with the added handicap of a French surname), Grenier learned early on to handle whatever came his way. He was also an exceptional student. He graduated from Manhattan College at age 20, then served two years in the Air Force before moving on to Harvard Law. At Harvard he wrote and edited materials for the Law Review, including a note by Antonin Scalia, who was one year behind him in the law school.

Grenier organized the Georgia Industrial Group in 1970, natural gas shortages were beginning to develop in the interstate market. A large amount of gas was being kept in the producing areas because its price was controlled at the federal level. But there were no controls at the intrastate level. Shortages and curtailments worsened, and regional animosities began to flare. (Those who lived through this period might well remember the mantra, "Let the Yankees freeze in the dark!")

The first major federal case for the electrical side of the energy practice came in 1975, when Grenier's team represented Kaiser Aluminum in a major proceeding. After this case Grenier's team branched out into other states, with a good deal of work coming out of Pennsylvania and North Carolina. They also began advising General Motors on propane and oil allocation rules.

GENERAL MOTORS

Natural gas regulation had a rather unusual origin. In 1954 the U.S. Supreme Court ruled that the rates charged by gas producers were subject to regulation. This upset President Eisenhower, and Congress soon passed a bill reversing the decision. However, after Ike got word that an attempted bribe had taken place while the bill was being crafted, he vetoed it in order to remove the taint of impropriety. His decision to allow regulation to continue effectively set the stage for many of the energy problems of the ensuing decades. Congress only began the slow process of deregulating in 1978. On a more positive note, Eisenhower's veto created a great deal of work for American lawyers.

The Sutherland energy group's connection to General Motors began with the federal curtailment cases. The Natural Gas Act provided that the Federal Power Commission (FERC's predecessor) would regulate all natural gas transported or resold in interstate commerce, though the commission could not regulate production. In the wake of the first gas shortages, the FPC in 1971 issued its first supply curtailment order. This set the groundwork for years of litigation over the correct way to apportion gas to industrial customers during shortages.

Grenier quickly became an expert in the allocation of natural gas, and his participation in one early hearing in which these allocation formulas were being determined led to a fortunate contact. Lou Flax, a Washington lawyer who later joined the Sutherland firm, had been asked by General Motors to represent them in a curtailment case. Flax had a conflict, so he recommended Grenier. Grenier met with the General Motors people, and this meeting spawned the most dramatic growth in a practice area that the Sutherland firm has ever seen in such a short time.[5]

GM was using gas for a variety of industrial purposes. In Grenier's first curtailment case for the company, he concluded that if the local gas distribution companies' plan was approved, most of GM would shut down within a few weeks. The other U.S. automobile manufacturers would be adversely affected as well. So

The Energy Crunch

Contrary to popular memory, President Nixon was one of the most heavily regulating presidents of the 20th century. Many of the Nixon-era regulations were unraveled in a limited way during the presidency of Jimmy Carter, while Ronald Reagan took deregulation even further. Ed Grenier told of one amusing incident while working for GM during the Nixon years: "GM heard a rumor that the government was about to seize propane because the supply was so short. So I asked them, 'Where's the propane?' And they said, 'On tank cars.' And so I said, 'Well, keep 'em moving! They can't seize them if they're moving. Keep 'em moving!' That turned out to be a false rumor."[11]

Grenier brought in some high-powered consultants and worked out a model curtailment plan, which GM then agreed to put into that case and other gas curtailment cases in which it participated at Grenier's urging. In this way GM became the Sutherland firm's major energy client, while the Sutherland firm likewise became one of GM's major counselors. Tom Murphy, GM chairman and CEO, announced at the 1975 annual meeting that GM had paid more to the Sutherland firm for representation ($525,000) than it had paid to any other firm in the country.

THE ALASKA PIPELINE

The Alaska Pipeline proposal (1974-1979) was the biggest case ever handled by the energy group and one of the biggest ever handled by the firm. More significantly, the planned Alaskan Natural Gas Transportation System was, at the time, the largest privately financed venture in history. The energy group's work for GM had caught the attention of Bill Diener, general counsel of Northwest Pipeline Corporation, who asked Ed Grenier to represent Northwest in a major rate case. This was an unusual situation because lawyers do not normally represent both industrials and the pipeline. As the firm had no conflicts concerning Northwest, Grenier agreed, and the relationship between Sutherland and Northwest developed from there.[6]

Meanwhile, the natural gas shortages were spurring interest in the huge gas reserves off Prudhoe Bay in Alaska. Two groups filed applications with the Federal Power Commission to transport the gas from the North Slope to the lower 48 states. The first group, Arctic Gas, proposed a pipeline across the Alaska wildlife range, down the McKenzie Delta, and through to the lower 48. This plan was problematic, though, for it involved a protected wildlife range. The second group,

El Paso, put together what they called the "all American plan." They planned to send the gas through a pipeline to Valdez, Alaska, liquefy it, put it on ships, and unload it at Port Conception in California. This plan had *two* major problems: Valdez was on the worst earthquake fault in North America, and Port Conception was the location of a sacred Indian burial ground.

After two years of FPC hearings, Northwest Pipeline filed a third application. As Grenier recalled, his team had to claw its way into the hearings, and they "were not at all welcome after two years!" Theirs was going to be the "environmental" plan: Their pipeline would follow the oil pipeline right-of-way and the Alcan Highway, cut through Canada, then terminate in Chicago.

Congress had meanwhile passed a special statute, the Alaska Natural Gas Transportation System Act, which the Sutherland lawyers jokingly referred to as "ANGST." Under that statute, the FPC was to issue an advisory opinion at the end of the Alaska natural gas hearings, with the final decision ultimately to be made by the president of the United States. On decision day the commissioners voted two to two, with two favoring Arctic Gas, two favoring Sutherland client Northwest, and all four agreeing that El Paso would be a good second choice. The split decision left a good deal of legwork ahead of Grenier's team, and they spent the next few years cajoling and lobbying many agencies to get a favorable result. President Carter eventually chose Northwest, much to the satisfaction of the entire Sutherland energy group.

But although thousands of hours had gone into the research, hearings, arguments, and lobbying, the pipeline was never built. Several factors contributed to this inaction. To begin with, overall cost estimates ran to upwards of $20 billion, with the unreported "real" number even higher. In addition, none of the teams had solved the frost heave problem, whereby a warm underground pipeline tends to buckle when it meets with frozen arctic ground. But the chief cause of the project's cancellation was the realization that there really was no gas shortage in the continental U.S. Once the 1978 Natural Gas Policy Act broke down the distinction between the interstate and intrastate markets, gas started flooding through the interstate system. (The perceived shortage had been so great that at one point in the mid-1970s Kansas City came within hours of losing its gas service.) By the time President Carter approved the Alaska Pipeline, gas was pouring in and prices were plummeting. Grenier's consultants had long predicted that deregulation would lower prices, and their prediction was finally coming to pass.

RECENT DECADES

The Sutherland energy practice's reputation was so strong that the work continued to roll in through the 1980s, leading to even greater industrial representation. GM did not want to be alone in many of their cases, so in 1977 the company joined

Electric substation

with Nabisco and Cone Mills to form the Process Gas Consumers group (PGC). The PGC eventually grew to include 17 members, and the Sutherland team served as its legal representative.[7]

By the early 1980s the energy practice was generating a quarter of the Washington office's income and 15% of the combined offices' revenues. As the energy practice grew, so did the number of lawyers involved. In addition to those already mentioned, some of the other prominent lawyers in the early years of the practice were Rich Noland (in Austin, Texas), Richard Pierce (later a prominent professor of law), Bob Clark, Bob Morrow, William Penniman, and Glen Howard. Later additions included Earle O'Donnell, Rob Skinner, Gail Gilman, Kathy Yarbrough, Jim Bushee (from GM), Fred Aman (later a law school dean), Ron Levin, and Chris Hagy (in Atlanta). Grenier and Hagy worked together on a number of Georgia cases, and Hagy handled the Georgia Industrial Group's electrical needs. Hagy went on to become a federal magistrate judge. Another key acquisition in the early 1980s was Jan Vlcek, who came on as a lateral from Gardner, Carton & Douglas. He brought legislative skills to the energy group, but unfortunately he died young from a brain tumor. These players were the real driving force behind both the energy group's creation and its success. As Sutherland partner Herbert Elsas said, "We fell into some aspects of [the energy work], but you cannot give too much credit to Ed Grenier and his crew for making it really grow into an enormous practice."[8]

Two major acquisitions and expansion into Texas further augmented the group's capabilities in the early 1990s. In 1991 a group including Keith McCrea and Paul Forshay came over from the firm of Squire, Sanders & Dempsey. Two years later, partner Rich Noland moved to Austin to open the firm's branch there, and he was soon joined by four lawyers from the Austin office of New York's Varet & Fink. Sutherland was then the only Atlanta-based firm with a Texas office. At about the same time, the energy group made another major acquisition with the addition of Peter Rodgers, Jacob Dweck, and Beverly Rudy. Their inclusion broadened the scope of the practice beyond industrials. Rodgers, a Stanford Law graduate and Woodrow Wilson Fellow in Economics, had practiced environmental, energy, and commodities law in Washington since 1974. Dweck, who was also a veteran of Washington energy law, had worked with Rodgers since 1975.[9]

Rodgers's group came to the firm because they wanted to merge their abilities with the Sutherland firm's strong regulatory expertise. Before coming to the firm, the group did work for the financial players in the energy markets, including trading companies like Goldman-Sachs and Morgan Stanley. These clients wanted to move into trading natural gas and electrical power, and they asked Rodgers and his colleagues questions the lawyers could not handle. Rodgers's group therefore decided to look for a firm that had a strong presence at FERC. When they came to Sutherland in 1993 they immediately brought the Sutherland Washington office's regulatory lawyers in to help their clients, an arrangement that worked very well for all parties.

Also in the 1990s, the Atlanta office developed a recognized practice for electric cooperatives through the acquisition of a group of lawyers headed by Barrett Hawks. Hawks's team assisted electric utilities in the rural electric system, a heavily subsidized scheme established to get electricity to rural areas. They oversaw the financing and restructuring that took place as the government weaned these customers from the dole, and in the process they built electric cooperative representation into a premier national practice.

Grenier and his colleagues had a huge impact on federal energy policy throughout this entire period. The firm got into many kinds of curtailment cases, advancing the same basic plan that curtailments should be based on the ultimate end uses of the gas. Before 1993, upwards of 20 Sutherland lawyers were representing natural gas end users, principally at the federal level. These end-user groups essentially pushed through the deregulation of gas by forcing the separation of the transportation and commodity functions. Pipelines remained regulated because they were fundamentally monopoly entities.

By the early 1990s the most important work in gas deregulation was accomplished, which made electrical power the new focus of deregulation efforts. The Sutherland energy group adjusted its efforts accordingly, but although natural gas deregulation had been a great success, power deregulation was not. Several factors made electrical deregulation more difficult. Gas deregulation succeeded in part because government and industry ultimately cooperated to make it work. Gas was also a commodity that could be stored, while power could only be stored indirectly, and in a limited capacity. In addition, gas markets were more national, while power was more regional. Finally, very powerful, entrenched utilities in some regions fought to stay with the traditional model of electrical power distribution. These utilities had enough clout to prevent state legislatures from making changes.

One of the firm's most significant electric power clients after 2000 was Calpine, an independent, California-based producer. When the California electricity crisis of 2000-2001 drove up prices, power sellers began to pull in record profits. Calpine grew to be the ninth-largest electricity producer in the world, and many other producers saw similar growth. The combination of the electricity crisis and the producers' profits led to a public demand for investigations into power sellers' practices. Coincidentally, some of Enron's trading practices came to light at this time, and this did much to turn public opinion against the power producers. Calpine approached Sutherland in November of 2000, and the firm agreed to represent the company in these investigations. The Sutherland energy group put together a team that included Keith McCrea, Peter Rodgers, Jim Bushee, Paul Forshay, Dan Frank, and Mike Bradley. FERC established a cost-based ceiling of prices for the period in question, and in the end Calpine was found to have virtually no culpability. As of 2006, appeals were still pending in federal district court. Meanwhile, the Sutherland energy group continued to represent Calpine in FERC proceedings, including those that addressed Southern electricity deregulation.[10]

The energy group also made a successful foray into liquefied natural gas. The group represented the Norwegian company Statoil in their entry into the American energy market through the acquisition of capacity in Maryland. Much of that venture's success followed the group's achievement of regulatory approval over the potential objections of competitors. The energy group had the necessary combination of skills to pull this off at the regulatory, policy, and legislative levels. The group also solicited the skills of lawyers in the Atlanta corporate group who understood the energy business and were able to draft complex agreements for Statoil's investment. Collaboration of this sort became common.

By 2005, the group's leader, Peter Rodgers, was calling Sutherland energy "a very multifaceted, fairly eclectic practice." Rodgers pointed out that although "the Washington norm is to think of an 'energy firm' as one whose lawyers only work at FERC or state regulatory agencies," the Sutherland energy group did not follow that model. True, some Sutherland lawyers worked only at FERC, but there were "a lot of lawyers, including young lawyers, who on a given day might do an environmental project, at the next moment a trade project, the next day be involved with a FERC proceeding, and perhaps be involved in traditional litigation as well. It ranges across many levels." With its unique skill set, the group was pulling in some of the largest companies in the energy business.

∽

A tanker loaded with liquefied natural gas is readied for transport

Francis M. Gregory outside the Chicago Bar (Omaha)

Omaha Indemnity

The Mutual matter consisted of dozens of cases and eventually touched, directly or indirectly, just about everyone in the litigation group, as well as many of the firm's partners.

CHAPTER TEN

MUTUAL OF OMAHA'S REINSURANCE TROUBLES

The Mutual of Omaha cases (1986-1994) marked the most significant stage in the development of the modern firm-wide Sutherland litigation practice. The Mutual matter was at the time the biggest set of cases the firm had ever handled, and it involved an immense marshaling of resources across the firm. The team saved or recovered a vast amount of money for Mutual of Omaha, and this herculean effort over nearly a decade helped make litigation the firm's largest practice area. The work also gave a shot in the arm to both offices at a time when litigation work was diminishing. The Washington practice in particular grew tremendously.

The Mutual matter consisted of dozens of cases and eventually touched, directly or indirectly, just about everyone in the litigation group, as well as many of the firm's partners. Frank Gregory took the lead, and he and John Bonds, together with paralegal specialist Lena Hinton, spent most of their time in Omaha until the cases wound down. The core Omaha team also included Sheila Carpenter, Nick Christakos, and later Jim Clinger, whose frequent-flier miles to and from Omaha were only a notch behind the others'. Additional Sutherland lawyers who also spent considerable amounts of time in Omaha included Carey DeDeyn, John Fleming, J.D. Fleming, Al Lindseth, Steuart Thomsen, and others too numerous to mention.

This was also a period that saw its share of tragedy, both in the litigation group and in the firm as a whole. First came the death of Mac Asbill, Sr. and Mac, Jr. in 1992. The younger Asbill's death after a brief fight with cancer was particularly surprising, for he seemed to be in very good health before he was stricken. In fact, he had gone on a ski trip only a few months earlier, and he worked until only 10 days before his death. The next unfortunate turn of events took place the following year. First, John Bonds was sidelined by a heart attack while working in Omaha. Then, to everyone's shock, Frank Gregory died of a heart attack.[1]

CASE SUMMARY

As with many of the firm's other significant cases, its involvement in the Mutual of Omaha matter grew out of an existing relationship.[2] The Sutherland firm's ties to

(clockwise from left) John W. Bonds, Jr., Jenny Jensen (FBI), Jim Clinger, Francis M. Gregory, Larry Harr (holding handcuffs), Dan Stewart (KC US Atty's office), Nicholas T. Christakos, Sheila J. Carpenter and Lena Hinton

Mutual dated back to the 1950s, when Laurens Williams brought the company along as a client. This relationship was nurtured over the next few decades largely out of the Washington office, though it remained a somewhat modest association. The firm achieved greater visibility with Mutual when, in the early 1980s, Frank Gregory successfully defended the company and its subsidiary, United Benefit, in an important stockholders' suit.[3]

Through Gregory's work on that case, he came to the attention of Mutual CEO V.J. Skutt. In 1986 Skutt asked Gregory for assistance on a major matter concerning a number of reinsurance contracts entered into by a Mutual property/casualty subsidiary. Mutual had acquired this subsidiary, Omaha Indemnity Company (OIC), to serve as a convenient entity through which Mutual's life and health policyholders could buy other forms of insurance (for example, homeowner's and auto policies). The subsidiary was not a major player in this area, but it was licensed in all 50 states. Skutt explained to Gregory that OIC had a serious problem with one or more reinsurance contracts entered into by a pair of Kansas City-based agents, and that he feared the problem ran even deeper than a handful of questionable contracts. As it turned out, these agents had traveled the world writing not just a few but hundreds of huge reinsurance contracts that were well beyond the subsidiary's means. Mutual was at risk with virtually all of these hidden contracts, and the reinsured were beginning to demand payment.

Gregory agreed to take on the work, though he could not have known that Skutt had only discovered the tip of the iceberg when he called in Sutherland. Gregory would eventually need nearly eight years, an onsite firm-wide team, and a huge amount of support from both offices before the problems were solved. John

Bonds came along as the second lead partner, and the pair added Sheila Carpenter and Nick Christakos from the Washington office. Once the team got into the matter they realized just how much was at stake.

The matter began when Frank B. Hall, one of the nation's best-known brokerage firms, introduced a small Kansas City-based company called World American Underwriters (WAU) to OIC's management. WAU was very small, and not well known, but it was a part of the reputable Financial Guardian Network. OIC was not very profitable, given the limited role it played in the Mutual organization, and OIC's management was looking for a way to generate a modest underwriting profit. WAU appeared to have the answer.

Simply put, James R. Wining and Willie A. Schonacher, the two WAU principals, decided to rip off OIC. With this goal in mind, Wining and Schonacher offered the OIC leaders a deal. If OIC would give them the power to commit OIC as a reinsurer of a modest amount of property and casualty business developed by agents around the country, the arrangement would create risk-free income for OIC, in that OIC would in turn be reinsured for most of the risk and would reap a respectable underwriting profit on the business written. OIC, they explained, would be protected while it made money on the deal. This seemed like an easy choice for OIC's management, so they agreed. Wining and Schonacher then began

---

Reinsurance

Reinsurance is effectively the transfer of risk to another insurance company, or "insurance of the insurer." It allows insurance companies to leverage their business and protect themselves in the long run by sharing risk with other insurers. When an insurance company writes business to insure risk, state laws and basic accounting principles limit the amount they can write vis-à-vis their capital and surplus. Insurers typically work from a three-to-one ratio of business premium to capital and surplus, and since that ratio is quite small, they quickly hit the ceiling. So in order to write more business, they reinsure policies they have already written, which frees up their capital and surplus for more business. An auto insurance company, for example, may write a policy for a consumer, then have a reinsurer pick up all or some percentage of the risk of all car insurance the company writes in a region of the U.S. Anything that fits the parameters of that treaty will be picked up by the reinsurer. If the insurance company writes $100 million in premiums and works out a treaty of reinsurance for half of that, the amount that goes against the company's capital and surplus is $50 million, not $100 million. The company can write more business with the extra funds. Reinsurers can also reinsure themselves, and a single policy may involve a chain of multiple insurers and reinsurers.

to do quite well, and they created their own company called Royal American Managers (RAM) so that they could directly profit from the arrangement rather than just make money for the Financial Guardian Network. The key to the scheme was to convince Mutual's management to issue what became known as the surplus additions letter, which promised the companies contemplating doing business with OIC that Mutual would stand behind its subsidiary with any additions to OIC's surplus that were necessary to make the reinsurance program a success. This essentially opened the door to Mutual's assets.

From that point on, Wining and Schonacher really took advantage of OIC. WAU, through these two rogue agents, wrote about $300 million worth of reinsurance policy premiums, most of which were undisclosed writings, against OIC's capital and surplus of only $20 million. This represented about $700 million in ultimate losses after an initial appearance of a modest underwriting profit. (Wining and Schonacher reported only a few million dollars a year over a two-year period.) Although these two were at the center of the scandal, a nationwide network of producing agents and brokers did much of the legwork by drumming up business around the country. A great deal of what they brought in was very high risk in nature, such as insurance for taxi and truck drivers. The only way the principals could continue the scam was to hide the enormous sums of money through an elaborate scheme that included vacation homes in the Caribbean and sham overseas brokerage subsidiaries, through which they could siphon off commissions. Mutual of Omaha at the time had a net worth of about $750 million, so this scam could have finished the company.

Once Frank Gregory and the rest of the Sutherland team saw the extent of Mutual's predicament, they realized that the work was going to take more than just a few months. The problems seemed so insurmountable, in fact, that when the Sutherland folks arrived in Omaha, Mutual's lawyers were exhibiting the "thousand-yard stare" of combat veterans. V.J. Skutt eventually asked Gregory to move to Omaha, but Gregory nixed that idea, saying he preferred to commute each week. And for the next eight years he and most of the others did exactly that. The lead lawyers and associates flew to Omaha on Sundays and returned on Thursday evenings or Fridays. They stayed in Mutual of Omaha's Educational Service Center, which was much like a university dormitory for traveling Mutual agents, and eventually got permanent rooms. Their daily work routine was grueling as well. Gregory and Bonds generally worked from 6 a.m. to 8 p.m. At that point they would usually head across the street to the Chicago Bar to do more work over a few drinks. This was their schedule for several years, except when the team traveled to a different city for work related to the case. They routinely billed 3,500 hours per year.

This schedule was brutal, but it was nothing the Sutherland team could not handle. John Bonds, for one, was already battle-tested, having flown KC-135s and C-123Ks in Vietnam. He later recalled that he realized the Mutual case was going to be a long one when Mutual decided to build offices for the Sutherland lawyers. He joked with the Mutual management that it was not a *real* lawyer's office unless it had an English hunting print on the wall. The next time he returned to Omaha, he saw that they had put one up.

Nick Christakos, who went on to contribute to the growth of the Washington litigation practice, was another important player in the Mutual case. He had spent four years doing antitrust legal work at the Washington boutique of Bergson, Borkland, Margolis & Adler in the 1980s, and when antitrust work began to drop off ("when Reagan stopped enforcing the antitrust laws," as Christakos liked to put it) that firm dissolved and he decided to join Sutherland. He later noted that, although the Mutual work schedule was grueling, Frank Gregory did give him a week off to get married. "Frank was very generous!" he joked.

The two main issues for the Sutherland team were how to deal with the mass of contracts Wining and Schonacher had entered into as agents for OIC, and the pursuit of an arbitration award against the two men and litigation against other responsible parties. In the early months of Sutherland's involvement in the case, Mutual of Omaha was receiving demand letters on a weekly basis from companies the Mutual insiders had never heard of, many of whom were threatening to sue. (The letters were arriving with such merciless regularity that Nick Christakos likened this stage of the case to the siege of Troy.) Around 300 contracts were at issue, so John Bonds decided the team had to prioritize the 30 most important. This list would represent about 90% of the known losses. A different Atlanta or Washington partner could then take primary responsibility for each of the cases, and assemble a team to handle the matter, with support from the core Omaha team as necessary.[4]

In the conflict between OIC and the reinsureds (also known as the ceding insurance companies because they ceded the risk to OIC as reinsurer), the key issue was to decide who was ultimately responsible for paying the claims. The Sutherland team argued that OIC had been swindled by crooks who assumed rotten business with known losses in the name of OIC, filed false reports, and stole much of the hidden money, with the knowledge and active involvement of the ceding companies themselves. In one case involving insurance for cab drivers in Philadelphia, for example, the ceding company readily took advantage of the willingness of Wining and Schonacher to cheat OIC and dumped a large portion of lousy business on OIC through one of these reinsurance contracts. OIC, meanwhile, thought it got a much smaller amount of the business than it actually got, and its managers had no idea at the time that known losses were being foisted upon it by its own trusted agents, as well as by ceding companies all too willing to solve their own underwriting problems by transferring them to OIC. While many of the ceding companies presented themselves as innocent contracting parties looking to get the benefit of their bargain with OIC, several of them simply could not get away with playing the victim. As the Sutherland team got into the matter they saw the pattern in these cases: One ceding company after another had gone along for the ride with Wining and Schonacher, at OIC's expense.

Downtime in Omaha

Despite, or perhaps because of, the high stress environment, the lawyers working the case also found time for some much needed R & R. The epicenter of the team's downtime was the Chicago Bar, conveniently located across the street from both the lawyers' "dorm" and the Mutual of Omaha offices. It soon became the group's unofficial after-hours headquarters. It was here that Frank Gregory held court like Plunkitt of Tammany Hall, singing Gilbert and Sullivan tunes with John Bonds (usually way off key) and occasionally getting unceremoniously ejected from the bar at the end of the night. To the bartender's credit, joked Nick Christakos, "they were the worst singers." Bonds later admitted that the duo's singing was subpar, but he respectfully added, "Frank had a wonderful facility to remember all the lyrics."[5]

Any disrespect encountered in the Chicago Bar was doubly disconcerting to Gregory because, the way he saw it, he owned the bar. And in a way he did. Mutual of Omaha owned the lease, and at one point the company decided to close the bar to build an employee parking lot. Gregory then told Mutual's CFO, perhaps only half-jokingly, "We need that bar; you close it, we're gone." Mutual therefore decided to renew the lease as long as the Sutherland lawyers were working on the case, and whenever Gregory met a new bartender or waitress, he told them, "I'm your landlord!" Few believed him.

A tale recounted by Nick Christakos shows just how proprietary Frank Gregory could be about the Chicago Bar:

> They had an indoor basketball hoop that you'd pay to use. Every night Frank would get a roll of quarters and we'd go to the back and shoot baskets. Well, the insurance agents would come from around the country for training, and one night we were in the back, and these guys, 10 or so, were acting like they owned the place. As a general rule, insurance agents are mostly ex-football players, so they're big. They were getting a bit rough with the machinery because they were missing too many baskets. Anyway, Frank started getting hot because he didn't want them to break the machine, so he went over and asked them to quit abusing it. They didn't comply, so he reached into his pocket and slammed an entire roll of quarters on top of the machine and said, "Dammit, I'll pay for every game you play for the next three hours. Just quit screwing around with the machine!"[6]

This bold salvo nearly occasioned a brawl, but the situation was defused when another of the far outnumbered (and outmuscled) Sutherland lawyers began to small-talk the insurance men. Cooler heads soon prevailed.

(left to right) Larry Harr, Sheila J. Carpenter, Kimberly J. Smith, Lena Hinton, Scott Hoyt, Lyman Larsen (Kennedy Holland), John W. Bonds, Jr., Francis M. Gregory, and John Sturgeon

CULMINATION

The Mutual matter reached its climax when the firm brought an arbitration case against RAM, the company formed by Wining and Schonacher. The Sutherland team asked for $225.6 million, though the conventional wisdom held that arbitration panels usually award only half of a requested amount. Gregory and his team should not have worried, though, for in the end they got a $225 million judgment against RAM – the largest reinsurance arbitration in history. The arbitration panel clearly established that the entity had defrauded OIC, though the Sutherland lawyers later joked that they never learned what happened to the remaining $600,000.[7]

The team then filed a federal suit against Wining and Schonacher, arguing that the arbitration award should be extended to the individuals because they were the alter egos of the company they used to defraud OIC. (The two men were not parties to the arbitration, but of necessity the arbitration decided the issue of their liability.) The team satisfied the test for applying that theory, and the federal court also entered a $225 million judgment. Collecting that money was another matter, however. Wining and Schonacher had put huge amounts of unreported money into Caribbean homes, a corporate jet, offshore accounts, and the like. Consequently, Mutual was able to recover some money, but not the full amount.

The defendants were quite colorful, to say the least. "They weren't professional criminals," noted Bonds. "They were not even particularly gifted amateurs." Wining hired famed Las Vegas mob lawyer – and later Sin City mayor – Oscar Goodman, onetime barrister to such organized crime notables as Meyer Lansky and Chicago crime boss Anthony "Tony the Ant" Spilotro. Goodman argued that his client had to remain free in order to look after his mentally disabled son. An odd defense, to be sure, but good enough to receive a suspended five-year sentence. Wining also had a sense of humor about what was, in reality, no laughing matter. He regularly wrote checks to Mutual of Omaha for tiny amounts, always adding, "In partial satisfaction of debt …" Schonacher was not as lucky. U.S. District Judge Dean Whipple gave him a two-year sentence, of which he served just over half.[8]

Many were disgusted at just how easily the pair had gotten off. Federal law provided a maximum sentence of 10 years for their crimes, but the judge apparently felt this would be unduly harsh. An editorial in one Omaha newspaper expressed the anger felt by both Mutual of Omaha employees and the Sutherland firm lawyers:

> *Judge Whipple's leniency is appalling. It's no wonder some people have lost confidence in the justice system…These weren't small-time con men. They persuaded people who worked with them that they had millions of dollars in backing that they didn't have. Wining told a Mutual of Omaha subsidiary that he was a former deputy to the chairman of Lloyd's of London, which wasn't true. He and Schonacher diverted millions of dollars to new companies that they created in the Caribbean. When Mutual grew suspicious and told them to stop accepting new business, they agreed to stop. But that was a lie, too. They continued to write new business. Twenty-one months in prison for one of them. Five years on probation for the other. Whatever became of the idea that the punishment should fit the crime?[9]*

Despite the Sutherland firm's success, the rigors of the case took their toll. The troubles began when John Bonds suffered a heart attack in January of 1993 while working in Omaha. At that time the cases were winding down and the litigation group was transitioning to other matters. Frank Gregory was on his way to Japan when he heard about Bonds's condition, and he changed his plans in order to visit his partner. The firm was then dealt a major blow when Gregory died in his sleep of a heart attack.

Gregory's tragic death notwithstanding, the outcome of the Mutual cases was a huge success for Sutherland. Although the partners' long-term plan to develop a niche in the reinsurance litigation business did not pan out as expected, Mutual kick-started the modern form of the Sutherland litigation practice while bringing in or saving a huge amount of money for the client. This was the first case to involve a massive cooperative effort between the offices in the pursuit of a bet-the-company case, and it spurred Sutherland to create a firm-wide litigation group (which Gregory headed until his death). This case also saw the development of a sophisticated document data base that was years ahead of its time and served as a model for many cases to come. Altogether the Sutherland team recovered about $100 million for Mutual from various sources and upwards of $200 million through the successful reduction of liability. The Sutherland team's work was integral to Mutual of Omaha's survival as a business entity.

BIOGRAPHY

FRANCIS M. "FRANK" GREGORY, JR. (1941-1993)

It would be impossible to understand the development of the Washington office from the 1970s to the 1990s without knowing about **Frank Gregory**. Gregory brought to the firm an energy and a knowledge of the business that few others possessed. Like Baxter Jones before him, Gregory built up an impressive résumé at a young age. And like Jones, Gregory died tragically young.

The New York native was educated at a rigorous Catholic high school and later attended the Notre Dame Law School, where he served as editor in chief of the *Law Review*. After graduating in 1966 he served for one year as a law clerk to Judge Carl S. McGowan at the U.S. Court of Appeals for the District of Columbia. He was then fortunate enough to garner a stint as law clerk to Justice William Brennan, Jr. at the U.S. Supreme Court, during which two landmark cases – *Ginsburg v. New York* and *Zwickler v. Koota* – were decided. In the years that followed it was often said that Gregory was Justice Brennan's favorite clerk. (Gregory later argued a case before the Supreme Court in which Brennan joined an opinion against Gregory's side. The decision prompted Sutherland partner Carey DeDeyn to joke, "I don't think Frank ever forgave Brennan for that!")[10]

When Gregory hit the job market, he asked Judge McGowan his opinion about Washington firms. The judge thought for a moment, then said, "The two best oral arguments I have ever heard in the DC Circuit were both by Mac Asbill, Jr." This was high praise coming from McGowan, who had certainly heard his share of arguments over the years. Gregory chose Sutherland largely on that basis. Shortly after Gregory joined the firm, Bill Sutherland wrote Elbert Tuttle and asked him to personally thank McGowan for his recommendation. Said Sutherland, "I know Judge McGowan is quite enthusiastic about Frank Gregory, and we certainly share his enthusiasm… He is really a most unusual boy, and I would like for Judge McGowan to know that…we are expressing our gratitude."[11]

While at the Sutherland firm, Gregory specialized in business and insurance litigation and arbitration, with an emphasis on corporate insurance and liability issues. He built a national reputation for his work in insurance law, and he frequently lectured at insurance conferences worldwide. He periodically published on litigation and insurance topics and held many leadership positions in the American Bar Association. But his most important role within the firm was as managing partner of the Washington office. While in this position he used his boundless enthusiasm and powerful business acumen to take the practice to new heights.

One of Gregory's most significant legal contributions came in the Mutual of

Frank Gregory Takes On the Mob

Frank Gregory could be a tough customer when he had to be. At one point during the Mutual cases he was given the rather thankless task of interviewing a seasoned criminal named Lou Mazzella, who was being forced to cooperate with the investigation as a term of his parole. When Gregory met Mazzella, the mobster was in no mood for tough questions. The ex-con was so hostile, in fact, that he mentioned having once broken a chair over a rival's head, in this way implying that he was more than willing to break a chair over *Gregory's* head. Upon hearing this, Gregory put down his pen, took off his glasses, and said, "Mr. Mazzella, I'll make you a deal. You can either *try* to break that chair over my head, or you can let me finish this interview and I'll buy you a beer." Mazzella sized up Gregory, gave the proposition some thought, and after an uneasy pause said, "All right, let's finish. I'll take the beer."[13]

Omaha cases. These helped establish the firm's litigation practice in its modern form, and they cemented Gregory's reputation as a tireless fighter for his clients' interests. Unfortunately these cases were also physically and spiritually grueling, and it was while working in Omaha that Gregory died of a heart attack. His passing at such a young age shocked the entire firm, and some of the most memorable tributes to Gregory came in the many stories told by the lawyers who knew him best.

Sutherland partner Glen S. Howard said of Gregory shortly after his death:

> The expression "larger than life" has become clichéd, but Frank Gregory was that rare person to whom the expression really did apply. He was the first SA&B lawyer I met – over 20 years ago in a law school interviewing room – and I knew a mere two minutes into that interview that this was a man who did everything with gusto. (This was confirmed, at least in part, that same evening at a local pub – before I put Frank on a train to a Notre Dame football weekend.)…His love for the law, his pride in his colleagues, and his dedication to this law firm were boundless.[12]

John Bonds got to know Gregory while working on the Mutual of Omaha matter, and he had similar memories of a man with a tremendous lust for life. Gregory may have died young, said Bonds, "but he lived over one hundred years in that short time." Bonds noted that Gregory was also a great lawyer, and that the other lawyers on a case always knew where they stood with him. Gregory made it a point, for example, to negotiate in his opponent's office, because this put the negotiations on Gregory's terms. "Frank had a real gift," added Bonds, "in his ability to earn his adversaries' respect."

Gregory regularly paired his hard-driving personality with his love of Notre

Dame football. On one occasion around 1990 a group of Sutherland lawyers headed to South Bend to take in one of the last great Notre Dame-Miami games. When a Notre Dame fan at the game shouted his disapproval of the team's defensive coverage, a near brawl ensued between the fan and Gregory. "We thought Frank was gonna throw the guy off the top of the stadium," said eyewitness and fellow Sutherland partner Carey DeDeyn, "because he dared to criticize the Notre Dame player. But that's just the kind of person Frank was. He was larger than life."

As for Gregory's contributions to Sutherland, he should perhaps be remembered most for his almost superhuman ability to make contacts, build the practice, and sell the firm to numerous prospective clients. "Frank had a strong personality," recalled DeDeyn, "and he was great with people. People picked up on his energy, so he had a very positive impact on the law firm." Ed Grenier added that Gregory "put the rest of us to shame" with his work ethic. DeDeyn's final thoughts are worth recounting in full: "People underestimated how intelligent he was. A lot of the time you think a person like that is just a strong personality and nothing more. But Frank was an extremely smart guy, very accomplished. He worked hard, he played hard, and he was just a pleasure to be around."

∾

A B-29 flies over the Bell Bomber Plant in Marietta, Georgia

Pat Patterson became the Atlanta office's sixth lawyer when he joined the firm in 1950, and over the course of a few decades he created one of the city's most successful real estate practices.

CHAPTER ELEVEN

REAL ESTATE

Like most of the Sutherland firm's major endeavors, the real estate practice grew from rather humble beginnings. Indeed, the real estate group is perhaps the clearest example of a Sutherland practice developing from a purely local, one company, tax-driven practice to that of a major national and international practice.

Many talented lawyers contributed over the years, but the growth of the real estate group cannot be understood without reference to Pat Patterson. Patterson became the Atlanta office's sixth lawyer when he joined the firm in 1950, and over the course of a few decades he created one of the city's most successful real estate practices. As an associate he handled tax planning for clients involved in real estate investment and development, and that work soon spiraled into more direct real estate-oriented work such as negotiating purchasing agreements. Over time he became as much a real estate specialist as he was a tax specialist.

Patterson's first major real estate project involved the construction firm of Wilson & Henderson. W&H was a major player in developing the workers' communities at the Bell Bomber plant during World War II (later Lockheed Martin in Marietta, Georgia). This area desperately needed rental properties for plant employees. The American industrial economy had worked wonders during wartime, but it did not provide much in the way of a housing or construction base. Wartime entrepreneurs seemed uninterested in building rental houses. Consequently there was a huge demand for housing with little in the way of supply or infrastructure to support new construction.

Wilson & Henderson received government funding to develop living communities in the area, and these were considered projects with little lasting value. But even the price controls then in effect could not restrain market forces. The builders and sellers made big profits, and their need for tax help led them to the Sutherland firm. Federal income tax rates were incredibly high, so the challenge for Patterson was to find ways to get the client's income subjected to lower rates.

Patterson acquired a reputation from his work for Wilson & Henderson, and this naturally led to more projects. He went on to handle general business matters for real estate companies, including creating pension and profit-sharing plans, and soon he was also assisting with the planning and negotiating of land purchase agreements and construction arrangements. Cousins Properties became one of his

Perimeter Place, Atlanta, Georgia (Sembler)

– and the firm's – most important clients in the 1950s and 1960s. Tom Cousins was high in the hierarchy of National Homes and Knox Homes, companies that built prefabricated housing. Patterson served on Cousins's board of directors and gave him general business advice through the 1960s.

Patterson developed this practice on his own, but he later credited Jim Wilson with mentoring him in various legal and business methods. "It would be difficult to overestimate the importance of Jim Wilson," said Patterson, "to the growth of our practice and the growth of our capabilities in those early days." Tuttle and Sutherland were great lawyers, but they knew little about real estate or pension and profit-sharing plans. Wilson was the firm's expert in these areas before Patterson came on the scene, and Patterson later said that Wilson "taught me a ton about drafting those things. Those were drafting skills that have worked to my benefit ever since."[1]

By the early 1970s other lawyers at the firm were also getting involved in the real estate practice. Patterson brought in Robert Brown and Loran Johnson as the firm's first real estate associates. Pat Hyman (whose brother, Tom Hyman, subsequently joined the corporate group) and Ed Hales also joined the real estate group. Much of the group's energy in these years was focused on representing New York banks, Northeastern life insurance companies, and other out-of-state financial institutions that were loaning money to Atlanta-based real estate entrepreneurs. The real estate group also represented some of these Atlanta entrepreneurs. Several Sutherland lawyers were involved, but Patterson was still at the center of things, training the newcomers, developing the work, and bringing in nearly all the clients.

In 1973-1974 the group experienced a significant blow. Clay Long, who had moved to real estate after working with Jim Wilson in corporate, decided to start his own firm, which later became Long & Aldridge. To make matters worse for the

Sutherland real estate group, Long & Aldridge was founded primarily with Sutherland lawyers, including John Aldridge, Bill Stevens, Bill Sumner, and Mike Pope. The real estate group then had to recreate itself with the three main lawyers who remained: Patterson, Hyman, and Hales. Jim Paulk moved in from corporate and Kent Frazier from the tax group. The newly hired associate Al Adams also came aboard.

Around this time, largely through the efforts of Paulk, Frazier, and George Cohen, the group was successful in developing two important client relationships that significantly affected the growth and focus of the practice. BF Saul and GAMI were nationally prominent mortgage real estate investment trusts (REITs), and although the firm was not general counsel to either company at the time, the firm's lawyers handled some of the companies' loan forms and loans nationally. This was the beginning of the transition from a regional practice to a national one.[2]

The departure of Clay Long and the others was followed by another unfortunate event for the group. An economic downswing in 1974 signaled the beginning of the first major real estate recession to hit the Atlanta area since the 1930s. This recession took much of the life out of the earlier boom. Investment decreased, and older clients found they had less legal work to pass to the Sutherland firm. Even when the market bounced back in the 1980s, investor confidence remained shaken. The group also suffered a personal and professional setback when Kent Frazier died of a heart attack at the age of 41.

REAL ESTATE AFTER THE 1970S

The real estate practice underwent many changes after the 1970s, with steady expansion its overriding characteristic. By Al Adams's description, "The depth and the geographic scope, the variety of industry groups, and certainly the depth of the practice, have grown by a huge multiple since I came to the firm in the mid-70s." By 2005 the group had 35 lawyers, including five in Washington (which had no real estate lawyers until the 1990s) and three in New York.

The growth of the practice had much to do with changes in the cities of Atlanta and Washington. Atlanta was still somewhat provincial in the 1970s, but it became more international in the ensuing years. As a result the city saw a great deal of inbound foreign investment and Fortune 500 companies relocating into North Georgia. This benefited the firm tremendously. "Our practice has grown with Atlanta," said Adams, "and now we have financial institutions that are either based here or have substantial presence here. We have national and international real estate developers and businesses that are located here, and that has caused our practice to be national in scope."[3]

Needless to say, Washington was always more of a government town than Atlanta. But the DC metropolitan area also became a significant commercial center, which spurred the Washington office's corporate and business practice growth beginning in the 1980s. The firm's goal of establishing firm-wide practice groups led the real estate group to expand into Washington in the 1990s by bringing in Lisa Rosen and Mark Jackson as partners. Washington's growing attractiveness to developers and investors helped sell the practice group as a national practice, one that could represent big players like UBS Realty Investors, GMAC, and TIAA-CREF on a multi-jurisdictional basis.

The Sutherland real estate group was able to expand as a national player once the real estate market recovered from the recession. Among the more significant new clients in this period, the firm represented Executive Affiliates in the acquisition and financing of projects in over 20 states. On the finance side, the group represented a number of life insurance companies that were then the primary source of debt financing for large real estate transactions, including John Hancock, Prudential, and Travelers. The group also established an extensive equity formation practice, representing American Express in the private placement of equity capital. Real estate's syndication work in the 1980s ended with the passage of the Tax Reform Act of 1987, but the group continued to handle nontax-driven private placement transactions, including the formation of several equity funds for the Shoptaw Group.

At the same time that Sutherland was reaching out to national markets, national players were relocating to Atlanta. Two important representations in the 1970s and 1980s grew out of this trend and helped the group expand its scope and reputation. The first involved Mobil Land Development, a subsidiary of Mobil Oil, which came to Atlanta in 1977. The company contacted Patterson and told him they were interested in acquiring 4,000 acres in and around what was then the tiny town of Alpharetta. The firm represented Mobil in the acquisition, and over the course of several years the land was turned into hundreds of commercial and residential units. This was the first of several major Mobil master plan developments that the firm helped establish throughout a 20-year relationship, and it helped put the real estate group on the map nationally. Many Mobil Land employees later moved to other companies, and the Sutherland real estate group went on to do work for those companies as well.[4]

The second important client at this point was Vantage Properties, a major Texas-based developer that came to Atlanta in the mid-1980s. At a time when Atlanta-based developers and financial institutions were still a bit conservative in the aftermath of the recession, Vantage became one of the city's most prominent office developers. This was a major representation that helped increase the firm's prominence and its connections to several big players in Southeastern real estate. And as with Mobil Land, the firm continued to represent many of Vantage's alumni in other companies.

Mall of Georgia, Buford, Georgia (Ben Carter Properties)

MODERN PRACTICES:
TIMBER, HOSPITALITY, RETAIL

The timber and forest products practice was among the real estate group's most successful ventures. This practice dated back to the 1930s, when Bill Sutherland gave tax assistance to major Southern timber owners. The connection to timber companies continued through the years, with Sutherland, Joe Brennan, and Randolph Thrower handling tax cases involving large tracts of land, percentage depletion issues, and capital gains. Brennan, Thrower, and Herbert Elsas took on an important case for the Douglass family of Augusta, Georgia – owners of Augusta Hardwood – in the 1960s and 1970s, and this matter bridged the gap between the earlier years and the modern practice.

The modern timber practice grew largely out of timber-related real estate and finance transactions, as well as the firm's tax practice (timber being a tax-favored investment). In the 1970s Pat Patterson and Jim Paulk began to represent insurance companies in their loans for large tracts of land. Most notably, they agreed to represent John Hancock and Travelers Insurance in the companies' Southeastern timber investments. The pair soon became known for their expertise in timber, and this developed into a very profitable practice. The real estate group became nationally prominent in the 1980s and 1990s, representing wood products producers and various investors in huge transactions. Sutherland's national timber and forest products group was formed in the early 1990s, with Haynes Roberts, Victor Haley, and Bill Bradley at the helm. Together with Jim Paulk, these men brought the practice to a new level. Through 2005 the timber practice had represented clients in timberland transactions worth over $8 billion.[5]

Hospitality work also expanded tremendously. The group's efforts in this area grew primarily from the equity formation matters for RH American Express, and the lawyers' expertise led to lucrative work for TIAA-CREF in real estate investment. Sutherland had been providing significant insurance, securities, and regulatory advice to TIAA-CREF, but not real estate investment advice. The group ultimately assisted TIAA-CREF in the disposition of a large portfolio of hotels and

Legacy Place, Palm Beach Gardens, Florida (Sembler)

hospitality transactions. The group was also chosen to represent several resorts and hotels in the 1980s and 1990s, including InterContinental Hotels and the Four Seasons in Puerto Rico.[6]

The retail real estate practice expanded in the early 1990s, when the group started to represent major national and regional developers of retail centers, including Ben Carter Properties, Hendon Properties, Simon Properties (an Indianapolis-based developer that owned more malls than any other company in the world), and the Sembler Company. The firm represented the Atlanta-based international retailer Home Depot in deals involving more than 20 stores in the U.S. and nearly 40 in Mexico. Finally, Sutherland was chosen as one of two firms to represent TIAA-CREF in all their legal work, not just real estate. To celebrate, the group represented TIAA-CREF in their $200 million purchase of the Pinnacle Office Building and the adjacent Two Live Oak Center in Atlanta's Buckhead neighborhood, the second-largest office deal in Atlanta in 2004. And if that were not impressive enough, the group also handled the largest deal: a $247 million acquisition of the Wildwood Office Park by UBS Realty Investors.

Other major changes in the real estate industry in the 1990s and 2000s were driven by the rapid consolidation of the insurance industry, the inability of many of the remaining insurance companies to compete effectively, and the accumulation of vast amounts of capital in public and private pension funds. Due in large part to Sutherland's reputation as a national firm with the ability to handle major transactions, the firm was routinely representing many of the major institutional real estate investors and advisory firms in the U.S. on a national basis, including UBS, Morgan Stanley, and L&B Realty.[7]

BIOGRAPHY

WILLIAM R. "PAT" PATTERSON (1924-2007)

Pat Patterson is widely credited with having established the firm's real estate practice. In fact, it is generally agreed that the real estate practice essentially *was* Pat Patterson until well into the 1970s and 1980s. Patterson was born in Wathena, Kansas, and his storm-weary parents (Pat had been born during a 25-below-zero blizzard) relocated to the warmer climes of the North Carolina Piedmont when he was 18 months old. He went on to study at Lenoir-Rhyne College, taking a break from school to serve in the Navy in the Pacific Theater during World War II (see Ch. 5).

Although Patterson knew no lawyers when he was growing up, he overcame an early interest in business and decided instead to enter Duke University Law School. He graduated in 1950 and joined the Sutherland firm that year on the recommendation of his professor Charles Lowndes. Lowndes, who was an old friend of Joe Brennan, suggested the Sutherland firm to Patterson because he knew the young man was interested in tax law. Patterson took his tax law skills to Sutherland and went on to perform many services in the legal profession, including stints as president of the Atlanta Tax Forum, chairman and president of the Southern Federal Tax Institute, president of the Georgia Tax Conference, and president of the American College of Mortgage Attorneys.

Patterson is also credited with helping expand Sutherland's high profile at Duke Law School. He was the first "Dukie" to join what was then a Harvard- and Emory-dominated Sutherland firm. In the ensuing years, he spent a great deal of time and effort maintaining contacts at Duke, lecturing on real estate and tax law, and serving on Duke Law's Board of Visitors, which he chaired from 1977 to 1987. His efforts to give Sutherland a high profile at Duke benefited both the firm and the university.

Al Adams, the real estate group's leader beginning in 1992, summed up Patterson's legacy for the practice and the firm as a whole:

> *We owe a lot to Pat Patterson. I worked with Pat for 25 years and never saw him raise his voice; I never saw him lose his temper. He was always so calm in a crisis, just a great mentor, and he set a great tone and atmosphere of collegiality for our group. A wonderful sense of humor. A great person to have founded our real estate practice.*[8]

Sutherland is the only firm to have five partners lead the ABA Section on Taxation –
Mac Asbill, Jr., William A. Sutherland, Randolph W. Thrower, N. Jerold Cohen, and
Herbert N. Beller

As the field became more competitive,
the Sutherland firm adapted. Its reputation
has been greatly enhanced when its lawyers –
including IRS "draftees" Randolph Thrower,
Jerry Cohen, and Peggy Richardson – have
spent time in government.

CHAPTER TWELVE

The Modern Tax, Insurance, Financial, and Corporate Practices

I t goes without saying that the Sutherland tax practice has served as the firm's anchor since its founding. The first generation of Sutherland, Brennan, and Tuttle was followed by a second group of very able tax lawyers, including Randolph Thrower, Jim Wilson, and Mac Asbill, Jr. These early partners established the firm's reputation for excellence in the tax field, while the next generation – those hired in the 1950s and 1960s, especially Jim Heffernan, Laurens Williams, Ed Schmuck, Jerry Libin, and Jerry Cohen – took the practice into its modern form.

The newer tax specialists had to come to grips with a wide variety of changes in the tax field from the 1960s to the 2000s. Jerry Libin, for one, witnessed the evolution of both the Sutherland tax practice and the field as a whole beginning in the 1960s. The tax field "became vastly more complicated" after the 1960s, said Libin, as practitioners "were expected to have much more specific knowledge of very detailed rules." One significant trend that began in earnest in the 1960s was the phenomenon of tax lawyers entering government for short periods in the tax area and then returning to practice with a weightier résumé. Many experienced tax practitioners in this period spent a few years in government and later became notable competitors in Washington and elsewhere.

Libin also noted a critical change in client/firm relationships. Although these had once been quite solid, the revolving door of lawyers into and out of government frequently led existing clients to seek other experts on particular matters. Consequently, loyalties began to change. Older relationships were also weakened when top lawyers switched firms, a phenomenon that began in the 1970s and accelerated thereafter. These trends came about through a combination of personal ambitions and client needs. "You realized that a firm client was no longer a firm client for life, and that nothing is forever," lamented Libin. "That's a theme all lawyers should keep in mind."[1]

As the field became more competitive, the Sutherland firm adapted. Its reputation has been greatly enhanced when its lawyers – including IRS "draftees" Randolph Thrower, Jerry Cohen, and Peggy Richardson – have spent time in government. Several other tax partners have declined significant government opportunities over the years. Another firm strategy was to begin training new associates in their desired practice area at the outset. Adaptive strategies like these were partially client driven. Beginning in the 1980s, the firm got on a roll of tax

Internal Revenue Service Commissioner – and former Washington office partner – Margaret Milner Richardson hands out tax forms at a local subway station in downtown Washington, Friday, April 14, 1995.

litigation at the behest of some key clients, and this new dimension turned out to be very lucrative. Some fortuitous acquisitions also dramatically expanded the scope of the practice. Lateral hires Paul Freeland and Bill Corey came to the Washington office in 1983, and they were instrumental in bringing several major corporate clients to the firm. This enabled Sutherland to expand the general tax practice significantly. Corey later became the managing partner in Washington.[2]

In the 1990s the firm was again forced to deal with outside events in order to maintain its competitive position. Accounting firms were trying to dominate the tax field by aggressively hiring lawyers from tax firms, which unfortunately led to some losses for Sutherland. Determined to remain a major force in the tax field, Jerry Libin and his cohorts found some strong replacements, and the firm emerged from this period with its national tax reputation as strong as ever, if not stronger. The accounting firms eventually reduced their aggressive efforts, and soon the Sarbanes-Oxley legislation had a profound effect on how accounting firms could practice tax law.

GM's Tax Emergency

A few notable cases underscore the tax group's work since the 1960s.[3] One of the most significant, involving General Motors, was to have long-term consequences for the group. In 1977 GM was under investigation for a potential criminal tax violation. The company retained another firm to handle the matter, but the

Jerome B. Libin

management also decided, for the first time ever, that they would bring in outside tax counsel to review their entire tax situation. The company eventually agreed in July 1977 to have the Sutherland firm do a complete review of the company's tax situation in relation to its 1976 tax return.

The criminal investigation was a wakeup call for GM. "Before," said Jerry Libin, "GM never really worried much about its federal tax obligations. It was making so much money at that time, it did not focus on ways to reduce taxes." Because the tax return had to be filed in September, the Sutherland tax group had only two months to come to grips with the tax status of the largest industrial corporation in the world. This was a massive undertaking, with Asbill, Libin, and a large number of other partners and associates taking up temporary residence in Detroit in order to pore over documents and interview GM employees. Although the Sutherland lawyers were told that this would be a one-off project, GM management was so impressed that they continued the relationship. For many years thereafter the Sutherland tax group regularly advised GM on a variety of matters.

Bell Telephone's $100 Million Deposit Fight

The tax group was at the center of a huge tax litigation case following the breakup of AT&T in the 1980s. The matter began when the IRS demanded a tax payment on deposits paid to the company by telephone customers. These deposits were customarily untaxed because they were eventually paid back to the customer with interest. The amount requested by the IRS per deposit was small, but the aggregate amounted to around $100 million. Utilities across the country also took in deposits, and as a result many eyes were on this case.

Thrower and Libin had earlier handled a matter for Pacific Telephone when the utility was part of the AT&T system, and all seven of the Bell companies hired Sutherland to handle the deposit case. Early in their investigation, the Sutherland lawyers learned that an Indiana utility company, Indianapolis Power, had a similar case involving only about $20,000 in taxes. The Sutherland lawyers were very worried because this small utility was ahead of them in litigating the same issue. The Bell companies offered to pay Indianapolis Power's tax in order to move it to the sidelines, but the company president thought it was important enough on principle to continue the suit. Fortunately, the small utility won its case in the tax court before the Bell companies' case could be presented. Indianapolis Power's lawyers also accepted help from Sutherland in order to preserve their victory in the Seventh Circuit. By then, the Bell companies had also won in the tax court and were expecting an appeal by the IRS to the Second Circuit.

Then came an unexpected "gift" that brought a smile to the face of every Sutherland tax lawyer. The IRS had 90 days to appeal the Bell case, but the 90th day came and went, and still the Sutherland tax team had not been notified of an appeal. One of the lawyers contacted the liaison at the IRS to ask if an appeal had been filed, and all hell broke loose on Constitution Avenue. The IRS had forgotten to file the appeal! They were so sure they were appealing the case that they had marked it on their calendar as soon as the case was decided. Unfortunately for them, nobody followed through. It was an oversight of such staggering proportions that Peter Jennings actually reported it that night on the ABC evening news.

The IRS was then successful in getting the U.S. Supreme Court to review the Indianapolis Power case. Because the issue was one of ongoing importance to all utilities, Sutherland remained involved by assisting the small utility's lawyers and filing an amicus brief on behalf of the Bell companies. The utility won its case in the Supreme Court, putting an end to the dispute. Sutherland's work for the Bell companies in the customer deposit case led to other work for individual telephone companies in later years.

Philip Morris, Procter & Gamble, and Significant Atlanta Tax Representations

Two of the major clients Paul Freeland and Bill Corey brought to the firm in 1983 were Philip Morris (later known as the Altria Group) and Procter & Gamble. Freeland and Corey had been happy to practice with a smaller firm until they realized that they could not effectively handle the caseload of these two large corporations. The two men decided to join Sutherland because, as Corey put it, the firm "had the best vision of how to handle all the work and also expand the two relationships." Over the years, Sutherland lawyers have handled a wide range of very significant tax planning matters for both companies. Cliff Muller, who joined as an associate in the early 1980s, became the lead tax partner on Altria matters, while Giovanna Sparagna, who came aboard in the late 1980s, took the lead on P&G matters.

The Atlanta office lawyers also did tax work for a number of important textile companies, including Springs Mills (later Springs Industries). As U.S. textile production began to decline, however, the firm could no longer count on that industry to provide it with a solid client base in the Southeast. The formation of Coca-Cola Enterprises as a separate bottling company arm of the Coca-Cola operation gave Sutherland an opportunity to capture a new client with a broad base of operations. In the 1990s and 2000s, CCE became one of the Atlanta office's primary tax clients, along with Temple-Inland, Spectrum Industries, and UPS.

Much of the Atlanta office's tax work in the 2000s was in the tax controversy area. Jerry Cohen spearheaded a series of efforts to resolve major disputes with the

IRS involving transactions entered into by large groups of taxpayers on the advice of accounting firms and other promoters. A number of these matters went unsettled and thus ultimately made their way to litigation.

INSURANCE

Unlike some of the firm's modern practices, insurance was an area of planned growth. Unsurprisingly, the insurance practice developed from the firm's handling of insurance companies' tax issues in the 1940s and 1950s. Growth in this area was deliberate, but significant, after the 1950s. When Laurens Williams came to the firm in 1956, none of the Sutherland lawyers had insurance experience, but by 1984 Sutherland was recognized as the preeminent Washington firm active in the practice of law for life insurance companies.[4]

Williams was the key figure in the early years. He arrived with a wealth of experience from his time in the Nebraska Bar Association and the Treasury Department. He had worked on stopgap legislation and regulations applicable to life insurance companies, so he was well versed in contemporary insurance tax law. Williams's first accomplishment was getting the Sutherland firm involved in tax work relating to Mutual of Omaha's deferred compensation agreements between the company and its agents. No insurance expertise was required in these matters, but this work led to other insurance connections, including Aetna and MassMutual. The young associate Jim Heffernan was also very active in this area. The firm was able to parlay this expertise in insurance taxes into work handling various other problems encountered by insurance companies.[5]

The 1960s saw continued growth in the insurance practice. The partners routinely moved into SEC matters after working with companies on the tax side, and some new clients were brought into the fold when the firm made lateral additions. When Ed Schmuck joined in 1963, for example, he brought Travelers Insurance Company with him. Schmuck would later head the firm's insurance tax practice. Jim Heffernan, meanwhile, became the firm's chief securities lawyer for insurance companies. In the late 1960s Jim Jorden became the Washington office's first true securities lawyer. A few years later, David Woodward joined as an associate under Jorden, while Bob O'Sullivan was hired to do general corporate securities work. The firm also got into the variable annuity field quite early for several clients and began to edge into the equity product aspect of the life insurance industry's operations. By the time Sutherland celebrated its 50th anniversary in 1974, 15 of the 50 largest life insurance companies were using its services in one area or another.[6]

Two valuable additions at the turn of the 1980s brought the insurance practice to the next level. In 1978 Bill Harman, executive vice president of the American Council of Life Insurers (then called the American Council of Life Insurance, ACLI), joined the firm as a lateral to replace the retiring Ed Schmuck as head of the insurance tax practice. Three years later, Paul Mason, chief counsel of securities at ACLI, came along as well. Harman came because he thought Sutherland was a great firm with a leading insurance tax practice, while Mason came largely because of Harman. This pair brought a great deal of insurance expertise and a great number of contacts.[7]

Far more firms had an insurance tax practice in these years than in the 2000s. The Sutherland firm had half a dozen or more young partners working in the insurance tax area in the late 1970s, including George Abramowitz and Carolyn Chiechi, who went on to become a judge on the U.S. tax court. The nature of the work then changed because the industry no longer needed some of the outside legal services that had spurred the practice's growth. The group lost some talented people in the 1980s and 1990s, in part because of a division within the industry between the stock life insurance companies and the mutual life insurance companies.

Financial Services

The financial services practice grew out of the insurance tax practice, with Jim Heffernan, Jim Jorden, and David Woodward among the key players. Steve Roth (Yale J.D. 1976) was a valuable addition to this team. He joined the firm in 1977 and ultimately headed the practice. When Roth arrived, the firm had from four to six lawyers doing corporate and securities work at any given time. Half of that work was for insurance companies, and most of the insurance work involved the companies' securities business. The securities matters were grouped into an area that would eventually come to be called "financial services," which comprised variable insurance products, mutual funds, and the like. By 1980 Roth was working full time with Jorden and Woodward on securities work, including a great deal of insurance product development, which became a core aspect of the financial services practice.[8]

The hiring of Bill Harman and Paul Mason also helped to expand financial services. Harman was a tax lawyer, but he increased the firm's attention to financial services securities work. Mason was also an important player in the evolution of the practice, as he knew the general counsels and lawyers of the major life insurance companies. He had a broad enough reputation so that he was also able to develop noninsurance work. He got involved, for example, in a high-profile SEC enforcement action involving junk bond trader Ivan Boesky. He was retained to serve as special counsel in connection with that case, and he brought along some other Sutherland lawyers for good measure.

The practice continued to be heavily focused on the insurance industry, but the lawyers were also successful in broadening their clientele. Jorden, Woodward, and Mason did a small amount of work outside of insurance in the 1980s, and beginning in the 1990s Steve Boehm helped the group build its business development company, college savings plans and hedge funds practice.

The practice centered on product development from 1980 to the mid-1990s.

Life insurance companies in the 1980s began to compete in the financial services platform, and they needed assistance to offer their securities products. A large portion of Sutherland's financial services practice was therefore aimed at helping insurance companies develop new securities products and establish distribution systems. By the late 1980s the securities practice far outweighed the insurance tax practice in terms of volume of work and number of lawyers. The firm's subsequent move into the corporate side – mergers and acquisitions, reinsurance transactions, and the like – was largely attributable to the explosive growth in the securities area in the late 1980s and 1990s.

Stephen E. Roth

Beginning in the mid-1990s the group began to focus more attention on the distribution of securities products. This work involved many of the same client organizations, but the financial services group provided more services for broker/dealers and investment advisers, including national firms like Merrill Lynch. This was initially in the insurance product area, but the group soon broadened its advice to include mutual funds and other investment products and services. Susan Krawczyk was the first lawyer in the firm to devote considerable time to this area.

In the late 1990s the group began to develop work for Washington-based Allied Capital in the areas of business development and college savings plans. Allied was the largest such organization in the country and was the firm's first business development client. Behind Steve Boehm's leadership, the financial services group took on other business development clients, with the result that Sutherland soon became the leading Washington firm in this area.

Much of the growth in the securities practice came from the Sutherland lawyers' efforts at business development. Steve Roth traveled to road shows in the 1980s to develop relationships with actuarial firms, and his hard work led to additional relationships beyond the firm's core client list. In later years the lawyers broadened beyond financial services and into securities enforcement. The SEC and NASD enforcement practice, carried out by the likes of Neil S. Lang, Brian L. Rubin, and Peter J. Anderson, grew largely from the relationships developed by the financial services group.[9]

By 2006 financial services was a diverse practice, intimately entwined with the firm's other practice areas. The tax and securities lawyers developed a fair amount of work for each other, as each group helped "sell" the other's services to their clients. As Steve Roth pointed out, although financial services was really a securities regulatory practice, it included lawyers in the tax, litigation, and corporate groups, all of whom worked for financial services clients. Furthermore, enforcement lawyers had relationships that led to regulatory work, and the "deal" lawyers who worked on the corporate side brought in both regulatory and tax work.

The Corporate and Business Practice

Although the firm had little in the way of a federal securities practice for many decades, the partners established a business practice shortly after the firm's founding. Herbert Elsas became the business expert after he joined in 1935, and the addition of Baxter Jones in the 1950s further expanded the business practice. Jones, who was entrepreneurial by nature, came to the firm at a time when the partners were looking to increase Sutherland's business presence. The partners began to invest in businesses after World War II in order to get active in this field, and from that time forward the firm represented several businesses in which the partners had an equity interest.[10]

In the 1950s and 1960s the business and corporate practice began to handle public offerings for real estate investment and life insurance companies. Clients who tapped the firm for this service included Atlanta Motor Lodge and Liberty Life Insurance Company. As the firm got more active in the securities field, many of the lawyers started working in this area. George Cohen, who was known for his abilities as a tax lawyer, eventually became the firm's chief securities and corporate lawyer.

The textile manufacturer Springs Mills was another important representation. The firm had worked with the Springs family of Fort Mill, South Carolina, since the processing tax cases of the 1930s, and the family naturally contacted Sutherland for advice on how to take the company public in the 1960s. Randolph Thrower and Herbert Elsas took the lead on advising the family on operations restructuring, with George Cohen handling much of the securities work. The relationship between Springs and Sutherland continued for many more years. Elsas even served on the company's board of directors from 1970 to 1981.

In the 1980s and 1990s the corporate and business practice saw measured growth under Cohen's leadership. Many in the firm became active in the corporate area, and the organizational structure changed as the group grew. Corporate and business returned to a single group with both firm offices working closely together. In this period the group did work for NYSE companies Royal Crown, West Point Stevens, Riegel Textile, and Liberty Corporation, among others. Sutherland's stable of public companies was reduced somewhat through the industrial consolidation trend, but major representations continued.

First Financial Management Corporation (FFMC)

FFMC was a subsidiary of the Georgia Railroad Bank of Augusta that did data processing for the bank, its affiliates, and other customers in multiple states. The firm got involved with FFMC in 1981 when both Georgia Railroad and First National Bank of Atlanta attempted to take over Columbus Bank and Trust. The Columbus Bank management preferred to merge with the railroad bank, but First

Atlanta was aggressively courting them. On the recommendation of a Columbus lawyer, Columbus's management sought out Jim Wilson for representation, and Wilson in turn asked George Cohen to handle the matter because of his corporate experience. Cohen and the Sutherland firm successfully merged Columbus Bank with the railroad bank, despite a hostile tender offer made by First Atlanta. Cohen worked out a merger agreement that was authorized by the Columbus board, and thus defeated the tender offer.[11]

George L. Cohen

The firm's success in the merger led the Georgia Railroad bank to ask Cohen to handle the IPO of their subsidiary. The public offering took place in 1983, and that was the beginning of the firm's relationship with FFMC. In 1995, when First Financial merged with First Data Corporation, the consideration for the merger was $7.2 billion in stock. The Sutherland firm had essentially taken a company whose capitalization was less than $100 million in the 1970s and represented it to the point where it was worth $7.2 billion.

FFMC's business changed noticeably along the way. Cohen was on First Financial's board of directors until it was sold to First Data, and from 1983 to 1995 he worked with FFMC on securities offerings, buyouts, mergers, stock issues, and cash acquisitions of other companies. Their most significant acquisitions included NaBANCO – a company that handled hundreds of millions of dollars in merchant processing for credit card transactions – and the check verification company Telechek.

FFMC also acquired Western Union in the early 1990s. Western Union's parent company was in bankruptcy at the time, a situation that led a federal judge to decide that Western Union should be liquidated at auction. FFMC decided to get involved in the competition, as did First Data (with which FFMC ultimately merged) and the company of investment entrepreneur Ted Forstmann. When the final bids were made at a hearing in New Jersey, FFMC won with a price of $1.1 billion. Thereafter, Western Union became a major part of FFMC's business, and it was later a major part of First Data's.

The Sutherland firm went on to handle Western Union's trademark work in more than 150 countries. Washington partner Libby Langworthy supervised the establishment of a database to handle renewals of one of the best-known trademarks in the world. After FFMC was acquired by First Data, the company continued to use Sutherland for work of this nature. Another Sutherland partner, Louise Adams, became an expert in handling merchant credit card processing transactions, which were multiple hundred million-dollar blocks of business for banks like Wells Fargo and credit card companies.

The W. R. Grace Building, 1114 Avenue of the Americas, New York — offices are on the 40th floor

*The partners decided that a strong
New York presence would be a key element
in a reinsurance growth plan.*

CHAPTER THIRTEEN

WATERSHED MOMENTS, 1980-2005

Just as the postwar years saw a debate over expansion into new practice areas, the 1980s and early 1990s witnessed sharp internal debates over mergers, national expansion, and the division of profits.[1] On a few occasions these debates escalated into conflicts that threatened to split the firm in two. This period also saw the passing of much of the firm's first generation, including Bill Sutherland (1987), Elbert Tuttle (1996), Joe Brennan (1991), Mac Asbill, Sr. (1992), Mac Asbill, Jr. (1992), and Ed Schmuck (1990). Fortunately the firm's leaders weathered these troubles and Sutherland, Asbill & Brennan emerged with a great deal of promise as it entered the new century.

THE FIRM BREAKS INTO NEW YORK

The Mutual of Omaha matter led Frank Gregory to believe that the Sutherland firm could become a major player in the reinsurance area. Some partners agreed, and they decided that a strong New York presence would be a key element in a reinsurance growth plan. Because New York is the financial capital of the world, they argued, a firm does not have international client credibility without an office there. Furthermore, the litigation group had long considered getting together with some New York lawyers. But although the benefits of a New York presence were clear, establishing such a presence took much longer than the Sutherland partners had expected.[2]

The partners decided to absorb the firm of Boyle, Vogeler & Haimes, which had been specializing in reinsurance litigation similar to Sutherland's Mutual work. The decision seemed like a good one, but circumstances at both the Boyle and the Sutherland firms prevented the merger from succeeding.

Various factors contributed to the merger's eventual failure. The New Yorkers' major international clients were French, and France went into a recession. The Boyle firm's reinsurance work also tapered off at around the same time that the Sutherland firm's Mutual work wound down. These factors, in combination with Frank Gregory's untimely death just after the merger became final, arrested the momentum. Without Gregory's energy behind the consolidation, it just could not work. The merger was undone in 1996.

William H. Bradley

A few years later the partners decided to take another crack at the big city, and this second effort proved successful from the start. Sutherland's New York office opened in earnest in 2002, with most of the original staff of lawyers arriving in early 2003. Two partners and two associates went to New York from Atlanta that year, and the firm also began to rotate in some people from Washington on a part-time basis. Bill Bradley, managing partner of the Atlanta office from 1991 to 1995, became partner-in-charge in New York. His time spent there might well be compared with Bill Sutherland's 1946 move to Washington, after which the Washington office took off. By 2005 the firm had 17 lawyers in New York, with plans for more growth in the future.

TRANSITIONS

A rocky relationship developed between the firm's Washington and Atlanta offices in the late 1980s. Fortunately the partners exercised enough restraint and foresight to quell the unrest and to emerge from this period stronger than ever.[3]

The root of the conflict was the simple fact that the firm had two main offices, with separate leadership, in two cities. This was rather unusual for its time. As Jerry Libin was fond of saying, "We had two offices when most firms had only one, and we had two offices when most firms had five or six." Despite the "two offices, one firm" philosophy, lawyers in each office naturally developed an affinity for those around them. Against this backdrop, the immediate source of the conflict was the issue of dividing profits. As in any business, the firm had seen periods of investment and periods of payoff, and the debate about growth and expansion was intense.

Another source of friction was the lawyers' competitive nature. Neither office wanted to be "second" in the firm, of course. Sutherland had long had two managing partners, and the executive committee was typically composed of equal numbers from both offices. The idea of having two managing partners and an even number on the executive committee was, it later became clear, a recipe for trouble. It created a certain territoriality for each of the managing partners, who would naturally go to bat for those in their own office. In John Fleming's words, because decisions were made with two constituencies in mind, "the fact that the firm stayed together through it all is really a credit to the great relationships the lawyers had."

In the mid-1990s things finally changed at the organizational level. Bill Bradley and Jerry Libin headed a strategic planning committee to seek out the roots of the troubles and devise solutions. Inspired in part by the drastic nature of earlier proposals, the committee recommended that the firm go to one managing partner

Offices at 1275 Pennsylvania Avenue, Washington, DC

and that more power be given to group leaders. These recommendations were viewed with suspicion by some, for the firm's tradition of "loose" management was what had attracted many lawyers to the firm in the first place. Nevertheless, the firm went through with the committee's recommendations, and Jim Henderson became managing partner in 1995.

By almost every account, the plan worked extremely well. The firm got all the lawyers moving in the same direction, which freed them up to do their jobs rather than worry about internal matters. The plan also reaffirmed Sutherland's commitment to being a *national* firm, as opposed to one that merely served two regions. In the final analysis, the older structure may have limited operations somewhat, but things eventually worked to the Sutherland firm's advantage. A few other Atlanta and Washington firms grew more quickly in the 1980s and 1990s, but some of these others also grew beyond their means and very few entered the 21st century as well-positioned in each practice area as the Sutherland firm.[4]

THE ANDREW LEGARE CASE

Yet another of the firm's major pro bono cases in more recent years concerned the hotly debated topic of the juvenile death penalty. In 1980 John Fleming was contacted by Diane Wood, a former colleague who was practicing in Washington. Wood told Fleming that her firm had handled a certiorari petition for a Georgia prisoner who had been convicted of murder and sentenced to death. The Georgia Supreme Court had affirmed the ruling, and certiorari was denied by the U.S. Supreme Court. Wood needed a Georgia lawyer who could handle a state habeas proceeding, and she asked Fleming if he would be interested.[5]

Fleming had never handled such a case, so he asked Jim Wilson for advice. Wilson suggested he take the case but told him to avoid criticizing the trial judge, Joseph Duke, whom Wilson knew. (Fleming agreed, though as the case progressed he showed no mercy toward the judge in his efforts for the client.) When Fleming took the case, he was informed that the trial judge had scheduled the execution for 10 days hence. So with the clock ticking, he put together a team and got to work.

As they got deeper into the matter, the details became clear. Andrew Legare, the defendant, was a runaway from Massachusetts with a troubled background. He had served time in the youth detention center in Milledgeville, Georgia, and had broken out at the age of 17. The state argued that Legare had then killed 54-year-old George Hill, Sr. with a crowbar and stolen his car. Legare denied it all along, saying he had gone in a different direction after escaping. But upon reviewing the case Fleming could see that physical evidence placed Legare at the scene. It was quite clear that Legare had not only committed the crime, but also committed perjury during the trial.

Another significant factor also came to light: Legare was white and the victim was black. This was important because plaintiffs in a separate Georgia case were seeking to invalidate the state's death penalty convictions on the grounds of state bias. The plaintiffs' argument in that case – that the death penalty was disproportionately meted out when perpetrators were black and victims were white – essentially gave the state a vested interest in executing Legare. To make matters worse, Joe Briley, the district attorney in Legare's case, was known for seeking the death penalty whenever possible. Joe Duke, the trial judge, was also a death penalty advocate.

So it seemed to Fleming that the only way Legare could beat the death penalty was to own up to his crimes. "Nobody could look at the evidence," Fleming later recalled, "and think Legare should be exonerated." At the habeas hearing the Sutherland team ended up with a scene straight out of *Perry Mason* as Fleming managed to extract an in-court murder confession. Unfortunately, it was from his own client.

The Sutherland team also pointed out the failure of Legare's trial lawyers to enter any mitigating evidence. The original trial had simply gone from the guilty verdict to the sentencing phase. This had taken place the Wednesday of Thanksgiving week, which led Legare to muse, "They wanted to get home and cook their turkey, but they cooked this turkey first." The original jury had returned from their deliberations with little more than a verdict of death and a few verses of the Bible. But by the time the

Sutherland firm got involved, the Supreme Court was considering cases in which it was suggested that the defense should be required to lay out mitigating circumstances. In Legare's case these mitigating circumstances would have included, among other factors, his abusive foster care and his exceptional intelligence.

The trial judge denied the writ, so Fleming's team took it to the Georgia Supreme Court. Unfortunately this court declined to hear it because they had issued a lengthy opinion on the direct appeal saying that Legare was guilty and the death penalty was appropriate. The Sutherland team then took a certiorari petition to the

John H. Fleming

U.S. Supreme Court at the same time that one of the mitigating evidence cases was being heard. The Court granted certiorari in the other case, arguing that there was an obligation to put on mitigating evidence, and a week later the Court also granted certiorari in the Legare case. This sent it back to the Georgia Supreme Court to be reconsidered in light of *Eddings v. Oklahoma*, in which the Court vacated a juvenile's death sentence on the grounds that the trial court had failed to consider additional mitigating circumstances. The Court in the *Eddings* case held that the chronological age of a minor is a relevant mitigating factor that must be considered at sentencing.

This gave Fleming more time to gather witnesses and experts. The trial was once again held in Milledgeville, and Briley and Duke were again the respective prosecutor and judge. The unfortunate result was another death sentence. Fleming's team then took it back to the Georgia Supreme Court and argued that there had been errors in the charge to the jury. This enabled them to get a reversal before that court. At a third hearing back in Milledgeville, Fleming's team tried again with a slightly different cast of witnesses and experts. But once again Briley was prosecuting and Duke was presiding, and once again the jury recommended a death sentence. This seemed like a fatal blow to Legare's chances.

Still seeing a slim chance of success, the team took the case back to the Georgia Supreme Court. At this point Joe Briley told Fleming that if the latter was able to get the case reversed again, the state would not pursue a fourth death sentence. In front of the Georgia Supreme Court, Fleming brought objections to the questions given to potential jurors. In a fortunate coincidence, he sent his secretary to pull a case from the library as he was preparing his argument. She pulled the wrong case, but the one she pulled was exactly what he was looking for with regard to the jury questions. This enabled Fleming's team to win this third appeal.

Briley then informed Fleming that, contrary to his earlier claim, he would indeed seek the death penalty again. A fourth trial was scheduled for January 1992, but this time it was to take place in Madison, Georgia, with a different judge. Briley was still the prosecutor, and Fleming and Charles Mathis took the lead for the defense. This trial was the most sensational of all and was shown live on the television network *Court TV*. The story was particularly fitting for television because Legare's formi-

2-16-05

Dear John,

It is wonderful and extraordinary, but I am sitting here at a table watching cars and people pass by — no fences, no concertina wire, no "guard" standing by. Nothing but an opportunity for a life that might matter. In the parking/entrepot area of Jackson Diagnostic right before putting on hand cuffs for the last time I about broke down and cried. I hoped this day would come, or a day like it, but I never knew it or trusted that it would, even though the last several months it began to seem so. And now, as I sit and see real life happening around me, I know it.

I have a month of orientation and - for me - real adjustment, and then I'll start going to work and start the transition to the work-a-day world. (There are 150 men here and all in various stages of transition) Then, after 6-9 months, parole. (Though they may at that time parole me to a private half-way house). For now, I'm just soaking it in. It is wonderful and amazing and I'm loving every minute of it. And so very thankful.

I hope you're doing well John, and I think you know that I've always appreciated what you did for me, but at this point I hope you know also that I won't ever give any cause for you to regret it. This is the only chance I'll ever get and I cannot and will not allow myself to fail.

Thank you again for all you did.

Sincerely,

Andrew

Andrew Legare #394788
Macon Transitional Center
1100 Second Avenue
Macon, GA   31201

P.S. Could you send me a copy of the 1977 or 1980 Death Warrant that was signed/ordered in my case?

"...an opportunity for a life that might matter." Andrew Legare thanks John Fleming for his help in overturning a death sentence.

dable letter-writing talents had garnered him numerous female admirers while he was on death row. (The television producers made much of the fact that Legare had married an Atlanta area schoolteacher while in prison a year earlier.)

The trial was tough for all parties, but for John Fleming it was even tougher. His best friend committed suicide during the trial, and Fleming had to forge on with this tragedy weighing heavily on his mind. In the end his team succeeded in getting the jury to recommend a life sentence rather than death.[6]

Legare served 13 more years and was released on parole in 2005 at the age of 45. He was by then well on his way to becoming a productive member of society. His defense had taken hundreds of hours and had included numerous Sutherland lawyers over the years. "It was in the Elbert Tuttle tradition," said John Fleming upon reflection, "and that commitment to public service has always been an important part of the firm."

$\sim$

Herbert Elsas and *Gone with the Wind*

One of Herbert Elsas's higher-profile legal roles was as trustee to the estate of *Gone with the Wind* author Margaret Mitchell. This relationship began when Stephens Mitchell, Margaret's brother and heir to her *Gone with the Wind* interests, asked Elsas to join longtime Mitchell lawyer T. Hal Clarke and Paul Anderson in managing the family's ongoing interests in the book. Clarke had worked for Stephens Mitchell for many years and once protected Mitchell's rights over sequels in a federal case brought by MGM Studios.

Shortly before Stephens Mitchell's 1983 death, he authorized his legal team to allow a sequel. In this way he hoped to preempt unauthorized sequels from flooding the market once the *GWTW* copyright expired. Elsas, Clarke, and Anderson had absolute authority to make decisions for the estate after Stephens Mitchell's death, and in 1988 the trio sanctioned a long-awaited sequel. They interviewed a dozen authors before eventually settling on Alexandra Ripley, whose 1991 novel *Scarlett* would sell more than three million copies. The trustees read several outlines and drafts, and they had final approval over the finished product. They later exercised similar control over a television miniseries, the rights for which cost producer Robert Halmi, Jr. a record $9 million.[7]

Supporters, reporters, and onlookers during the deliberation in the presidential ballot dispute leave the Supreme Court, Washington, DC, Dec. 12, 2000. The nine justices ruled 5-4 to stop the hand counting of ballots in Florida.

Several Sutherland lawyers were heavily involved in the litigation that followed the contested 2000 presidential election, as a team headed by Teresa Wynn Roseborough handled two separate 11th Circuit cases on behalf of Vice President Al Gore.

CHAPTER FOURTEEN

SPECIAL PROSECUTIONS
AND POLITICAL CONNECTIONS

Some of the firm's most compelling cases have been special assignments from local governments. Members of the Sutherland firm have been called upon many times to act as special prosecutors in criminal investigations and trials, or to otherwise give aid to law enforcement officials. This legacy of service began in the early years of the firm, when Tuttle, Brennan, and Sutherland had already built up a regional reputation. In the firm's eighth year Elbert Tuttle and several other Atlanta lawyers represented the county prosecutor in proceedings to enjoin the unauthorized practice of law by several corporations and to punish the defendants for contempt (*Atlanta Title and Trust Co. v. Boykin, Solicitor General*, 172 Ga. 437 (1931); *Boykin, Solicitor General v. Hopkins*, 174 Ga. 511 (1932)). Tuttle later served as solicitor pro tem to investigate charges of irregularities in the office of the solicitor general. Much later Baxter Jones led a grand jury investigation into the possibility of corrupt practices involving some government agencies, including the public prosecutor's staff.[1]

THE ROBERT CARPENTER CASE

But perhaps the most unusual case of this sort in the firm's early decades was the 1949 case of Judge Robert Carpenter of the civil court of Fulton County. Carpenter had chased and shot a lawyer, John Lockwood, whom he suspected of having an affair with his wife. The wound was superficial, but Carpenter was indicted for assault with intent to murder. The Fulton County solicitor general then asked Elbert Tuttle to serve as special prosecutor when Carpenter was charged with attempted murder.

Given the sensational circumstances of the crime, the case attracted widespread interest. Rumors in the community tended to conclude that a high-ranking judge like Carpenter would receive special treatment from the "Courthouse Crowd." Even newspaper editors suggested that Judge Carpenter would be protected by his friends on the solicitor general's staff. The solicitor general thus drafted Tuttle as a means of allaying these suspicions. Because Tuttle had no political ties whatsoever with the county courthouse, a group of prominent Atlanta lawyers recommended him without reservation. The solicitor general announced that he had chosen Tuttle "because of his outstanding character and ability, and because of his willingness to render public service."[2]

Observers noted that the case was prosecuted flawlessly and that the trial was fair. The jury rendered a verdict of not guilty because, according to Randolph Thrower, "the unwritten law prevailed." However, said Thrower, Tuttle "did bring to light the judge's sordid life, and that was widely recognized as a great contribution." The Atlanta Bar Association publicly chastised both Carpenter and Lockwood, and Carpenter was summarily removed from his judicial position.[3]

THE ATLANTA POLICE CHEATING SCANDAL

Nearly 30 years later, Randolph Thrower was asked to take the lead in another high-profile Atlanta case. In 1977-1978 Mayor Maynard Jackson appointed Thrower co-counsel on a pro bono basis to conduct a major investigation of alleged cheating on promotion examinations in the Atlanta Police Department. Thrower was chosen for his superlative ethical and legal reputation and because he had gained some investigative experience while in the FBI during World War II.[4]

Mayor Jackson had run for office on a platform that included an effort to increase the number of black officers in leadership positions. Some of his appointed officials did not seem to realize, however, that he wanted these promotions done by the book. Police promotions in those days were based on standardized test scores, not performance, which had led one APD officer who had been denied a promotion to file suit against the city. This officer claimed that influential officers had provided exam answers to other candidates in advance. The plaintiff further asserted that the scandal went all the way to the top, and he implicated Atlanta Public Safety commissioner Reginald Eaves and deputy police director Eldrin Bell. (Interestingly, another whistleblower in this case was Atlanta City Police homicide detective Sidney Dorsey. Dorsey would later be elected the first black sheriff of Dekalb County, Georgia. In 2002 he achieved an entirely different level of celebrity when he was convicted of murdering Dekalb County sheriff-elect Derwin Brown.)

The police cheating scandal became a local media sensation, leading Mayor Jackson to name Randolph Thrower and Felker Ward, a lawyer from outside the Atlanta area, as special investigators with full subpoena power. Jackson publicly gave them a free hand in the investigation and instructed them to "let the chips fall where they may." Thrower later said of Ward, "I had misgivings [at first] because I didn't know him, but before it was over I realized he was a giant, just tremendous." Sutherland firm lawyers Bill Bradley and Mary Yates (then Mary Mitchell) and several other Sutherland employees directly assisted Thrower over the course of the three-and-a-half-month investigation. The team recorded more than 100 sworn statements and conducted more than 100 polygraph tests with officers at all levels of the Atlanta Police Department.

On February 28, 1978, the special prosecutors filed a detailed 250-page report with findings on a person-by-person basis. They corroborated the original claim that Commissioner Eaves had authorized another officer to circulate advance copies of the questions and answers "for the benefit of certain candidates favored for promotion." Thrower and Ward stated that Commissioner Eaves "knew throughout…that there was extensive cheating. He in fact had authorized it in order to aid in the promotion of certain officers." The investigators also stated that Eaves had attempted to foil the investigation and to stymie their efforts to give him a polygraph test. In addition to Eaves, the report implicated Captain A.L. Cardell, who was a longtime friend of the mayor, and 22 other officers who either participated in the cheating scandal or attempted to block the investigation. As Thrower later recalled, one central aspect of the scandal was that it was not a case of black against white. Indeed, the investigation brought out some of the worst elements of the entire Atlanta police bureaucracy, casting light on an environment more reminiscent of Thomas Hobbes's philosophical "war of all against all."[5]

The report hit the streets like a bomb and forced the mayor to take a hard line. Eaves and Cardell lost their jobs, and several others were either fired or demoted. Bell managed to keep his position, though the investigative report declared that he was "immature" and should have known about the cheating. (Bell's son, Justin Guarini, would later achieve a modicum of national fame as runner-up in the first season of the television program *American Idol*.) The image of both the mayor and the police department greatly improved after the report was issued and the corrupt insiders were removed.[6]

Thrower later recalled that the entire investigative team was inspired by the weight of their task. One brief anecdote helped him bring this to light: "Afterward one of our outstanding secretaries, who'd worked all night on the matter – we'd borrowed her from the litigation practice – came to see me…I expected a complaint, but she thanked us for letting her participate in such a meaningful case."[7]

POLITICAL CONNECTIONS

The Sutherland firm has never been identified with any political party or ideology, though some of its lawyers have been active in politics from time to time. This activity has run the gamut from legal representation of parties and candidates to Sutherland lawyers who themselves actually held elective office.

The first such explicitly political task for a Sutherland lawyer came in 1933, when President Roosevelt named William Sutherland the first solicitor general of the Tennessee Valley Authority (TVA). Sutherland organized the TVA's law department, and he set up the basic plans for valuation of the vast areas of land that were to be condemned. He accepted the appointment with the understanding that he would be free to devote a reasonable amount of time to his law firm, but he

Appointed by Eisenhower — Elbert P. Tuttle and W. Roscoe Tucker won seats at GOP Convention Meeting, July 1952.

quickly found that he was spread too thin. He resigned and returned to the firm after eight months on the job. He had earned only $582 a month with the TVA – all of which was put back into the firm – but in the long run he and the firm gained substantially from his experience and enhanced reputation.[8]

Some years later two of the firm's lawyers ran for Congress in Georgia's Fifth District (Atlanta). In 1952 C. Baxter Jones made an unsuccessful bid for the Democratic nomination for the Fifth District seat. He won the popular vote, but owing to the traditional system of county unit voting he lost the election on county unit votes. Elbert Tuttle reportedly comforted Jones by pointing out that he actually had the best of both worlds: He had won the election but did not have to serve.[9]

Two years later Randolph Thrower got the Republican nomination for the same district post, but he lost to his Democratic opponent, James C. Davis, in the general election. Thrower made a strong showing, however, polling more votes in the Fifth District than President Eisenhower. Thrower later noted that "race was very much an issue" in this election. His opponent was "a courtly Southern gentleman, former judge, former member of the Ku Klux Klan, and a Neanderthal on racial issues." *Brown v. Board of Education* had been decided earlier that year, so a good deal was at stake. In the general election Thrower received an estimated 98% of the black vote, though the general election meant less than the primary. In his words:

> *It was all decided in the primary, and I had a group of enthusiastic young supporters, many of whom were not registered. But it was a spirited race, and the firm was fully supportive. I didn't enter until August, which was quite late in the day. But we activated a campaign and actually got about 48% of the vote with a very large percentage turnout, and I felt rewarded by that. My wife and I made friends throughout the three counties, including Martin Luther King's father and mother…many of which continued until today.[10]*

Other Sutherland lawyers have served in elected or appointed positions. Michael J. Egan remained active in the firm while he served as a Republican member of the Georgia House of Representatives from 1965 to 1977. He decided to run for office after the *Gray v. Sanders* case ended Georgia's county unit system. When Fulton County suddenly had 21 new seats to fill, the Georgia Republican Party scrambled to find qualified candidates. Egan was elected and eventually worked his way up to become minority leader of the House. He also served as a state senator from 1989 to 2000. Also in the late 1970s, Floyd Propst, a valued Sutherland associate, was sought by leading members of the bar to assume the position of probate judge of Fulton County. With the bar's support Propst ran successfully in the Democratic primary and in the general election. Another partner who served in elective office was David Adelman, who represented Dekalb County for many years as a Democratic state senator. Finally, Teresa Wynn Roseborough served as deputy assistant attorney general in the Office of Legal Counsel of the Justice Department from 1994 to 1996. Roseborough also served on the Georgia Judicial Nominating Committee in 1999 at the behest of Governor Roy Barnes.[11]

Others have come to the firm after serving in a governmental capacity. Douglas Rosenthal joined the firm in 1980 after serving as chief of the Foreign Commerce Section of the Antitrust Division of the Justice Department. Jan Vlcek was minority counsel to the House Commerce Committee in the 1970s before joining Sutherland. Vlcek was also a member of President Reagan's transition team for the Department of Energy. Lovida Coleman served as deputy general counsel of the Bush-Quayle 1992 reelection campaign before joining the Washington office.[12]

Still other lawyers have withdrawn from the firm, either permanently or for short periods, to serve in non-elective public office. Don Moorhead left Sutherland in 1975 to serve as chief minority counsel to the Senate Finance Committee. He returned to the firm after passage of the Tax Reform Act of 1976. Washington

---

Jim Wilson on Elbert Tuttle's Republican Affiliation

Elbert Tuttle's position of leadership in the Georgia Republican Party led to numerous meetings with high-level functionaries, including an unannounced weekend visit to the offices of Sutherland, Tuttle & Brennan by Secretary of State John Foster Dulles. The young associate Jim Wilson recalled that he was not equally impressed with all of Tuttle's political connections. In Wilson's words:

Elbert was always a staunch Republican. On one occasion I was expressing some disapproval of Richard Nixon, and Elbert said, "Well if you knew him personally you'd feel differently." Well, I never knew him personally, but I surely never felt differently.[24]

Randolph Thrower on Elbert Tuttle's Role in the 1952 Election

In a 1999 interview, Randolph Thrower described Elbert Tuttle's role in the 1952 Republican nomination process that put General Dwight D. Eisenhower on the path to the presidency:

> *Elbert was very enthusiastic about General Eisenhower and his presidency, and he was one of those who undertook to organize the Southern delegates [of the Republican Party]. The Georgia delegation was split.[25] Some contended they were the true delegates, Elbert's group contending they were the three delegates of the state. That had to be determined by a special committee at the convention. Tuttle led the debate for the Eisenhower supporters. A prominent automobile dealer here in [Atlanta] had promised to support Eisenhower – the convention was, I believe, in Detroit – and this gentleman was courted by the major automobile manufacturers who were supporting Taft, and he defected at the last. Elbert was outraged and expressed this…over radio and television, and he led the debate and was successful in the matter. The Eisenhower delegation was seated, and that was credited with having broken the back of the Taft forces, who needed the Southern support, or at least beginning the landslide toward Eisenhower.[26]*

The Tuttle-led "revolt" against the Republican establishment in Georgia had a significant impact on Georgia politics, and in retrospect it helped make the Republican Party a more agreeable alternative for moderate Southern voters. Tuttle's role in Eisenhower's nomination was noted by the party's South Carolina chairman, who wrote to Tuttle shortly after the convention, "A history making revolution has taken place in the Republican Party. The Old Guard is out…. You must find extreme satisfaction in the knowledge that you have had a part in writing one of the pages of this historic chapter." The day after the general election that brought Eisenhower to office, Sutherland firm associate Mac Asbill, Jr. echoed these remarks in a letter to his "Uncle Tut," saying, "I am certain that the Republican turnout was more than sufficient to destroy the political complacency in Georgia which you have so long fought."[27]

partner Margaret Richardson served temporarily on the IRS commissioner's Advisory Group, and like Randolph Thrower before her, she left the firm in 1993 when President Clinton named her commissioner of Internal Revenue.[13]

Mike Egan temporarily withdrew from Sutherland in 1977 to accept appointment as associate attorney general in the Carter administration, a move that made him the third-highest-ranking member of the Department of Justice and the

Dwight Eisenhower thanks Elbert P. Tuttle for his staunch support

highest-ranking Republican in the Carter administration. Egan and the other Georgia Republicans had supported many of Governor Carter's moves against the state's Democratic establishment, and the newly elected president and his attorney general, Griffin Bell, decided to retain Egan's services in Washington. While in this position Egan oversaw civil law functions and presidential appointments within the Justice Department. He rejoined Sutherland's Atlanta office in 1979.[14]

But surely the two most prominent departures from the firm were those of Elbert Tuttle and Randolph Thrower. Thrower withdrew to accept appointment as commissioner of Internal Revenue in 1969. He resigned this post and rejoined the Sutherland firm after two years (see Ch. 7). Tuttle's departure, however, was permanent. As state chairman of the Georgia Republican Party for the 1952 election, Tuttle was an important figure in the Southern conference for Eisenhower at the Republican convention. Many later said that if it had not been for this conference, Eisenhower would not have won the Republican nomination (see sidebar). Eisenhower returned the favor by appointing Tuttle general counsel of the United States Treasury, where he served for two years before his appointment to the Fifth Circuit Court of Appeals (see Ch. 7).

On other occasions the firm's lawyers have participated in litigation having a definite political flavor. In 1951 Baxter Jones was at the forefront of the challenge to the county unit system as lead counsel in the case of *Cox v. Peters.* This was an action for damages brought by a voter who claimed that the county unit system operated to devalue or discount his vote in relation to the total number of voters in the state in the 1950 primary. Under the county unit statute, six unit votes were allocated to each of the eight most populous counties, four each to the next 30 most populous, and two each to the remaining 121 counties. In a party primary the candidate who received a plurality of the vote in any county was given the number of unit votes allocated to that county. The system was designed to give the rural areas of the state more voting power than the urban areas.[15]

Unfortunately, the Georgia courts held that a party primary was not an election within the constitutional provisions on which the plaintiff relied, and the plaintiff's appeal to the United States Supreme Court was dismissed for want of a substantial federal question. (342 U.S. 936 (1952)). Jones lost the case, but his argument was vindicated when the county unit system fell a decade later through the decision in *Gray v. Sanders* (372 U.S. 368). (Incidentally, the *Gray* case was heard by Elbert Tuttle, who was then serving on the Fifth Circuit bench).

LESTER MADDOX'S "TRIUMPH": MORRIS V. FORTSON

Randolph Thrower took a leading role in litigation over the hotly contested 1966 Georgia gubernatorial election. This was one of the tightest races in the state's history, and the combination of old antagonisms and vitriolic debates over the future of the state and the South made for an intriguing climax.

The controversy began with the Democratic primary. Lester Maddox, Jimmy Carter, James Gray, and former governor Ellis Arnall all finished with more than 150,000 votes. Arnall received a plurality but not a majority, thanks to unexpectedly strong showings by Carter and Gray. Maddox and Carter came in second and third, respectively. Maddox's strong showing ensured even more fireworks, for he had rocketed to national prominence a few years earlier when he chose to close his Pickrick Restaurant in Atlanta rather than serve black patrons. Televised images of Maddox chasing away black customers with a pistol symbolized to many the worst that Georgia had to offer, while his adoption of the axe handle as a symbol of segregationist defiance endeared him to others. At any rate, few suspected he could win either the runoff primary or the general election.[16]

But Maddox had a few aces up his sleeve. Supporters of Georgia political heavyweights Eugene and Herman Talmadge were still livid over Arnall's 1942 defeat of Eugene, as well as his role in the "three governors controversy," wherein three men laid claim to the governor's seat after Eugene Talmadge's death. To Talmadge supporters, Arnall was a far too liberal urban lawyer who represented the Atlanta establishment. As governor in the 1940s he had challenged the rural power structure of the state by, among other things, introducing a merit system for state employees and abolishing the poll tax. These disaffected Talmadge supporters cast their lot with Maddox in the primary. Maddox was further assisted by a large Republican crossover vote. Republican strategists wanted Maddox as their opponent because they thought he would be too repugnant a candidate for moderate Democrats in the general election. Maddox thus defeated Arnall in the runoff primary.[17]

Winning the general election would prove more difficult. Here Maddox faced the moderate Republican textile heir Howard "Bo" Callaway and, unsurprisingly, Ellis Arnall, who had thrown his hat into the ring as a write-in candidate. Callaway seemed on track to become the state's first Republican governor since Reconstruction, as polls showed him leading by a wide margin. But Arnall received enough votes to play spoiler, preventing either of the party regulars from getting a majority. Callaway narrowly won a popular plurality with 47.07% of the vote to Maddox's 46.88% and Arnall's 6.05%. Maddox's surprising showing perhaps suggests that most voters in the "Solid South" were still wary of voting for a Republican, even though the Democratic candidate was so objectionable. Given the lack of a clear majority, an 1824 Georgia constitutional provision gave the general assembly the right to elect the governor from the two candidates receiving the highest number of votes. Led by Speaker George Leon Smith II, they chose Maddox.[18]

At this point a Sutherland team comprised of Randolph Thrower, Jim Paulk, Mike Egan, Laurence Walker, and Dick Ritsch brought an action on behalf of a group of voters to secure the right to select their governor in a direct popular election. Two issues lay at the center of the controversy: whether Georgia could have a constitutional provision that took the vote away from citizens; and whether the Georgia legislature could act to decide an election while it was still "malapportioned" due to the now-unconstitutional county unit voting system.[19]

Thrower and the others focused on the argument that a malapportioned legislature could not decide an election. To their great satisfaction, a three-judge federal district court panel held that the Georgia constitutional provision for election by the general assembly in such a situation was repugnant to the equal protection clause of the 14th Amendment. This court further enjoined the secretary of state and others from seeking to cause the election by the general assembly (*Justice et al v. Fortson, Secretary of State*, consolidated with *Morris v. Fortson*, 262 F. Supp. 93 (1966)).

The case was then brought on appeal to the U.S. Supreme Court, which decided to hear all of the Georgia election cases together. The Supreme Court reversed the district court's judgment in a five-to-four decision (385 U.S. 231 (1966)), and the general assembly elected Lester Maddox governor. Considering just how close the primaries and election had been, it is perhaps fitting that the

Court's decision was close as well. One of the dissenting opinions argued that the general assembly was "concededly malapportioned" and was "under a federal court order to reapportion itself" (385 U.S. at 244). But in the earlier case so holding the Court had held that the general assembly could continue to function until 1968 (*Toombs v. Fortson*, 384 U.S. 210, affirming 241 F. Supp. 65).

Bush v. Gore: The 2000 Election

Several Sutherland lawyers were heavily involved in the litigation that followed the contested 2000 presidential election, as a team headed by Teresa Wynn Roseborough handled two separate 11th Circuit cases on behalf of Vice President Al Gore. Roseborough argued in front of the Florida Supreme Court and sat for an argument in front of the U.S. Supreme Court. The team did exemplary work for 17 days, including several all-nighters, until the Supreme Court ended the process by calling off the vote recounts.[20]

The firm first got involved through Roseborough's contacts with Ron Klain, a senior Gore adviser with whom Roseborough had worked at the Supreme Court and in the Department of Justice. When a complaint was filed by then-governor Bush's attorneys in federal court in Florida just days after the election, Klain asked Roseborough whether the Sutherland firm would be willing to represent Gore in the 11th Circuit.

Roseborough was understandably intrigued, and she and the other partners discussed the pros and cons of taking the matter. Needless to say, they had much to consider. The political nature of the case led some to fear that the firm would be judged by the politics of its prospective client, Vice President Gore, but the vast majority were very pleased to have the matter in the office. Even some lifelong Republicans adamantly insisted that the firm take the case. Once the managing partner, Jim Henderson, gave Roseborough the green light, she proceeded to assemble a team. Several Sutherland lawyers, secretaries, and paralegals signed on, and they essentially put their lives on hold for more than two weeks to work on these cases.

The Bush supporters' initial complaint was an emergency motion for a stay of the vote counts in some Florida counties. The judge in the Southern District of Florida, Donald Middlebrooks, set a hearing for the Tuesday after the election and ordered the Sutherland lawyers to file their response by Monday. The Sutherland team thus had to scrutinize the complaint and assemble experts and affidavits within a period of about two days.

The hearing took place in a chaotic courtroom packed with reporters from all over the world. Around 40 attorneys were representing the Gore side, while only three were representing Bush. The reason for this disparity was that the pro-Gore side represented a variety of interests, including the canvassing boards from counties in which recounts were taking place, the Florida Democratic Party (the Sutherland client), and groups of voters who were intervening on the side of the defendants to let the recounts go forward. Despite these differing interests, those on Gore's side shared the singular goal of forcing recounts. Many participants noted that despite the partisan passions involved in the election itself, the opposing attorneys got along remarkably well.

At the end of this first hearing, Judge Middlebrooks ruled from the bench that the recounts should go forward. The following morning the plaintiffs filed notice of appeal and an emergency motion for a stay in the Middle District of Florida. In addition, a separate suit – *Touchston v. McDermott* – was filed by a separate set of Florida voters, so there were now two cases in the 11th Circuit. Sutherland partner John Fleming volunteered to take over the second case. The Sutherland team filed briefs in opposition to the motions to enjoin the recounts in both cases, and in both cases the courts denied the motions for a stay. That is to say, the Gore side won those judgments. However, the courts also granted motions for expedited review, so Fleming, Roseborough, and their colleagues were still very busy.

While this was happening, hearings were being held in the Florida courts on the issue of recounts, and Sutherland lawyers watched on television as the Florida Supreme Court ruled in the case of *Siegel v. LePore* to let the recounts go forward. This led the Bush side to file a certiorari petition the day before Thanksgiving asking the U.S. Supreme Court to consider the Florida Supreme Court decision. This turned out to be an intense few days because the Supreme Court ordered Gore's counselors to file their briefs in opposition to the certiorari petition that day. So the Sutherland team worked on the brief all Wednesday night and early Thursday, with some participants pausing to catch a few minutes of sleep on a spare couch or floor. It was only one of several all-nighters that the team pulled over the course of the matter, leading Roseborough to muse, "We could have made a list for future reference of all the best couches in the office for sleeping."

The U.S. Supreme Court granted certiorari with respect to the Florida Supreme Court decision but denied it with respect to the cases then pending in the 11th Circuit. The weekend after Thanksgiving, then, the Sutherland lawyers had to do an enormous amount of work. They ended up splitting the team, with the Atlanta office handling the 11th Circuit matter and the Washington office supervising the process of filing merits briefs and Supreme Court briefs. David Adelman and James Orr went to Washington, while John Fleming and Teresa Roseborough stayed in Atlanta. The Sutherland lawyers also supported some Florida lawyers who were working on related Florida cases.

In the first oral argument before the Supreme Court, which took place on December 1, Larry Tribe and Ted Olson handled the arguments for Gore and Bush, respectively. Because the Supreme Court was unclear as to whether it had jurisdiction, it denied the stay and remanded the case to the Florida Supreme Court. That shifted the focus to the 11th Circuit, which scheduled its oral argument for December 4. The Sutherland team therefore had a very busy weekend preparing for both cases. The Sutherland side then won the 11th Circuit case, which set up a second oral argument in front of the U.S. Supreme Court. At this second oral argument, David Boies took Tribe's place for the Gore side, and Al Gore personally asked that Teresa Roseborough be seated at the counsel table during the argument.

Things then got even more intense, as contest proceedings were now taking place in Florida. The Florida trial court ruled that there could be no recount while these proceedings were under way. That matter went to the Florida Supreme Court, which on December 9 ordered a statewide recount. (Ironically, aspects of this decision were agreeable to both parties. The Gore side wanted a recount, while the Bush side believed that any recount – if deemed necessary by the courts – should take place in every county.) That night, the trial court judge set the rules that would govern the recount, and by the next morning most of the counties had enthusiastically begun recount procedures.

George W. Bush's lawyers then applied to the U.S. Supreme Court to stay the recount decision, and this was granted as a writ of certiorari just hours after the recount had begun. The Sutherland team had to respond to the application for a stay and then file their briefs in opposition to the writ. Then, to the surprise of all, the Supreme Court issued a ruling that no further recounts could be undertaken, which effectively meant that Vice President Gore had lost the 2000 election. By the terms of the Court's ruling, the statewide recount could not possibly be completed by the time the Florida statute said it had to be finished. Gore conceded the following evening.

After so much hard work, the Sutherland team was devastated. They saw no legal justification for stopping the recount, as they felt that the Supreme Court had not shown that a recount would cause "irreparable harm." The Sutherland lawyers were also incensed that the Court had placed the decision into the terms of Florida's statute on a recount deadline.

Despite the heartbreaking outcome, these lawyers had much to be proud of. Some put in several hundred hours over the course of the matter, and their work was met with approval by observers from across the political spectrum. Litigation surrounding the 2000 election also meant a great deal for the firm as a whole. It boosted the firm's reputation and increased internal competence and operational abilities, while also augmenting trust and respect between lawyers. Teresa Roseborough summed up the feelings of many of her colleagues when she said of the case:

> *I think that all of us felt that we were in a historic moment that was unlikely to be duplicated in our lifetime and that this was really something that had the focus of the world. The notion of a presidential election coming down to a battle of hundreds of votes in a single state was a rema rkable thing. There was a real sense that you were deciding not only the fate of what the law was going to be, but the fate, in a practical sense, of who the president was going to be. It was exciting and exhilarating and stressful all at the same time; when people decided they were going to work on this case, they gave it 100%.*

FROM STATE BONDS TO GUANTANAMO BAY

The Sutherland firm's bond practice has also handled work of a political nature. In 2002 the Georgia attorney general's office tapped Sutherland's bond lawyers for their expertise in the use of bonds for transportation funding. Governor Roy Barnes was committed to funding a huge mass transit reform package that was to include a variety of construction and improvement projects. The plan would have cost the state upwards of $1.9 billion, which was far beyond what the state could borrow on general obligation (G.O.) bonds. The state therefore sought expert advice on the use of GARVEE bonds, through which the state government could borrow large amounts of money by pledging rebates or refunds on the federal fuel tax.[21]

The firm accepted the work, and a team comprised of Bill Barwick, John Mobley, Matt Nichols, Tom Farnen, and Laurance Warco worked to prove the constitutionality of GARVEEs. Former Georgia attorney general Michael Bowers, meanwhile, was representing Georgia property owners who opposed the Northern Arc, a major tollway that was planned for the counties north of Atlanta. Bowers, a major supporter of then-gubernatorial challenger and Northern Arc opponent Sonny Perdue, filed suit on behalf of the landowner group to prevent the state from issuing the GARVEE bonds.

When the GARVEE issue was tested in the courts, Judge Rowland Barnes of the Superior Court of Fulton County found the bonds permissible, and accordingly he ruled in favor of the Sutherland firm's client. (Incidentally, Judge Barnes was later killed in the 2005 Fulton courthouse shooting.) The opposition appealed, but before their case could be heard in the Georgia Supreme Court, Sonny Perdue upset Roy Barnes in the 2002 gubernatorial election. Notwithstanding Perdue's criticism of the Barnes transportation plan and its heavy use of GARVEE bonds, the Sutherland team was instructed to defend the GARVEEs regardless of the election outcome. A few months after the election, Barwick and Mobley won a seven-to-zero Georgia Supreme Court affirmation of the Fulton County judge's ruling. This final victory was somewhat ironic, for Barwick's team had begun doing their work when Roy Barnes was in the governor's mansion, and they finally got the bonds approved when a critic of the GARVEE program – Sonny Perdue – had replaced Barnes. Nevertheless, the Sutherland team's work was strong enough to pass the test of the courts. The GARVEE bonds remained on the table for state lawmakers for the foreseeable future, and in 2005 the Sutherland team was again retained to bring State of Georgia GARVEEs to market, this time under the Republican administration of Sonny Perdue.

At around the same time, some other Sutherland lawyers got involved in a completely different kind of political matter, one that fell solidly within the Elbert Tuttle tradition of pro bono civil liberties work. In 2005 a group of Sutherland lawyers volunteered to represent five Yemeni nationals who were interned at the U.S. Navy detention center at Guantanamo Bay. This representation began when the New York-based Center for Constitutional Rights asked the American College of Trial Lawyers for volunteer lawyers for Guantanamo detainees. Three lawyers each from the Atlanta and Washington offices – John Chandler, Rick Murphy, Beth

President Ford's notes on the list of prospective Supreme Court nominees; James Wilson is included

Tanis, Kristin Wilhelm, John Anderson, and Greg Smith – answered the call and agreed to represent the five detainees pro bono. Although the politically sensitive nature of the internments led some at the firm to question this involvement, the firm's leadership was solidly behind the team's work.

As these lawyers got deeper into the matter, they overcame whatever misgivings they may have harbored at the outset. They soon found that the Yemeni internees had not been taken prisoner on the battlefield; they had been picked up for bounties and held without formal charges for more than four years. The lawyers traveled to Yemen to meet with the clients' families, and they videotaped the meetings in order to win the trust of their detained clients. Throughout this period, even the most basic representation work was made all the more challenging because so much of the information concerning the detainees was classified. For example, the lawyers had to file suit before the government would even acknowledge that these clients were held at Guantanamo, and before the lawyers were even allowed to meet the detainees. The lawyers later found that it often took weeks for government authorities to declassify their notes from interviews with their clients.

John Chandler, an Army veteran, called the experience both "fascinating" and "horrible" because he was convinced that his clients were entitled to a hearing before an impartial fact finder to determine whether they should be detained or released. He also took pride in knowing that American lawyers were at the forefront of an important public awareness issue. They were the ones most responsible for keeping the public apprised of what was going on in Guantanamo. Chandler's final thoughts go far toward explaining the Guantanamo controversy's place in the classic conflict between liberty and security in a democratic society: "At its core, Guantanamo is about us; about our country and whether we will countenance the long-term detention without trial of human beings just because the executive branch says so."[22]

Jim Wilson Makes the Supreme Court Shortlist

Throughout Jim Wilson's career at the Sutherland firm, his reputation often put him at the top of the list when a leadership position needed filling. A notable example of the esteem in which Wilson was held was his inclusion on the list of possible appointees to replace the retiring Supreme Court justice William O. Douglas in 1975. When Douglas vacated his seat, President Ford's aides, including future vice president Dick Cheney, put together lists of possible nominees in an effort to influence the administration. Ford then asked his attorney general, Edward Levi, to compile a thorough list of possible appointees, taking into account the political context of the times. Levi's list of 18 who were worthy of consideration included Judges Robert Bork, Arlin M. Adams, and John Paul Stevens (who was eventually nominated and confirmed); Senator Robert P. Griffin; and several leading legal scholars and practicing lawyers. Jim Wilson was included in this final category. Also on the list was Antonin Scalia, whom President Reagan would appoint to the Court in 1986. In the end, for political reasons, Wilson did not make the final cut, but he was in quite good company to say the least.[23]

*By 1991 the intellectual property litigation
subgroup had put together what amounted
to a full stable of true IP cases, and it was
nearly doubling its business every year.*

CHAPTER FIFTEEN

TECHNOLOGY AND INTELLECTUAL PROPERTY

It should come as no surprise that the roots of the technology and intellectual property practice lay in the tax field. Joe Brennan's tax work for kaolin producers in the 1930s and 1940s was so well regarded that these companies naturally came back when they had a contractual dispute or a product liability issue. These were some of the firm's earliest technology cases.

The "Square D" cases of the 1960s – so called because one of the first was brought against the company Square D – were the firm's first substantial technology cases. These involved very broad patents on exterior electrical meter boxes that were claimed to cover products of the major electrical equipment suppliers. The most significant such matter was a patent infringement case handled for General Electric in the 1960s. In this case, the patents were invalidated by the patent owner's public sale of boxes to Georgia Power and other users more than a year before the patent application was filed (the "on-sale bar" of Section 102(b) of the Patent Act; *Strong v. General Electric Co.*, 305 F. Supp. 1084 (N.D. Ga. 1969), aff'd, 434 F.2d 1042 (5th Cir. 1970)).

GE took this matter to the Sutherland firm because the firm had previously done some work for the company, and because some of the firm's lawyers had other GE connections. Most notably, Joe Brennan's son was working for GE, and Brennan's wife, Catherine Ginn, also had family connections at the company. Since the case was being tried in the U.S. District Court for the Northern District of Georgia, the company naturally asked Sutherland to act as local counsel.

Carl Strong, the plaintiff, claimed he had designed and patented a home electrical meter box and that GE had infringed upon his patent by building several such boxes. The one-month trial was presided over by the well-known judge Newell Edenfield. Francis X. Doyle took the lead for GE, while Joe Brennan stood as lead local counsel. The pair mounted a defense centered on the patent claim itself, and they brought several patent law experts into the court to testify as to the validity of Strong's claim. The main flaw in Strong's case, the team argued, was that GE's boxes had been put into public use more than a year before Strong filed. In order to back their claim, they searched through Georgia Power's records in an attempt to find houses on which the GE box had been installed before Strong filed the patent application. They found their smoking gun in Albany, Georgia, where the city records revealed that a house had been outfitted with the box before Strong filed.[1]

Despite the firm's success in this matter, such cases were rare, and it would be

J.D. Fleming, Jr.

a long time before Sutherland would put together a true technology practice.

The modern IP practice grew largely from the efforts of J.D. Fleming. It is perhaps fitting that Fleming spearheaded the development of a cutting-edge practice, for he had taken a rather unconventional route to the legal world. The Georgia native earned a Ph.D. in chemical engineering from Georgia Tech and went on to join the faculty there. While working as a professor, he also did outside consulting work, including a long stint as staff consultant for the nuclear materials program at Oak Ridge, Tennessee. Over time Fleming found that more and more of his consulting clients were lawyers and that the "language barrier" between the legal and scientific fields was forcing him to spend far too much time learning what these clients wanted and then explaining the work he had done. He decided to enter the Emory Law School in order to bridge this communication gap. Still, he had no intention of ever becoming a lawyer, in part because the "experts" did not consider science and law to be a good match.[2]

Fleming's modest legal ambitions notwithstanding, on the recommendation of some colleagues he interviewed at the Sutherland firm. Like many before and since, he and his wife, Sid, were both very impressed when they traveled to Washington for the interview. They were so impressed, in fact, that Sid told J.D., "You're going with this firm." Fleming later recalled, "This was a surprise to me," for he had not yet decided to become a lawyer, let alone join a law firm. He added, "I wouldn't say that she got me to come to Sutherland, but she had some very good insights about the people. I have to say that, but for her reaction, I probably wouldn't be at Sutherland, and I wouldn't be in law at all." He soon resigned from Georgia Tech and joined Sutherland.

When Fleming came aboard in 1967, IP law did not exist in the Southeast. Soon thereafter, though, the firm got involved in cases with IP characteristics. The Hollingsworth case, for example – the largest individual U.S. tax case the firm has ever handled – included an unpatented textile manufacturing process. The firm also began to take on a large number of tech-related cases, including numerous infringement actions. One set of these cases, concerning Burlington Industries' patents and trade secrets, was very important for the firm in the 1970s and 1980s. Sutherland partner Jim Wilson had long been a friend of Burlington president and future Callaway Golf company founder Ely Callaway, and he and Pat Patterson were instrumental in bringing in Burlington as a client. Other IP clients from this early period included Pabst Brewing, GAF, Dow Chemical, and Rohm and Haas. The firm continued to represent Rohm and Haas (best known for having developed Plexiglas during World War II) for many years in technology cases in the Southeast.

EXPANSION

As the 1980s approached, one major question for the Sutherland partners was whether the firm would expand into areas in which it did not already have lawyers to build the business. In earlier years, of course, a Southeastern firm would not court another law firm's business. Patent cases, for example, were handled by Northeastern patent firms to whom the older Sutherland partners had long farmed out this kind of work. Despite these traditional constraints, the partners decided to make some moves toward building up a patent prosecution practice, and they took their boldest step in this direction by hiring John Behringer as the firm's first true patent lawyer in 1977. But while Behringer's work was commendable, the firm was unable to attract a large enough group of patent lawyers to make the practice self-sufficient in the 1980s and early 1990s.

Despite this setback, the litigation/IP lawyers continued to build up their client list. In the 1980s they built on their earlier relationships by adding companies as diverse as Riegel Textile and Chemical Products Corporation. Meanwhile, litigation lawyers like Patricia Cunningham and Libby Langworthy continued to do work in trademark litigation and trademark prosecution. John North (Emory J.D., cum laude, 1987) was brought in as an associate in 1987, and he would later be instrumental in creating and heading the IP group. Yet at the end of the 1980s, although some of the firm's litigators had long been doing IP-related work, there was still no formal IP group to speak of.

By 1991 the intellectual property litigation subgroup had put together what amounted to a full stable of true IP cases, and it was nearly doubling its business every year. Up to that point J.D. Fleming had borrowed associates from the litigation practice, but he had never hired dedicated IP lawyers. Things began to change when Fleming and North took on trade secret cases in the 1990s. A major case for TDS Healthcare led North to make a permanent move from the securities practice to IP litigation, and in the meantime the IP cases continued to get bigger. The subgroup's multimillion-dollar *Graham* case was one of the firm's largest in the 1990s.

IP law nationwide grew tremendously later in the 1990s. An increase in the rate of patent grants combined with other factors to make IP the top billing area according to the 1996 Law Office Management and Administrative Report. As a result, many general service law firms expanded their IP resources, with most of the larger firms creating substantial IP groups. Mergers between general service firms and small, specialty law firms – intellectual property "boutiques" – also became common. Before the mid-1990s a good deal of IP work had been sourced out to the engineers and patent experts at these boutiques. But when the larger firms realized that IP was a high-growth area, these firms worked aggressively to attract the best IP talent.[3]

The Sutherland firm made its boldest move toward bolstering the practice after a key partners' meeting in 1997. Here the IP litigation subgroup presented a heavily researched summary of the state of the field and a plan for future growth. Although the field was growing rapidly, the Sutherland firm had not targeted IP as an area for development. IP litigation resources, though substantial, had evolved for the most part in response to the needs of existing clients who had decided to turn to the firm when they encountered an IP controversy. The team therefore made a strong pitch in favor of reorienting the practice and setting targets for growth. The fledgling IP team's leaders also realized they needed additional IP-capable lawyers. They had put together a team of roughly a dozen lawyers – including Pete Burke, Libby Langworthy, Bob Levy, Steuart Thomsen, Bob Clark, Karen Grimm, Lovida Coleman, Jeff Belkin, John Fleming, and Pat Cunningham – but they knew that the learning curve would force a true IP practice to take on more-specialized associates.[4]

The IP subgroup's pitch was well received, but the partners were concerned that the firm would lose some of its tax clients if it got more formally involved in IP. This was a reasonable fear, for IP-oriented firms had long passed tax work to Sutherland. But by this point the nature of business relationships had changed. Large firms had long since begun to poach at the smaller firms, and it was reasonable to expect that trend to continue.

In the end the partners decided to embark on an ambitious plan of growth. Fortunately Sutherland was already well placed among IP firms, so it was able to succeed almost from the start. Nevertheless, the IP group and the partners had to be cautious in hiring, for patent and IP lawyers generally had a different brand of legal résumé. Because most of them spent time working in the sciences and technologies, they did not have the kind of traditional résumé that would catch the eye of law firms. This made it even more important that the new hires were never viewed as second-class lawyers who happened to be in a hot field. J.D. Fleming and John North made a concerted effort to pursue lawyers who were first-class academically, intellectually, and personally.

Creation of the IP Group

Going into the year 2000, the firm had a small group of dedicated IP lawyers and a few associates. The practice then scored a major acquisition when Dan Warren and Bill Warren decided to leave the boutique of Jones & Askew. Dan Warren was a good friend of some of the Sutherland lawyers, and he brought along Pete Pappas, some associates, and a long client list. These lawyers were looking for a change of venue, and John North was instrumental in persuading them to come to the Sutherland firm. With this new set of lateral acquisitions, the Sutherland partners decided to form the IP group.[5]

From that point forward the IP practice grew dramatically. In fact, it seems that the Sutherland practice grew faster than its equivalent at almost any other firm, not counting the larger firms that had absorbed complete IP boutiques in the 1990s. The Sutherland team's preference for bringing in small numbers of people made for a more cohesive group than would have been possible had the firm

Although technical knowledge was very important in some of the scientific areas, the team was also successful in acquiring good litigators who could make technical concepts understandable to a judge and jury.

integrated an entire boutique. In this way the firm was able to avoid the pitfalls of some of the larger patent firms that expanded beyond their means too quickly.

The IP group's growth after 2000 was remarkable, and it soon caught the attention of top law school students and top talent from other firms. By the end of 2003 the group had more than 20 full-time lawyers, as well as many more associates doing part-time IP work. In 2003 the group set a five-year goal to remain well rounded, to establish a new focus on the cutting-edge field of biotechnologies, and to expand its presence in Washington. With regard to this final goal, the group's reputation soon brought about a fortuitous acquisition, as the Washington office acquired three IP litigation partners from the Pillsbury Winthrop firm. These lawyers helped the group expand its presence along the East Coast.

The Sutherland IP group soon stacked up to the IP abilities of almost any firm. As of 2005, it was close to reaching its five-year plan of being at the 50-attorney level, and it was representing a variety of clients, including Coca-Cola, Western Union, pharmacy giant Teva, and universities like MIT, the University of Georgia, and Emory. Because some IP fields required expertise in technical areas, the firm acquired several lawyers with advanced degrees. Although technical knowledge was very important in some of the scientific areas, the team was also successful in acquiring good litigators who could make technical concepts understandable to a judge and jury. The expanding scope of the practice and its increasingly international flavor led the IP lawyers to joke that Atlanta's best feature was its airport, through which they could fly anywhere at a moment's notice.

John North gave the lion's share of credit for this success to J.D. Fleming, whom he considered "a god in this field." Fleming was highly respected for his professionalism and the quality of his work. He was also a pioneer in the use of technology in the courtroom and in the legal field generally. Among Fleming's many other distinctions, he was perhaps the first to use a computer in a Georgia courtroom, and he was behind the firm's first use of online searching from a remote location for a case (see sidebar). He also facilitated the firm's first purchase of a true computer. The HP-85, acquired in 1980, was used to handle the calculations involved in partner distributions, which had always been done on paper with the aid of a simple calculator. The IP lawyers bought several more computers in the next few years, and by 1985 the firm as a whole had more than 20. These handled everything from partner distributions to partner performance statistics and capital adjustments. Fleming first used a database in court in 1984, and the firm's employment of databases greatly increased in the next few years, particularly in the Mutual of Omaha cases.

GEMSTAR COMMUNICATIONS

A few important cases illustrate the development of the IP practice in the 1990s and 2000s. The firm's work for California-based Gemstar Communications explains much of the energy and early growth of the IP group from the litigation side. The firm was contacted in 1998 for a limited role in the case, and the matter ultimately grew into a multiple series of cases in the Northern District of Georgia.

Gemstar, publisher of *TV Guide*, had many patents dealing with electronic guide technology, by which a television viewer can utilize an onscreen channel menu. Their portfolio covered many aspects of the patents for this technology. After Gemstar contacted the Sutherland firm, the IP litigation subgroup fielded a team from both offices in order to serve as co-counsel with some of the largest firms in the country. The case was so big that Sutherland had a team in California for upwards of 20 weeks just to handle document production. The Sutherland firm eventually became lead counsel, a position it held for several years before another firm took over that role. Through the Sutherland team's litigation efforts, Gemstar obtained settlements in excess of $250 million. The case was reported to be one of the largest patent cases in history, and Gemstar remained one of the firm's largest clients for a number of years.[6]

THE BEARINGS CASE

Perhaps the most important case to be handled by the IP group, working in tandem with the litigation group, was 2004's *In the Matter of Certain Bearings and Packaging Thereof, Inv.*, in which a Sutherland defense team led by Patricia Cunningham and Steuart Thomsen scored a landmark victory in a trademark investigation before the ITC. The case was significant in part because the ITC's decision addressed significant legal issues affecting trademark claims as to imported products. It was also a very intense case, forcing a team comprised of litigation, IP, and corporate lawyers to work seven days a week for more than a year.[7]

The matter began in 2002, when the American subsidiary of the Swedish company AB SKF filed a complaint to prevent New York-based Bearings, Ltd. and 13 other companies from importing SKF bearings into the United States. The case fell within a subarea of trademark infringement law that involves so-called "gray market" imports. These products legitimately bear the trademark of the parent company (in this case, SKF) because the products are made by foreign affiliates of the U.S.

company. The issue in this case, however, was that the products were imported by businesses other than SKF USA, which owned the American trademark rights to SKF. SKF argued that these products were being imported without their authority. The case fell under Section 337 of the Tariff Act of 1930, which allows the ITC to bar imports of products where the importation and sale is found to constitute unfair competition. The Sutherland team – which included Libby Langworthy and international trade specialist Mark Herlach – represented Bearings, Ltd.

The plaintiffs could have brought the case to a federal court but decided to bring it to the ITC for reasons of speed. Parties often take infringement complaints involving imports to the ITC because this commission brings its cases to trial much faster than the typical federal court. Indeed, by any measure the ITC is a very fast-track litigation environment. Whereas a federal court usually takes about three years to bring a case to trial, the ITC will do it in less than a year. The *Bearings* case, for example, was formally instituted in April 2002, and the trial began in December of that year. The commission accomplished this turnaround time by compressing all deadlines. (One Sutherland attorney described it as "litigation on steroids.") Several Sutherland associates and legal assistants joined the partners in handling this intense work, including Candice Decaire, Greg Kaufman, Rene Laforte, Kathleen Devereaux (who later joined the Illinois Office of Executive Inspector General), and John Anderson. In one round of briefing, the team put together a 200-page brief in seven days' time.

The trial had some interesting ins and outs. The courts and the ITC had developed a test for determining whether unauthorized imports infringe on a trademark. This was not infringement per se, but if a material difference between the authorized product and the unauthorized import caused confusion among consumers, it could be considered an infringement. This doctrine was developed in cases in which products were made physically different for foreign markets. SKF, in the *Bearings* case, alleged 15 or more material differences, and the Sutherland team had to disprove all of them in order to beat back the claim. Thomsen and Cunningham persuaded the administrative law judge to reject all but one, and both sides sought review on various issues by the commission. The commission remanded it for further fact finding, which required a second trial in December 2003. The ITC then ruled in favor of Bearings in May 2004, rejecting even the one difference that the administrative law judge had found. That decision was affirmed by the U.S. Circuit Court of Appeals in September 2005. SKF then filed a petition for certiorari, which kept the matter alive for the time being.[8]

Since the ITC does not award damages, it is difficult to measure the precise amounts involved. A different ruling could have prevented all the companies named from dealing in this popular brand of bearings. The case is also noteworthy because, although the ITC had handled many such gray market cases over the years, this was the first one in which the respondents won.

Technology in the Courtroom

Sutherland partner J.D. Fleming was responsible for what may have been the first use of a computer in a Georgia courtroom. The HP-97, which was then called a "programmable calculator," became the key factor in the firm's victory in the case of *OSHA v. Pabst Brewing Co.* in Ellaville, Georgia, in January 1978. The government's star witness in this case, acoustical expert Dr. Thomas H. Melling, was astonished to see that Fleming's team had written a program for the HP-97 that calculated the noise exposure under a variety of corrective measures proposed by OSHA, which was the controlling parameter in the case. While Dr. Melling's calculations with a slide rule and an adding machine took more than half an hour each, the HP-aided Sutherland calculations took less than one minute. After an afternoon's testimony, Dr. Melling admitted that the Sutherland lawyers' calculations were correct. Fleming's team thus won the case from the bench. The firm later retained Dr. Melling for similar cases, and with the one-two punch of the professor and the HP-97, Fleming's team so soundly refuted the government's experts that OSHA abandoned any further attacks on Pabst in the Southeast.

The firm first used online searching from a remote location in the 1984 patent antitrust case of *Brunswick Corp v. Riegel Textile Corp* (752 F.2d 261, 224 U.S.P.Q. (BNA) 756 (7th Cir. 1984), cert. denied, 472 U.S. 1018 (1985)). John Bonds won the case in the trial court, and Brunswick appealed to the Seventh Circuit Court of Appeals in Chicago. When J.D. Fleming went to the Seventh Circuit courtroom the day before the argument to find out who the panel judges would be, he saw Judge Richard Posner's name on the list. Because Fleming knew that Posner (who was later an unsuccessful Supreme Court nominee) was one of the most aggressive judges in the country in favor of antitrust plaintiffs, which was the opposite of the Sutherland firm's position in the *Riegel* case, he used an HP-110 in his hotel room to do an online search on Posner. As luck would have it, he found a Posner-authored case note in the *Harvard Law Review* that strongly supported the Sutherland position. In the courtroom the next day, Fleming went through the preliminaries and immediately cited the note, which elicited an enthusiastic reaction from Judge Posner. Since the opposing counsel had not heard of the note or the cases it cited, he could do little more than offer an ineffective rebuttal. Judge Posner ended up authoring a 17-page unanimous decision in favor of the Sutherland client.[92]

~

SUTHERLAND PARTNERS

(As of December 2006 — Current Partners in Bold)

George R. Abramowitz
Alfred G. Adams, Jr.
Bert Adams
F. Louise Adams
W. Susanne Addy
David I. Adelman
Joel A. Adler
John T. Adney
Dennis L. Allen
Robert R. Ambler, Jr.
Peter J. Anderson
R. Steven Anderson
Wright H. Andrews, Jr.
Kenneth F. Antley
Eric A. Arnold
Mac Asbill, Jr.
Mac Asbill, Sr.
Donald I. Baker
William D. Barwick
Marguerite C. Bateman
John W. Behringer
Frederick R. Bellamy
Herbert N. Beller

Daniel M. Berman
Jeffrey P. Bialos
Paul W. Bishop
Lester M. Bliwise
William Blumenthal
Steven B. Boehm
John W. Bonds, Jr.
George H. Bostick
Elizabeth W. Boswell
William C. Bowers
David R. Boyd
Roger Boyle
Michael S. Bradley
William H. Bradley
Joseph B. Brennan
J. Randall Buchanan
Dean Bunch
Lisa S. Burnett
James M. Bushee
Thomas M. Byrne
James M. Cain
Ann B. Cammack
Sheila J. Carpenter

John A. Chandler
Robert S. Chase, II
Francois M. Chateau
Carolyn P. Chiechi
William W. Chip
Nicholas T. Christakos
Reginald J. Clark
Robert W. Clark
Adam B. Cohen
George L. Cohen
Katherine M. Cohen
N. Jerold Cohen
Lovida H. Coleman, Jr.
W. Thomas Conner
Robert E. Copps
William S. Corey
Anthony J. Costantini
Thomas A. Cox
D. Robert Cumming, Jr.
Patricia B. Cunningham
Thomas W. Curvin
Jamie L. Dahlberg
William D. Darling

James D. Darrow
Lee C. Davis
Warren N. Davis
Peter H. Dean
Carey P. DeDeyn
Michael L. Denger
W. Eric Dennison
Nikola R. Djuric
B. Knox Dobbins
Arthur T. Downey
Jeffrey L. Dunetz
Jacob Dweck
Michael J. Egan, Jr.
Philip R. Ehrenkranz
Herbert R. Elsas
N. Beth Emery
Sarah B. Estes
Thomas A. Farnen
Eric R. Fenichel
Blair C. Fensterstock
Zori G. Ferkin
Louis Flax
J.D. Fleming, Jr.
John H. Fleming
Jennifer W. Fletcher
Paul F. Forshay
Ann G. Fort
Hamilton P. Fox, III
Peter A. Fozzard
Daniel E. Frank
Robert S. Franklin
Dorothy B. Franzoni
R. Kent Frazier
T. Paul Freeland
Jeffrey A. Friedman
Charles D. Ganz
Albert S. Gerstein
Stephen F. Gertzman
Thomas A. Gick
David A. Golden
Charles A. Goldstein
David S. Goldstein
Patricia A. Gorham

Francis M. Gregory
Edward J. Grenier, Jr.
Matthew J. Gries
Malvern U. Griffin, III
Karen L. Grimm
David A. Gross
James P. Groton
Philip P. Gura
Robert A. Gutkin
Cheryl L. Haas-Goldstein
C. Christopher Hagy
Burton K. Haimes
H. Edward Hales, Jr.
Victor P. Haley
William M. Hames
William B. Harman, Jr.
T. Alan Harris
James K. Hasson, Jr.
Barrett K. Hawks
James V. Heffernan
Deborah G. Heilizer
Walter Hellerstein
James L. Henderson, III
Walter T. Henderson, Jr.
Mark D. Herlach
Thomas C. Herman
Gerald D. Higdon
Joel E. Hoffman
Kendall L. Houghton
Glen S. Howard
Charles D. Hurt, Jr.
Randolph L. Hutto
J. Patton Hyman, III
Thomas B. Hyman, Jr.
Mark D. Jackson
Blair M. Jacobs
Paul D. Jacokes
Lisa C. Jern
E. Michael Johnson
Loran A. Johnson
Anne P. Jones
C. Baxter Jones
Kent L. Jones

James B. Jordan
James F. Jorden
Edward W. Kallal, Jr.
Edward R. Kane
Andrew M. Kaufman
Mark D. Kaufman
Sheldon M. Kay
Michael G. Kerman
Alicia M. Kershaw
Bennett L. Kight
Cada T. Kilgore, III
Paul W. Killian
Clifford Kirsch
Michael B. Koffler
Susan S. Krawczyk
Cynthia M. Krus
Dana S. Kull
Christopher T. Lamal
Thomas A. Lamar, Jr.
Neil S. Lang
David P. Langlois
Elisabeth A. Langworthy
Allegra J. Lawrence
Charles T. Lester, Jr.
Michael J. Levin
Robert G. Levy
Jerome B. Libin
Kenneth H. Liles
Alfred A. Lindseth
Clay C. Long
William F. Long
George G. Lorinczi
Daniel Marino
J. Dean Marshall, Jr.
Frank J. Martin
Paul J. Mason
David A. Massey
James M. May, III
Randolph J. May
F. Barry McCabe
Keith R. McCrea
James R. McGibbon
Daniel R. McKeithen

Michael R. Miles
John B. Miller, Jr.
Michael T. Mishkin
John H. Mobley, II
James R. Mogle
Philip H. Moise
Jennifer M. Moore
W. Henson Moore
Donald V. Moorehead
Robert R. Morrow
Clifford E. Muller
John R. Munich
Richard G. Murphy, Jr.
Alice Murtos
Matthew W. Nichols
Richard P. Noland
John L. North
Judith A. O'Brien
Earle H. O'Donnell
Cathy G. O'Kelly
Richard A. Oliver
James A. Orr
Harry S. Pangas
Peter G. Pappas
W. Henry Parkman
William R. Patterson
James R. Paulk, Jr.
Gordon O. Pehrson, Jr.
Gerald J. Pels
William H. Penniman
M. Celeste Pickron
Robert J. Pile
Lloyd Leva Plaine
R. Robinson Plowden
S. Lawrence Polk
Garner G. Prillaman, Jr.
Randall D. Quintrell
Peter C. Quittmeyer
David J. Rabinowitz
Margaret M. Richardson
Richard L. Robbins
Haynes R. Roberts
Peter H. Rodgers

Teresa W. Roseborough
Lisa A. Rosen
Douglas E. Rosenthal
Stephen E. Roth
William G. Rothschild
Robert M. Royalty
Brian L. Rubin
Barbara S. Rudisill
Amelia T. Rudolph
Beverly J. Rudy
Richard J. Safranek
Daniel H. Schlueter
Edward J. Schmuck
David Schwinger
Bradley M. Seltzer
John D. Sharer
Olivia Shay-Byrne
Michael J. Shea
Herbert J. Short, Jr.
Paul T. Shultz
Eric L. Sidman
Douglas L. Siegler
G. Anthony Smith
Holly H. Smith
James L. Smith, III
Kimberly J. Smith
William H. Smith
W. Mark Smith
Willis B. Snell
Giovanna T. Sparagna
Avital Stadler
Kenneth G. Starling
Douglas E. Stewart
Bibb L. Strench
Wade H. Stribling
William A. Sutherland
Elizabeth V. Tanis
Leonard B. Terr
Rocco E. Testani
Steuart H. Thomsen
Mary E. Thornton
Randolph W. Thrower
Willard K. Tom

Jeffrey J. Toney
Eric S. Tresh
Annette L. Tripp
C. Christopher Trower
Paul B. Turner
Elbert P. Tuttle
William A. Vaughan
Jan B. Vlcek
Alan R. Vogeler
F. Brook Voght
Lawrence A. Waks
William J. Walderman
Robert J. Walters
George H. Wang
Daniel J. Warren
Thomas H. Warren
William L. Warren
Mark D. Wasserman
Carol A. Weiser
Terry R. Weiss
Gail L. Westover
Larry J. White
Lewis S. Wiener
Dena E. Wiggins
William R. Wildman
Laurens Williams
James H. Wilson, Jr.
Mary Jane Wilson-Bilik
Thomas P. Wilson, Jr.
Walter H. Wingfield
Ronald L. Winkler
Don E. Wood
David R. Woodward
Roland C. Woodward
W. Scott Wright
David C. Wrobel
Katherine P. Yarbrough
Mary M. Yates
Harvey J. Yaverbaum
Kevin A. Zambrowicz
H. Karl Zeswitz, Jr.

A NOTE ON SOURCES

The information in this book has been collected from written sources, interviews, and judicial decisions. The author has cited material from court cases (via WestLaw and LexisNexis) using parenthetical notation in the text rather than in the endnotes. The following is a list of published sources, unpublished collections, and interviewees relied upon by the author:

Legal Indices
- *American Lawyer Guide to Law Firms*
- *Martindale's American Law Directory* (1917-1930)
- *Hubbell's Legal Directory* (1919-1930)
- *Martindale-Hubbell Law Directory* (1930-2000)
- *WestLaw*
- *LexisNexis*

Legal Journals and Periodicals
- *Cornell Law Review*
- *Georgia Bar Journal*, Vols. 1-15 (1938-1957)
- *The Georgia Jurist*, Vol. 1 (1938)
- *Georgia Law Review*, Vol. 1 (1927-28)
- *The Georgia Lawyer*, Vols. 1-2 (1930-32)
- *Legal Times of Washington*

Newspapers and Newspaper Databases
- *Atlanta Constitution* (1917-1990)
- *Atlanta Journal-Constitution*
- *LexisNexis Academic*
- *New York Times* (1920-2006)
- *The Washington Post* (1920-2006)

Collections and Private Papers
- The Elbert P. Tuttle Papers. Manuscript, Archives, and Rare Book Library (MARBL), Emory University, Atlanta, Georgia.
- The Fulton Bag and Cotton Mills collection. MARBL, Emory University.
- The Presidential Papers of Dwight David Eisenhower
(*http://www.eisenhowermemorial.org*)
- Records of the Watergate Special Prosecution Force. The National Archives, College Park, MD.

Secondary Sources
- Lea Agnew and Jo Ann Haden-Miller, *Atlanta and Its Lawyers: A Century of Vision, 1888-1988*. Atlanta: Atlanta Bar Association, 1988.

- Jack Bass, *Unlikely Heroes.* Tuscaloosa: University of Alabama Press, 1990.
- Mary J. Crolley, *Machinations: The Writings of Three Generations of Hollingsworth Women Telling of Wealth and Power – the Textile Machinery Empire and the Family Tragedy That Created a Billionaire.* Greenville: Mary Jane Hollingsworth Crolley, 1988.
- Mercer Cross & Elder Witt, eds., *Watergate: Chronology of a Crisis.* Washington, DC: Congressional Quarterly, Inc., 1975.
- John Dean, *Blind Ambition: The White House Years.* New York: Simon and Schuster, 1976.
- Charles H. Martin, *The Angelo Herndon Case and Southern Justice.* Baton Rouge: • Louisiana State University Press, 1976.
- Holland M. Smith and Percy Finch, *Coral and Brass.* Washington, DC: Zenger, 1979 (orig. 1948). Introduction by Mac Asbill, Jr.

Video Recordings (on file at Sutherland's Atlanta office)

- Elbert Tuttle, interview with Jack Bass (n.d.)
- Sutherland, Asbill & Brennan 75th anniversary video (1999)
- Randolph Thrower and Herbert Elsas, Sutherland 60th anniversary presentation (1984)
- Interviews, Teresa Wynn Roseborough and David Adelman – The *Gore v. Bush* Case (2001)

Interview Transcripts and Unfinished Manuscripts (on file at Sutherland's Atlanta office)

- Joseph Brennan, unfinished firm history excerpt (1979, unpublished manuscript)
- Mac Asbill, Jr. interview transcript, 20 March 1981. Stanley Forman Reed Oral History Project, Margaret I. King Library, University of Kentucky.
- Randolph Thrower interview transcript, 29 May 1990
- Randolph Thrower interview transcript, 1999

Interviews:

- Al Adams, 8 July 2005
- Bill Barwick, 24 February 2006
- John Bonds, 20 July 2005
- Bill Bradley, 20 May 2005
- John Chandler, 20 February 2006
- Nick Christakos, 9 June 2005
- George Cohen, 8 June 2005
- Carey DeDeyn, 27 May 2005
- Mike Egan, 5 December 2005
- Alan and Edith Elsas, 5 January 2006
- J.D. Fleming, 30 June 2005
- John Fleming, 1 July 2005
- Ed Grenier, 9 June 2005
- Jim Groton, 28 May 2005
- Jim Heffernan, 10 June 2005
- Jerry Libin, 10 June 2005
- Al Lindseth, 25 May 2005
- Keith McCrea, 20 February 2006
- John Mobley, 16 February 2006
- John North, 26 May 2005
- Pat Patterson, 28 May 2005
- Jim Paulk, 15 November 2005
- Peter Rodgers, 17 June 2005
- Steve Roth, 17 June 2005
- Steuart Thomsen, 10 June 2005
- Randolph Thrower, 25 February 2005
- Jim Wilson, 22 July 2005
- Walter Wingfield, 3 November 2005

NOTES TO CHAPTER 1

[1] "Attorney Sutherland Locates his Offices in Grant Building," *Atlanta Constitution* (hereafter *AC*), 16 January 1921, B8; Randolph Thrower, Sutherland 60th anniversary presentation (1984) (hereafter Thrower, 1984); idem, interview transcript (1999) (hereafter Thrower, 1999); preliminary draft, Sutherland firm description to The American Lawyer, 16 April 1982; interview with Jim Wilson (22 July 2005); Joseph Brennan, Sutherland firm history (1979, unpublished manuscript) (hereafter Brennan history).

[2] "Attorney Sutherland Locates his Offices in Grant Building," *AC*, 16 January 1921, B8.

[3] "New Firm Formed by Three Lawyers," *AC*, 4 January 1922, 8; "Miss Sarah Hall Weds Mr. Sutherland at Church Ceremony," *AC*, 7 June 1923, 14.

[4] Kin and Mary Hylton, "The Tuttle Brothers: Hawaii's Aviation Pioneers and First Glider Pilots," *Hawaiian Journal of History* 24 (1990) (available at *http://www.lava.net/~kelea/writings/tuttlepaper.htm);* *The Outrigger* (Honolulu), December 1993; Thrower 1999.

[5] Letter, Elbert Tuttle to Mac Asbill, Jr., 13 July 1965, "A 1954-65" folder, box 1, Elbert P. Tuttle Papers. Manuscript, Archives, and Rare Book Library, Emory University (hereafter Tuttle Papers).

[6] Thrower, 1984; Charles M. Elson, "Remembering Judge Elbert P. Tuttle, Sr." *Cornell Law Review* 82 (1996-97) ; Sutherland, Asbill & Brennan 75th anniversary video (1999) (hereafter 75th anniversary video); Louise Boyle, "The Tuttle Apartments: A Brief History," n.d., "Biographies" folder, box 5, Tuttle Papers.

[7] "Leading Attorneys Form New Law Firm," *AC*, 28 December 1919, 6; Brennan history.

[8] Much of this material comes from Randolph Thrower interview transcript, 29 May 1990 (hereafter Thrower, 1990). See also Anne S. Emanuel, "Lynching and the Law in Georgia, c. 1931: A Chapter in the Legal Career of Judge Elbert Tuttle," *William and Mary Bill of Rights Journal* 5 (1996-97), 220-221. Jack Bass, *Unlikely Heroes* (Tuscaloosa: University of Alabama Press, 1990), 32; idem, "Death of Judge Tuttle: A Hero of Desegregation," *Atlanta Journal and Constitution* (hereafter *AJC*), 25 June 1996, A9; "Judge Elbert Parr Tuttle," *Georgia State Bar Journal* 28 (August 1991), 20.

[9] Randolph Thrower once told an interviewer that the fee was $4,000 (Thrower, 1990). The reference to the Trust Company Building is from "New Firm Formed by Three Lawyers." Emanuel, "Lynching and the Law in Georgia," 221.

[10] Thrower, 1999.

[11] "Georgians to Share in Big Tax Refunds," *AC*, 28 December 1928, 2; Brennan history.

[12] Thrower, 1999; Brennan history.

[13] Brennan history.

[14] Quoted in 75th anniversary video.

[15] Brennan history.

[16] This story comes from Thrower, 1984.

[17] "Dekalb County Must Keep Faith, Says Court Rule," *AC*, 25 January 1924, 4; Brennan history.

[18] *The Washington Post* (hereafter *WP*), 12 November 1987, C14.

[19] This summary comes from Thrower, 1984. Other comments in this section come from interview with Ed Grenier, 9 June 2005.

[20] *WP*, 21 March 1953, 29. For Tuttle's connection to the firm after his departure, see, for example, letters, Herbert Elsas to Elbert Tuttle, 29 October 1953 and 17 March 1955, "23 (E 1953)" and "24 (E 1954-65)" folders, box 1, Tuttle Papers. Bill Sutherland also occasionally wrote to Tuttle to express his opinion about the latter's judicial decisions (cf. letter, Sutherland to Tuttle, 20 March 1958, "16 (S 1954-65)" folder, box 3, Tuttle Papers).

[21] Also named were Warren Burger and Herbert Brownell. Letter, Dwight D. Eisenhower to William P. Rogers, 17 September 1958, in *The Papers of Dwight David Eisenhower*, ed. L Galambos and D. Van Ee, doc. 857. WWW facsimile by the Eisenhower Memorial Commission (Baltimore: Johns Hopkins University Press, 1996), available at *http://www.eisenhowermemorial.org/presidential-papers/second-term/documents/857.cfm*

[22] See *Newsweek*, 20 October 1958, 25, 36-38; also, letter, Bill Sutherland to Elbert Tuttle, 13 February 1958, "16 (S 1954-65)" folder, box 3, Tuttle Papers.

[23] From untitled biographical sketch, Georgetown honorary Doctor of Laws pamphlet, "Biographies" folder, box 5, Tuttle Papers.

[24] Bass, *Unlikely Heroes*, 32-33, 41; John Minor Wisdom quoted in Wisdom, "My Friend and Chief: Elbert Tuttle," (1980), 12-14, "Reprints and Journals" folder, box 11, Tuttle Papers.

[25] Bass, "Death of Judge Tuttle;" idem, *Unlikely Heroes*, 33; Tom Bennett, "Led Court in Historic Era," *AC*, 24 June 1996, D6.

[26] Colin Campbell, "Recalling a Judge and a Journalist," *AC*, 20 June 1996, B1; "Biographical Note," from Finding Aid, Tuttle Papers.

[27] Thrower, 1999.

[28] Thrower, 1984; Wilson, 2005.

[29] Quotes come from interviews with Mike Egan, 5 December 2005, and Pat Patterson, 28 May 2005; Edith Elsas quoted in 75th anniversary video.

[30] Biographical information from *AC*, 4 March 1991, D4; "Brennan, Joseph Benjamin," entry in *Who's Who in America* (via LexisNexis).

[31] Former Tuttle clerk Charles M. Elson wrote that he "always ended each year's class reading (Tuttle's) speech to my students." Elson, "Remembering Judge Elbert P. Tuttle, Sr.".

[32] Quoted in Elbert P. Tuttle, "Heroism in War and Peace," *The Emory University Quarterly* 13 (October 1957), 138-139.

[33] This story comes from Wilson, 2005.

[34] This story is told in Hylton, "The Tuttle Brothers: Hawaii's Aviation Pioneers."

NOTES TO CHAPTER 2

[1] Thrower, 1990.

[2] Brennan history.

[3] Thrower, 1990, 1999.

[4] Thrower, "Is the Tax Bar Going Casual – Ethically?" *Tax Lawyer* 54 (Summer 2001), 798-799.

[5] Thrower, 1990, 1999.

[6] Thrower, 1984; Brennan history.

7   Thrower, 1990, 1999.

8   Thrower, 1990.

9   Ibid.; Patterson, 2005.

10 Thrower, 1990, 1984.

11 Thrower, 1999.

12 Except where indicated, this section is based on the Brennan history.

13 My retelling of the Bobby Jones tax case is based on Sidney L. Matthew's comprehensive account, "The Trials of Bobby Jones," *Litigation* 28 (Spring 2002), 53-74.

14 "Bobby Jones will get Quarter Million for Moving Picture Work, Authorities Say," *AC*, 18 November 1930, 1, 8; see also *The Atlanta Journal Magazine*, 23 October 1932, 6.

15 Lea Agnew and Jo Ann Haden-Miller, *Atlanta and Its Lawyers: A Century of Vision, 1888-1988* (Atlanta: Atlanta Bar Association, 1988), 119; "To Financial," *PR Newswire*, 16 April 1981; Ellen Howle, "Herbert Rothschild Elsas, Trustee for Margaret Mitchell's Estate," *AC*, 9 September 1995, 10C.

16 Patterson, 2005; Egan, 2005.

17 Some biographical information comes from the American Inns of Court website, *http://www.innsofcourt.org*

18 Joseph Wharton, "ABA Honors Randolph Thrower," *ABA Journal* 108, August 1993, 79.

19 William M. Ragland, Jr., "Courage Under Fire," *The Atlanta Lawyer* (March 2005), 3; See also Agnew and Haden-Miller, *Atlanta and its Lawyers*, 21.

20 Interview with Bill Bradley, 20 May 2005.

21 Thrower, 1999.

22 This story was published in Thrower, "Is the Tax Bar Going Casual – Ethically?," 797-809.

NOTES TO CHAPTER 3

1   Unless otherwise indicated, I am relying chiefly on the Brennan history for this section on New Deal cases.

2   Elbert Tuttle, "Control of National Agricultural Production and Consumption Through Taxation," *Cornell Law Quarterly* 23 (December 1937), 126 (note 36); Thrower, 1990.

3   Thrower, 1999, 1984.

4   Interview with Randolph Thrower, 25 February 2005.

5   Brennan history.

6   On the Hoosac case and the AAA, see "Cotton Awaits Supreme Court Tax Decision," *WP*, 21 July 1935, F7; "Text of Majority Opinion of the Supreme Court Ruling the AAA Invalid," *WP*, 7 January 1936, 4; "Cotton Industry Faces Confusion," *WP*, 12 January 1936, R10; "AAAbolition," *Time*, 13 January 1936.

7   Some of this discussion of the AAA comes from Elbert Tuttle's comments on the processing taxes and the AAA in his essay, "Control of National Agricultural Production," 117-130.

8   Thrower, 1999; Brennan history.

9   Thrower, 1999.

10 "Textile Trade Recovers with Vigorous Rise," *WP*, 11 September 1935, 16; Brennan history.

11 Thrower, 1999.

[12] Brennan history.

[13] "Silk Mills Fail in Fight on NRA," *WP*, 19 May 1934, 3.

[14] This section is from Thrower, 1999; Herbert Elsas, Sutherland 60th anniversary presentation (1984) (hereafter Elsas, 1984); and the Brennan history.

[15] Brennan history.

[16] Egan, 2005.

[17] This section is derived from Thrower, 1990, and the Brennan history.

NOTES TO CHAPTER 4

[1] Thrower, 1999. On their "society" connections, see Anne S. Emanuel, "Lynching and the Law in Georgia, Circa 1931: A Chapter in the Legal Career of Judge Elbert Tuttle," *William and Mary Bill of Rights Journal* 5 (1996-97), 222. Emanuel's study is the most comprehensive secondary account of the Downer case.

[2] Unless otherwise stated, I am relying on Elbert Tuttle's account of the Downer case in "Reflections on the Law of Habeas Corpus," *Journal of Public Law* 22 (1973), 325-334; Emanuel, "Lynching and the Law," 215-248; and the Brennan history.

[3] "Courageous Elberton Pastor Tells of Quieting Angry Mob," *AC*, 20 May 1931, 1, 6.

[4] "Tear Gas Bombs, Rifle Fire Used to Save Negroes," *AC*, 19 May 1931, 1.

[5] "The Elberton Victory," in ibid., 6.

[6] Thrower, 1999.

[7] Tuttle quoted in "Reflections on the Law," 327. For a brief but interesting synopsis of the early days of the Downer matter, see untitled editorial, *The Nation* 133, 4 November 1931, 474-475.

[8] Tuttle, "Reflections on the Law," 327.

[9] Tuttle felt that his involvement as a National Guard officer in the arrest and original trial might inhibit his ability to represent Downer effectively. He therefore asked Sutherland to act in his stead in the courtroom. Sutherland then read statements written by Tuttle. See Tuttle, "Reflections on the Law," 327, and "Asks Only Justice for Downer, Says Sutherland, Outlining Case," *AC*, 16 June 1931, 3.

[10] Elbert P. Tuttle, "Fall-Out from *Brown v. Board of Education*," *Emory Law Journal* 28 (1979), 913-914.

[11] Bass, *Unlikely Heroes*, 37. Anne S. Emanuel offers a good explanation of this defense in "Lynching and the Law in Georgia," 229-232.

[12] Quoted in Elbert Tuttle, "Reflections on the Law," 328-29.

[13] Unless otherwise noted, I am relying here on Tuttle, "Reflections on the Law;" Charles H. Martin, *The Angelo Herndon Case and Southern Justice* (Baton Rouge: Louisiana State University Press, 1976); and the Brennan history.

[14] A newspaper article at the time claimed that Herndon had "organized a march of about 1,000 families to the county court house to ask for relief." He was then arrested on a formal charge of "suspicion," after which his apartment was searched and communist literature was found. See Edwin Camp, "'Vagueness' Aids Herndon," *New York Times* (hereafter *NYT*), 15 December 1935, E11.

[15] Thrower, 1999; Bass, *Unlikely Heroes*, 37.

[16] Quoted in Martin, *The Angelo Herndon Case*, 75, 140-142.

[17] Brennan history.

[18] Thrower, 1999; Brennan history. See also Agnew and Haden-Miller, *Atlanta and its Lawyers*, 29-30, 32.

[19] Agnew and Haden-Miller, *Atlanta and its Lawyers*, 54.

[20] Camp, "'Vagueness' Aids Herndon;" Martin, *The Angelo Herndon Case*, 163; "Herndon Appeal Filed," *NYT*, 15 December 1935, N2.

[21] Martin, *The Angelo Herndon Case*, 169.

[22] "Herndon Set Free by Supreme Court," *NYT*, 27 April 1937, 1, 10; Edwin Camp, "Glad Herndon Case is Over," 2 May 1937, E7.

[23] This is from Martin, 164-165, and the Brennan history. While Herndon was in prison, he wrote a book, *Let Me Live* (New York: Random House, 1937). After he was freed by the Supreme Court, Herndon said he was going to continue to try to improve the lot of Southern sharecroppers. See Horace Gregory, "Two Generations," *The Nation* 144 (10 April 1937), 414-416; and "Herndon Set Free by Supreme Court," *NYT*, 27 April 1937, 1, 10.

[24] Bass, *Unlikely Heroes*, 38.

[25] Brennan history; Tuttle, "Reflections on the Law," 331.

[26] Tuttle, "Reflections on the Law," 332.

[27] Brennan history.

[28] See essay "Assistance of Counsel," *http://law.onecle.com/constitution/amendment-06/12-assistance-of-counsel.htm*

[29] The John Minor Wisdom citation comes from Wisdom, "My Friend and Chief: Elbert Tuttle," (1980), 12-14, "Reprints and Journals" folder, box 11, Tuttle Papers; Tuttle quoted in, "Reflections on the Law," 332.

[30] Elbert P. Tuttle, "Heroism in War and Peace," *The Emory University Quarterly* 13 (October 1957), 132, 135.

NOTES TO CHAPTER 5

[1] Brennan history.

[2] Thrower quoted in 75th anniversary video.

[3] Brennan history.

[4] Ibid.

[5] Ibid.

[6] Ibid.; Thrower, 1999.

[7] Jack Bass, *Unlikely Heroes*, 33.

[8] "Citation of 304th Field Artillery Battalion as Forwarded by 77th Division," n.d., "Brochures and Pamphlets" folder, box 5, Tuttle Papers. The brief story of Elbert, Jr.'s flight is from Jack Bass, "Judge Elbert Parr Tuttle," *Georgia State Bar Journal* 28 (August 1991), 22.

[9] Quoted in *Georgia Bar Journal* 8 (November 1945), 195-196. For more on Tuttle's views of the war, see Elbert P. Tuttle, "Heroism in War and Peace," *The Emory University Quarterly* 13 (October 1957), 129-139.

[10] This section on Thrower's war experiences is derived from Thrower, 1990 and 2005.

[11] Thrower, 1990.

[12] Interview with Alan and Edith Elsas, 5 January 2006.

[13] Ellen Howle, "Herbert Rothschild Elsas, Trustee for Margaret Mitchell's Estate," *AC*, 9 September 1995, 10C; Alan and Edith Elsas interview, 2006.

[14] This section is from Wilson, 2005.

[15] Ibid.

[16] The quotes and information on Asbill's relationship with General Smith come from Holland M. Smith and Percy Finch, *Coral and Brass* (Washington, DC: Zenger, 1979, 1948). See esp. the Asbill-penned introduction and pp. 261-263.

[17] This section is from Patterson, 2005.

[18] Unless otherwise noted, the details of this story come from Thrower 2005, 1990, and 1999.

[19] Thrower, "Is the Tax Bar Going Casual – Ethically?", 803.

[20] Brennan history.

[21] Thrower, 1990, 1999.

NOTES TO CHAPTER 6

[1] Unless otherwise noted, the first section of this chapter is from 2005 interviews with Jim Wilson, Jim Heffernan, and Jerry Libin, as well as the Brennan history.

[2] Mac Asbill, Jr. interview, 20 March 1981. Stanley Forman Reed Oral History Project, Margaret I. King Library, University of Kentucky.

[3] Thrower, 1999, 1984.

[4] Mac Asbill, Jr., 1981.

[5] The reference to Kane and Stallings is from the Brennan history.

[6] Thrower, 1999; Wilson, 2005.

[7] Egan, 2005; Elsas, 1984.

[8] Thrower, 1999.

[9] Heffernan, 2005.

[10] Thrower, 1999, 1984; Agnew and Haden-Miller, *Atlanta and its Lawyers*, 167-68.

[11] "Ex-Cabinet Aide Laurens Williams Dies," *WP*, 9 June 1975, C6; Brennan history.

[12] The information on Williams comes from Elsas, 1984.

[13] "Cards' Saigh Indicted for Tax Evasion," *WP*, 23 April 1952, 16; "Saigh of Cards Gets 15-Month Jail Sentence," *WP*, 29 January 1953, 1; Heffernan, 2005

[14] Heffernan, 2005.

[15] For a good perspective on how the law changed in Atlanta from the 1950s to the 1980s, see Agnew and Haden-Miller, *Atlanta and its Lawyers*, 167-68.

[16] Libin, 2005.

[17] Information for this section comes from Elsas, 1984; Patterson, 2005; and Libin, 2005.

[18] Wilson, 2005.

[19] Thrower, 1999; Wilson, 2005.

[20] Interview with Carey DeDeyn, 27 May 2005.

[21] Thrower, 1999, 1984.

[22] Egan, 2005.

[23] This section on the Asbills is from Mac Asbill, Jr. interview, 1981; 75th anniversary video; *WP*, 22 May 1992, C6; interview with Nick Christakos, 9 June 2005; interview with Steuart Thomsen, 10 June 2005; unpublished eulogy (filed in Sutherland Atlanta office); and letter, Frank Gregory to Mac Asbill, Jr., 19 May 1992 (filed in Sutherland Atlanta office).

[24] Mac Asbill, Jr., 1981.

[25] Ibid.

[26] Eugene Patterson, "Bright Arrows Across Eternity," *AC*, 4 June 1962.

[27] See Agnew and Haden-Miller, *Atlanta and its Lawyers*, 114-117.

[28] Ibid., 97-98.

NOTES TO CHAPTER 7

[1] The Sutherland firm's role in this case was described by Thrower, 1984, and in the Brennan history.

[2] Thrower, 1984.

[3] Wilson, 2005.

[4] Brennan history.

[5] Ibid.

[6] 75th anniversary video.

[7] Wilson, 2005.

[8] Brennan history.

[9] 75th anniversary video.

[10] Quoted in Jack Bass, "Death of Judge Tuttle: A Hero of Desegregation," *AJC*, 25 June 1996, A9.

[11] Cameron quoted in *The Florida Times-Union* (Jacksonville), 1 August 1963.

[12] Ibid.

[13] Bass, *Unlikely Heroes*, 31.

[14] For a discussion of the judges' methods, see ibid., 19-22.

[15] Quote from ibid., 217. Tuttle described some of the Fifth Circuit's methods, as well as the role played by the Supreme Court, in his article, "Fall-Out from *Brown v. Board of Education*," *Emory Law Journal* 28 (1979), 913-931.

[16] Bass, *Unlikely Heroes*, 20-21.

[17] "Elbert Parr Tuttle," entry in The New Georgia Encyclopedia, *www.georgiaencyclopedia.org*

[18] Bass, "Death of Judge Tuttle."

[19] Ibid.; Thrower, 1999.

[20] Thrower, 1999.

[21] Quoted in Bass, "Death of Judge Tuttle."

[22] Ibid.; Laura Williamson, "Hundreds Recall Judge Tuttle," *AC*, 30 June 1996, D1.

[23] Quoted in Bass, *Unlikely Heroes*, 215.

[24] I am relying here on an interview with Walter Wingfield, 3 November 2005, and the Brennan history.

[25] Unless otherwise noted, this section is from Thrower, 2005; Agnew and Haden-Miller, *Atlanta and its Lawyers*, 22; and "Nixon Names Lawyer as Tax Chief," *NYT*, 19 March 1969, 20.

[26] John Dean, *Blind Ambition: The White House Years* (New York: Simon and Schuster, 1976), 73.

[27] Memorandum, Richard Nixon to John Connally, n.d., no folder, box 3, Plumbers Task Force Investigation of Other Illegal Activities, Records of Watergate Special Prosecution Force, National Archives, College Park, MD.

[28] Memorandum, Henry Hecht to Jay Horowitz, 27 September 1973, "Investigation of IRS Witness Statements, Thrower, Randolph" folder, box 1, (same collection as previous note).

[29] Mercer Cross & Elder Witt, eds., *Watergate: Chronology of a Crisis* (Washington, DC: Congressional Quarterly, Inc., 1975), 177, 701.

[30] Unless otherwise noted, I am relying here on Bass, *Unlikely Heroes*, 205-222.

[31] Bass, "Death of Judge Tuttle."

[32] See Alfred C. Aman, Jr., "Honoring Judge Tuttle's Vision of the Law," *Cornell Law Forum* 10 (June 1983), 14-17.

[33] Brennan history.

NOTES TO CHAPTER 8

[1] Unless otherwise noted, this chapter has been compiled from interviews conducted in 2005-2006 with John Fleming, Carey DeDeyn, Jim Groton, John Bonds, Al Lindseth, Steuart Thomsen, John Chandler, and Nick Christakos.

[2] John Fleming, 2005.

[3] See Eleanor Kerlow, "No Free Lunch – or Soda," *Legal Times*, 25 March 1991, 6; Christakos, 2005.

[4] Christakos, 2005. The Ford explanation comes from DeDeyn, 2005 and John Fleming, 2005.

[5] Agnew and Haden-Miller, *Atlanta and its Lawyers*, 63.

[6] The description of the case comes from Groton, 2005 and Lindseth, 2005, except where noted.

[7] Raleigh Bryans, "Benchmarks in 8-Year School Litigation," *The Atlanta Journal*, 12 May 1980, A16.

[8] Angelo Lewis and Tyrone Terry, "Court Kills Metro Busing Suit," *AC*, 25 September 1979, A1; Peter Scott, "School Desegregation Suit Dismissed; Appeals Likely," *The Atlanta Journal*, 25 September 1979, A1.

[9] Ron Taylor, "Judgment is Affirmed," *The Atlanta Journal*, 18 May 1980.

[10] Mays quoted in Henry Eason, "Atlanta Cross-Busing Suit Crushed," *AC*, 13 May 1980, A1; "The Atlanta Case," ibid., A4.

[11] Josh Funk, "School-Funds Suits Drag On," *The Wichita Eagle*, 16 May 2004. See also Liz Austin, "Texas Latest State to Get Court Ruling on School Finance," *Associated Press*, 18 September 2004; Michael Dobbs, "Poor Schools Sue for Funding," *WP*, 7 June 2004.

[12] From Lindseth, 2005, and Bonds, 2005. See also Daniel Wise, "Sutherland, Asbill's Fees at $5M So Far in NY Education Battle," *Fulton County Daily Report*, 6 October 1999; Julia D. Gray, "Sutherland Team Vindicated in Reversal of NY Schools Suit," *Fulton County Daily Report*, 2 July 2002.

[13] David J. Hoff, "States on Ropes in Finance Lawsuits," *Education Week* 24 (8 December 2004), 1.

[14] Bonds, 2005.

[15] See Lindseth, "Suits Won't Fix School Woes," *USA Today*, 25 May 2004, 19A; idem, "Adequacy Lawsuits: The Wrong Answer for Our Kids," *Education Week* 24 (9 June 2004), 52, 42.

[16] Groton, 2005.

[17] DeDeyn, 2005; Thomsen, 2005.

[18] "Mark Lane," *Spartacus Biography Online*, *http://www.spartacus.schoolnet.co.uk/JFKlaneM.htm*

NOTES TO CHAPTER 9

[1] Herbert Elsas, 1984.

[2] See W. John Moore, "From Square One, Firm Built Ideal Energy Practice," *Legal Times of Washington*, 7 September 1981, 23, 27.

[3] Preliminary draft, Sutherland firm description to *The American Lawyer*, 16 April 1982.

[4] Elsas, 1984; Grenier, 2005.

[5] Elsas, 1984.

[6] Grenier, 2005; preliminary draft to *The American Lawyer*.

[7] Unless otherwise noted, I am relying here on interview with Peter Rodgers, 17 June 2005 and Grenier, 2005.

[8] Elsas, 1984.

[9] "Sutherland, Asbill Expands Austin Outpost," *Texas Lawyer*, 2 August 1993, 46.

[10] Interview with Keith McCrea, 20 February 2006.

[11] Grenier 2005.

NOTES TO CHAPTER 10

[1] *AC*, 22 May 1992, E9.

[2] Unless indicated otherwise, my description of the Mutual matter has been culled from interviews with John Bonds, Nick Christakos, and Carey DeDeyn.

[3] Preliminary draft, Sutherland firm description to *The American Lawyer*, 16 April 1982.

[4] Some of the cases are described in Paula L. Green, "Hall, Mutual of Omaha Settle $150 Million Suit," *Journal of Commerce*, 4 December 1987, 9A; see also "Hall Counterclaim," *World Insurance Report*, 7 August 1987; "RAM Syndicate-Omaha Indemnity Co.," *World Insurance Report*, 19 September 1986.

[5] Bonds, 2005; Christakos, 2005.

[6] Christakos, 2005.

[7] Bonds, 2005.

[8] Christakos, 2005.

[9] "Judge's Lenient Sentences Don't Fit Massive Swindle," *Omaha World Herald*, 2 February 1993.

[10] DeDeyn, 2005; Christakos, 2005.

[11] Letter, Bill Sutherland to Elbert Tuttle, 15 March 1969, "17 (S 1965-74)" folder, box 3, Tuttle Papers; Christakos, 2005.

[12] The quote is printed in the Sutherland Washington office's "Live from 1275" newsletter

(March 1993).

[13] Christakos, 2005.

NOTES TO CHAPTER 11

[1] Patterson, 2005; 75th anniversary video.

[2] Unless stated otherwise, the description of the latter years of the real estate group is from Ed Hales's comprehensive e-mail to the author, as well as the author's interview with Al Adams, 8 July 2005.

[3] 75th anniversary video; Adams, 2005.

[4] Adams, 2005.

[5] Preliminary draft, Sutherland firm description to *The American Lawyer*, 16 April 1982; Sutherland 2004 Annual Review; Paulk, 2005.

[6] Adams, 2005.

[7] Ed Hales, e-mail to author; Adams, 2005.

[8] Patterson, 2005; Adams 2005.

NOTES TO CHAPTER 12

[1] Libin, 2005.

[2] "Clinton Picks IRS Nominee," *The Houston Chronicle*, 24 February 1993, A5. The Associate Training Committee developed a comprehensive three-year curriculum for the training of the firm's lawyers in 1988-1989. See memo, Training Committee to All AO Attorneys, 7 June 1989, "Sutherland 1982-89" folder, box 13, Tuttle Papers.

[3] These are from Libin, 2005.

[4] This summary statement is from Elsas, 1984.

[5] Ibid.; Heffernan, 2005; "Nebraskan Leaves Treasury," *NYT*, 9 November 1956, 12.

[6] Elsas, 1984.

[7] Elsas, 1984.

[8] Interview with Steve Roth, 17 June 2005.

[9] Ibid.

[10] I am relying here on Cohen, 2005.

[11] Cohen, 2005.

NOTES TO CHAPTER 13

[1] The debate is explained in some detail by Eleanor Kerlow, "Sutherland, Asbill at the Crossroads," *Legal Times*, 11 February 1991, 1; and "No Free Lunch – or Soda," *Legal Times*, 25 March 1991, 6.

[2] Robb Mandelbaum, "Sutherland, Asbill's New York Divorce," *The American Lawyer*, December 1995, 18; Christy Harrison and Paul Kvinta, "Atlanta To Europe Via JFK," *The American Lawyer*, January/February 1993, 21; Bradley, 2005; Christakos, 2005.

[3] I am relying here on Kerlow, "Sutherland, Asbill at the Crossroads;" Bradley, 2005; Christakos, 2005; and unnamed sources.

[4] The successful turnaround of the late 1990s is documented in Jonathan Ringel, "Sutherland, Asbill on Comeback Trail," *Fulton County Daily Report*, 18 June 1998; and

Janet L. Conley, "Sutherland Asbill has Action-Packed Year of Litigation," *Fulton County Daily Report*, 27 June 2000.

5   John Fleming, 2005.

6   See Dennis Williams, "Inmate Gets Life in Third Sentencing Retrial," *AJC*, 11 January 1992, C8.

7   "Pair Protects 'Gone with the Wind' Copyright," *Associated Press*, 23 May 2001; Agnew and Haden-Miller, *Atlanta and its Lawyers*, 123-124; Jim Auchmutey and Jeffry Scott, "Gone with the Wind, its Sequels Earn Millions for Margaret Mitchell's Estate," *AC*, 17 November 1994, D8; Phil Kloer, "It's Another Day," *AC*, 23 November 1991, B2.

NOTES TO CHAPTER 14

1   "Comments on Recent Cases," *The Georgia Lawyer* 1 (May 1931), 274; Brennan history.

2   Thrower, 1984; Celestine Sibley, "Carpenter Questions Witness in Own Defense; Will Take Stand Today," *AC*, 16 September 1949, 1, 13; Brennan history.

3   Celestine Sibley, "Judge Carpenter Freed of Shooting Charges," *AC*, 20 September 1949, 1; "Bar Committee Deplores Lockwood, Carpenter Conduct," 5 October 1949.

4   I am relying in this section on Thrower, 1984 and Bradley, 2005.

5   Lyn Martin and Ken Willis, "Report: Eaves Authorized Cheating," *AC*, 21 February 1978, 1A; Thrower, 1984.

6   Ken Willis, "Bell Cleared; Two Others Punished," *AC*, 26 April 1978, 1A.

7   Thrower, 1984.

8   Brennan history.

9   The Tuttle quote comes from Agnew and Haden-Miller, *Atlanta and its Lawyers*, 37.

10 Thrower, 1999.

11 Egan, 2005; Agnew and Haden-Miller, *Atlanta and its Lawyers*, 40-42, 45; Brennan history.

12 Preliminary draft, Sutherland firm description to *The American Lawyer*, 16 April 1982.

13 "Clinton Picks IRS Nominee," *The Houston Chronicle*, 24 February 1993, A5.

14 Egan, 2005.

15 Brennan history.

16 "Lester Maddox," *http://ourgeorgiahistory.com/chronpop/2596*

17 "1966 Election for Governor of Georgia," *http://ourgeorgiahistory.com/chronpop/1000084*

18 Ibid.

19 Interview with Jim Paulk, 15 November 2005.

20 I am relying in this section on Stephanie Ramage, "Al Gore's Lawyer," *Georgia Super Lawyers*, March 2005, 20-23; "45 Under 45," *The American Lawyer*, January 2003; and a videotaped interview with Teresa Wynn Roseborough (2001).

21 The section on state bonds is derived from interviews with John Mobley, 16 February 2006, and Bill Barwick, 24 February 2006.

22 The section on Guantanamo is from Chandler, 2005 and Bill Rankin, "Lawyers Fight for Detainees," *AJC*, 30 November 2005, F1.

23 The inner politics of Ford's search for Douglas's replacement are revealed in David M. O'Brien, "Filling Justice William O. Douglas's Seat: President Gerald R. Ford's Appointment of Justice John Paul Stevens," *Supreme Court Historical Society 1989 Yearbook*

(Washington, DC: Supreme Court Historical Society, 1989), 20-39.

[24] Wilson, 2005.

[25] The Georgia GOP had been divided since 1944. Each faction had maintained separate committees; had operated under separate leadership; and had held separate conventions. At the 1952 convention, then, one faction supported Eisenhower, while the other supported Taft. See Paul T. David, Malcolm Moos, and Ralph M. Goldman, eds., *Presidential Nominating Politics in 1952, Vol. III, The South* (Baltimore: Johns Hopkins University Press), 85-103.

[26] Thrower, 1999. For more on Tuttle's role in the Georgia Republican Party and in Eisenhower's victory, see files 2-18, box 12, Tuttle Papers; and Bass, *Unlikely Heroes*, 23-29.

[27] Letter, W.A. Kimbel to Elbert Tuttle, 16 July 1952, "Republican Congratulations" folder, box 12, Tuttle Papers; letter, Mac Asbill, Jr. to Elbert Tuttle, 5 November 1952, "Personal Correspondence 1" folder, box 11, Tuttle Papers. For a contemporary description of the significance of the "revolt," see Joseph Alsop, "Matter of Fact," *WP*, 4 June 1952, 11.

NOTES TO CHAPTER 15

[1] The description of this matter comes from Paulk, 2005.

[2] Unless stated otherwise, the remainder of this section comes from J.D. Fleming, 2005.

[3] Memo, Intellectual Property Litigation Subgroup to John Bonds, et al, 15 December 1996 (on file in Sutherland Atlanta office).

[4] "Agenda: Intellectual Property Litigation Subgroup," Partners Meeting, 27 April 1997 (on file in Sutherland Atlanta office).

[5] The rest of this section is primarily derived from an interview with John North, 26 May 2005.

[6] Brenda Sandburg, "The Next Microsoft?," *Legal Times*, 12 November 2001, 25; Tatiana Boncompagni, "Opening Statements," *Intellectual Property World Wide* 2 (24 April 2002), 16; North, 2005.

[7] Thomsen, 2005; North, 2005.

[8] See press release on Sutherland website, "SAB Secures Win in International Trade Commission," 12 July 2004.

[9] J.D. Fleming, e-mail to author

Index

Note: *Italicized* page numbers indicate photographs.

PHOTO CREDITS

Pg. 3, 4, 10 (inset), 17, 19, 20, 23, 26 (inset), 72, 81, 90, 100 (top), 101, 112, 125, 148 (inset & background), 168 (William A. Sutherland) Sutherland Historic Archive; Pg. 6, 10 (background), 92 Courtesy of the Kenan Research Center at the Atlanta History Center; Pg. 8, 16, 26 (background), 32, 39, 42, 69, 102, 104 (inset & background) 115, Library of Congress; Pg. 12, 15, 73 Atlanta Directory Listings – Robert W. Woodruff Library, Emory University; Pg. 25 Pacific Commercial Advertiser; Pg. 34 Georgia Tech Archives (creator unknown); Pg. 37 Mr. Chip Simone (detail); Pg. 40, 167, 168 (Randolph W. Thrower) Michael Riggall; Pg. 44 (inset & background) American Stock/Hulton Archive/Getty Images; Pg. 56, 64, 111, 170, 192 AP Images; Pg. 58 (inset & background) Hank Walker/Time Life Pictures/Getty Images; Pg. 66 © Bettmann/CORBIS, 138 (inset) © Orjan F. Ellingvag/Corbis; Pg. 70 (inset & background) Damon Carter/Princeton Alumni Weekly; Pg. 77 Courtesy of Mrs. Elsas; Pg. 82 Courtesy of the Naval Historical Foundation; Pg. 86 (inset & background) Kiplinger Library of the Historical Society of Washington, DC; Pg. 93, 98, 129, 140, 168 (N. Jerold Cohen & Herbert N. Beller), 171, 175, 177, 180, 183, 206 Dupont Photographers; Pg. 100 & 168 (Mac Asbill, Jr./detail), 181 Carol Highsmith Photography; Pg. 113 Courtesy of the Richard B. Russell Library for Political Research and Studies, The University of Georgia Libraries; Pg. 121 National Archives; Pg. 122 (inset & background) Howard Sochurek/Time Life Pictures/Getty Images; Pg. 126 Courtesy of the Fulton County Daily Report; Pg. 138 Digital Vision/Punch Stock (background); Pg. 144, 168 & 204 (backgrounds) istock; Pg. 147 © Jack Picone/Alamy; Pg. 150, 155 Courtesy of Lena Hinton; Pg. 157 Chase Photography – Courtesy of the Gregory Family; Pg. 160 (inset & background) Courtesy of Kennesaw State University Archives; Pg. 162, 166 Courtesy of Sembler; Pg. 165 Courtesy of Ben Carter Properties; Pg. 178 (inset & background) NYC foto; Pg. 184-185 Courtesy of John Fleming; Pg. 188 (inset & background) Manny Ceneta/AFP/Getty Images; Pg. 195 the Elbert Tuttle Papers; Manuscript, Archives and Rare Book Library, Emory University; Pg. 204 Getty Images (inset); Pg. 202 Gerald Ford Library; Pg. 214 Precis Creative

Dust Jacket: *Front Cover, Sutherland Historic Archive; Back Cover, Library of Congress; Author's Photo, Michael Riggall*